TABLE OF CONTENTS

PREFACE

Nearly four years after the launch of the software program Publish or Perish, I am delighted to introduce to you the Publish or Perish book, your guide to effective and responsible citation analysis. The Publish or Perish software was first introduced in October 2006, partly as a response to my unsuccessful application to full professor that same year. I reasoned that if I was going to be successful, I would need to present a case that simply couldn't be rejected. Publish or Perish allowed me to do exactly that (see page 80), and I was promoted to full professor in 2007.

Even before I put in my second application for promotion, however, I realized that Publish or Perish might not only be able to help *me*, but also many other academics in a similar situation. I therefore made Publish or Perish freely available on my website, www.harzing.com. Over the years, I have come to realize that PoP can be used for many more purposes than I initially envisaged. This book documents its many and variable uses and shows you how to get the best out of the software program.

Citations are not just a reflection of the impact that a particular piece of academic work has generated. Citations can be used to tell stories about academics, journals and fields of research, but they can also be used to distort stories. This book is meant to help you create effective stories, but also to teach you to be a responsible user of research metrics. I hope you enjoy reading it and applying its content to good use.

Stories gain color through examples and this book contains many of them. Giving meaningful examples requires a detailed knowledge of the person or field in question. Therefore, many of the examples involve my own work as well as the broader field of Business and Management. However, wherever possible I have drawn from a broader discipline base, and I would be delighted to hear about your own stories for future editions of the book.

ACKNOWLEDGEMENTS

As this book is self-published there were few people beyond myself involved in its realization. However, I would like to thank my colleagues Christina Cregan and Joeri Mol as well as my PhD student Shea Fan for reading the final manuscript and providing thoughtful comments.

Most of all, however, I would like to thank Ron van der Wal of Tarma Software Research for his initial implementation and continuous improvement of Publish or Perish. Without his patience, dedication, and expert programming skills, Google Scholar's potential for citation analysis would still be unrealized.

Anne-Wil Harzing
September 2010
Melbourne, Australia

CHAPTER 1:
INTRODUCTION TO CITATION ANALYSIS

1.1   INTRODUCTION

This book is a companion to the software program Publish or Perish (PoP). PoP was designed in the first instance to calculate citation metrics for a variety of purposes. As is discussed in detail in Part 2 of this book, it can be used in many different ways. In Section 1.1.1., I provide a very brief summary.

In this first chapter, I will provide a brief introduction to citation analysis as well as an overview of the most popular data sources and metrics in use. The chapter will conclude with an overview of the remainder of the book.

1.1.1   THE MANY AND VARIABLE USES OF PUBLISH OR PERISH

Academics that need to make their case for tenure or promotion will find PoP useful to create reference groups and show their citation record to its best advantage. When evaluating other academics, PoP can be used as a 5-minute preparation before meeting someone you don't know, to evaluate editorial board members or prospective PhD supervisors, to write up tributes (or laudations) and eulogies, to decide on publication awards and to prepare for a job interview. Deans and other academic administrators will find PoP useful to evaluate tenure or promotion cases in a fair and equitable way.

PoP can also be used to assist when you are uncertain which journal to submit your work to. You can use PoP to get ideas of the types of journals that publish articles on the topic you are writing on, and to compare a set of journals in terms of their citation impact. Once you have decided on the target journal, it can also help you to double-check that you haven't missed any prior work from the journal in question.

PoP can help you to do a quick literature review to identify the most cited articles and/or scholars in a particular field. It can be used to identify whether any research has been done in a particular area at all (very useful for grant applications) or to evaluate the development of the literature in a particular topic over time. Finally, PoP is very well suited for doing bibliometric research on both authors and journals.

1.1.2   A CAUTIONARY NOTE

A word of caution before we start. This book provides lay users with an overview of how to use citation analysis in a more effective and responsible way. However, it is important to note that although high quality scholarship might be highly cited, citations are not in and of themselves a measure of quality. When assessing the quality of scholarship, there is no substitute for reading an academic's work.

Further, whether using metrics for counting publications or citations, another crucial question that should always be asked is: "Has the scholar asked an important question and investigated it in such a way that it has the potential to advance societal understanding and well-being?"

Governments worldwide, all of which have mandates to foster society's best interest, have introduced formal rankings-based research assessment processes. These national research evaluation systems reinforce universities' proclivity to systematically rank journals, scholars, and academic institutions.

In general we can distinguish two broad approaches to ranking: stated preference (or peer review) and revealed preference (Tahai & Meyer, 1999). Stated preference involves members of particular academic community ranking journals or universities (and less often academics) on the basis of their own expert judgments.

Revealed preference rankings are based on *actual* publication behavior and generally measure the citation rates of journals, academics or universities using Thomson ISI's Web of Knowledge. However, any source of citation data can be used. Publish or Perish is ideally suited to measure the impact of academics and journals with Google Scholar data.

If, after reading this book, you would like to learn even more about data sources, data metrics or any other aspect of citation analysis, you might be intrigued to know that there is a entire academic sub-discipline focusing on these topics: bibliometrics. Although bibliometrics is a multi-disciplinary field with relationships to the Sociology of Science and Science & Technology Studies, it is generally classified under Library and Information Sciences.

Journals most likely to publish articles relating to citation analysis are the longstanding *Scientometrics* (established in 1978) and *Journal of the American Society for Information Science and Technology* (established in 1950 as *American Documentation*), as well as the recently established *Journal of Informetrics*.

1.2.1   FROM RANKING JOURNALS TO RANKING ARTICLES

Traditionally, journal rankings were used to evaluate the research impact of individual academics. Hence, rather than measuring the impact of an academic's individual articles, universities and governments would use the ranking of the journal (based on stated or revealed preference) as a proxy for the quality and impact of an academic's articles.

Although this practice is still common, the realization that this might lead to sub-optimal conclusion is gradually beginning to take hold. Although on average articles in top-ranked journals can expect more citations (this is the very essence of the Journal Impact Factor, discussed in Section 1.4.1), there is a wide variance. Several articles have shown unambiguously that highly-cited articles can be published in lower-ranked journals, whilst many articles published in top-ranked journals fail to gather a substantial number of citations. Based on their research, Singh, Haddad & Chow (2007: 319) warn that:

> *"...both administrators and the management discipline will be well served by efforts to evaluate each article on its own merits rather than abdicate this responsibility by using journal ranking as a proxy for quality."*

This is a particularly important recommendation today when an increasing number of universities either require publications in the top three to five journals in a scholar's discipline or completely disregard publications in journals outside of those few identified as "top" (Singh et al., 2007; Van Fleet, McWilliams &

Siegel, 2000). Whereas there may be reasons to use journal rank as one indicator of article quality, there is no reason to use it as the only or even the best measure.

Using an academic's **actual** citation record rather than the journals he or she has published could also be argued to be a more objective way to measure research impact. Acceptance of an article for publication into a (top) journal is influenced by a very small number of gatekeepers (the editor and 1 to 3 reviewers). Although these gatekeepers can be expected to be dispassionate and well-informed experts, nearly every academic can relate experiences of bias in the review process. In contrast, citations to one's work are the collective "verdict" of the market, where a far larger number of users decide on the impact of one's work.

1.2.2   USE CAUTION WHEN APPLYING CITATION ANALYSIS

This doesn't mean citations are a panacea. Citations are subject to many forms of error, from typographical errors in the source paper, to errors in Google Scholar parsing of the reference, to errors due to some nonstandard reference formats. Publications such as books or conference proceedings are treated inconsistently, both in the literature and in Google Scholar. Thus citations to these works can be complete, completely missing, or anywhere in between.

When using Publish or Perish for citation analyses, I would therefore like to suggest the following general rule of thumb:

- If an academic shows good citation metrics, it is very likely that he or she has made a significant impact on the field.

However, the reverse is not necessarily true. If an academic shows weak citation metrics, this may be caused by a lack of impact on the field, but also by one or more of the following:

- Working in a small field (therefore generating fewer citations in total);
- Publishing in a language other than English (LOTE - effectively also restricting the citation field);
- Publishing mainly (in) books.

Although Google Scholar performs better than the Web of Science in this respect, it still does not provide a comprehensive coverage in capturing LOTE articles and citations, or citations in books or book chapters. As a result, citation metrics in the Social Sciences and even more so in the Humanities will always be underestimated as in these disciplines publications in LOTE and books/book chapters are more likely than in the Sciences.

1.2.3   WHAT ABOUT SELF-CITATIONS?

Whenever there is talk about citation analysis, the first concern always seems to be to exclude self-citations, i.e. authors citing their own work. It is generally believed that authors can inflate their citation records by excessive self-citations.

We will discuss this phenomenon in more detail in Section 9.2. However, I would like to categorically declare here that in my view the distrust of self-citations is completely misplaced. In most cases excluding self-citations is a huge waste of time and when done with ISI data has the potential to introduce more noise than it removes (see Section 14.2.2). To provide an illustration of this I looked at a group of nearly 250 editors of 57 Management and Marketing journals between 1989 and 2009. The average number of self-citations for these academics was 4.3% at the time they became editor. The higher proportions occurred for the editors with fewer citations overall.

For those with less than 100 citations, the self-citation rate was on average 8%. For those at the opposite end of the spectrum, more than 1000 citations, the self-citation rate was only 2.4%. However, in neither case would be the number of self-citations be problematic enough to completely change the assessment of someone's publication record.

Only 30 out of the 242 editors had a self-citation rate of more than 10% (10 of which had a self-citation rate of 11%). Only five out of the 242 editors had a self-citation rate of more than 20% and three of those editors had less than 15 citations overall. In these cases self-citations are not the problem. They are often a legitimate way to acknowledge the academic's previous research in the same field. What **is** a problem is a lack of non-self citations, i.e. the fact that other academics are not referring to these academics' articles.

1.3 DATA SOURCES FOR CITATION ANALYSIS

In this section we will provide a very brief overview of the three main sources for citation analysis: Google Scholar, Thomson Reuters Web of Knowledge, and Elsevier's Scopus. Here we will focus on the essentials only. In Chapters 13 and 14, we will provide a detailed analysis of the advantages and disadvantages of the two currently most important sources: Google Scholar and Thomson ISI.

1.3.1 GOOGLE SCHOLAR

Introduced by Google in 2004, Google Scholar has become a very popular alternative data source, not least through the fact that access is free and citation analysis programs such as Publish or Perish make bibliometric analysis easy.

Some academics are skeptical about its wider coverage. However, studies (e.g. Vaughan & Shaw, 2008) have found most of the citations to be scholarly. After a relatively slow start Google Scholar coverage is increasing, although Google still does not provide a list of its sources. Google Scholar is updated several times a week. For a more detailed analysis about Google Scholar as a source for citation analysis see Harzing & van der Wal (2008).

Google Scholar coverage is broader than that of both ISI and Scopus. It covers citations **IN** all academic journals. This includes academic journals that **are** ISI or Scopus listed, but also those academic journals that are **not** listed in these databases, but are available on the Internet. Google Scholar also includes citations in books, conference proceedings, white papers, and government reports.

Google Scholar also covers citations **TO** all publications, including academic journals that are and are not ISI or Scopus listed, books, conference proceedings, white papers, and government reports. Google Scholar also has a substantially higher coverage of foreign-language publications than either ISI or Scopus.

Thomson Reuters Web of Knowledge is a collection of databases and analytical tools relating to bibliographic and citation analysis. The two best known are the *Journal Citation Reports* and the *Web of Science*.

The Journal Citation Reports focus on the citation impact of **journals** and are discussed in Section 1.4.1. The Web of Science is most often used to search for publications and citations for individual **academics** and will be discussed in more detail below.

THE WEB OF SCIENCE

The Web of Science is generally known as ISI Web of Science or ISI. This is the traditional source of citation data, established by Eugene Garfield in the 1960s. Many universities still use this as their only source of citation data. It charges commercial rates for access and is generally updated once or twice a week.

The Web of Science has complete coverage of citations in the more than 11,000 journals that are ISI listed, going back to 1900. However, it only covers around 2,700 journals in the Social Sciences and Humanities. Although its worldwide coverage has been improving recently, it still has a North American bias.

The Web of Science has two main ways to search for citation data, the ISI Search and the ISI Cited Reference Search. The ISI Search function is the standard function selected when logging into the Web of Science. It has more extensive analytical functions than the Cited Reference Search, but has a more limited coverage of citations. The difference in coverage between the two functions is as follows:

- ISI Search = only includes citations **IN** ISI-listed journals **TO** publications ISI-listed journals. Only citations that refer **accurately** to the ISI Master record for the publication in question are included (see Chapter 14 for more details).

- ISI Cited by search = includes citations **IN** ISI-listed journals **TO** all publications (incl. non ISI-listed journals, books, conference papers, white papers, government reports). Citations that refer to a publication with small errors (stray citations) are reported separately. Even in the "cited by" search function ISI **ignores** citations for second and further authors for non-ISI publications.

1.3.3   SCOPUS

Introduced by Elsevier in 2004, Scopus aims to be the most comprehensive Scientific, Medical, Technical and Social Science abstract and citation database containing all relevant literature, irrespective of medium or commercial model. It covers nearly 18,000 titles from more than 5,000 publishers, but its coverage before 1996 is very limited.

Scopus claims worldwide coverage; more than half of Scopus content is said to originate from Europe, Latin America and the Asia Pacific region. It is updated daily and charges commercial rates for access.

Scopus has a substantially broader journal coverage than ISI. The contrast is particularly large in the Social Sciences and Humanities. For example Scopus has 1114 journals in Business & Management and 682 journals in Economics, Econometrics & Finance. This is in stark contrast with the less than 250 journals for both Business & Management (incl. Finance) and Economics in ISI. Although for Economics, ISI still has about a third of Scopus' coverage, for Business & Management, this is only about 20%.

Similar to ISI's Web of Science, Scopus has two different search functions. The General Search function is the standard function selected when logging into the Scopus. It has more extensive analytical functions than the Cited Reference Search, but has a more limited coverage of citations. The difference in coverage between the two functions is as follows:

- Scopus General search = citations **IN** Scopus-listed journals **TO** publications in Scopus-listed journals.

- Scopus More search = citations **IN** Scopus-listed journals **TO** all publications, incl. non-Scopus listed journals, books, conference proceedings, white papers, and government reports. Please note that even in the "cited by" search function ISI **ignores** citations for second and further authors for non-ISI publications.

Unlike the ISI Cited By search, the Scopus More search is not additive, i.e. in order to establish an academic's total Scopus citations, one needs to add up the results from the Scopus General search and the Scopus More search. Fortunately, unlike the ISI Cited By search function, Scopus **does** find citations for second and further authors for non-Scopus publications in the Scopus More search.

1.3.4   OTHER DATA SOURCES

In addition to the data sources described above there are a lot of other sources that focus on specific disciplines. Some notable examples are Harvard's Astrophysics Data System in Astrophysics, Citeseer in Computer Science, and PubMed in the Life Sciences.

Although these specialized data sources are often used frequently in their respective disciplines, they are not very useful for generic citation analysis as their coverage is very limited. In addition, not all of these databases provide citation information.

1.4   CITATION METRICS

The increased emphasis on research metrics has led to a virtual explosion of citation metrics, each focusing on slightly different aspects of an academic's citation record. Here, I will discuss the main metrics – the journal impact factor, Hirsh's h-index and its contemporary and individual variations, the m-quotient and the g-index – in a bit more detail.

1.4.1   THOMSON ISI JOURNAL IMPACT FACTOR

One of the earliest citation metrics that became widely used is Thomson ISI's (now Thomson Reuter's) Journal Impact Factor (or JIF). A simple short-hand explanation of the JIF is that it reflects the **average** number of citations that can be expected for an article in the journal in question within 1-2 years after publication.

A more formal definition is the number of citations in a particular year (e.g. 2009) to **all** items published in the journal in question in the two years before (e.g. 2007-2008) divided by the number of source items. Source items are regular articles, i.e. excluding letters, book reviews and editorials, conference abstracts. However, citations to non-source items are included in the numerator.

Thomson ISI publishes Journal Impact Factors in June every year for the previous year, i.e. JIFs for 2009 come out in June 2010. As typical citation patterns vary by discipline JIFs vary enormously by discipline. In the Social Sciences/Humanities impact factors above 2.0 are rare, in the Sciences they are quite common. This means that the average article in the Social Sciences and Humanities is cited less than once a year.

There are several commonly mentioned problems (see e.g. Seglen, 1997; Cameron, 2005 for a summary) with the use of the ISI Journal Impact Factor, the most important of which are the use of a 2-year citation window and technical issues related to the calculation of the JIF.

2-YEAR WINDOW IGNORES FIELD DIFFERENCES IN CITATION PATTERNS

When JIFs were introduced by Garfield in the 1960s, his focus was on biochemistry and molecular biology, disciplines that are characterized by a high number of citations and short publication lags (Cameron, 2005). Hence the use of a 2-year citation window might have been justified. However, this is not true for most other disciplines where knowledge takes much longer to be disseminated. Although Thomson ISI recently introduced a 5-year impact factor, the 2-year impact factor is still the most commonly used.

As Leydesdorff (2008) shows, impact factors can differ with an order of magnitude when comparing across disciplines such as Mathematics and Genetics. McGarty (2000) discusses the problems associated with the 2-year JIF for the Social Sciences in some detail. He shows that the publication lags for two important Psychology journals are such that for a typical paper published in these journals, two thirds of the literature that could theoretically be included in the JIF (i.e. papers published in the two years preceding publication of the referencing paper) was yet to be published at the time of submission.

A perusal of the last issue of 2007 of the *Journal of International Business Studies* shows that the problem is at least as severe in Business Studies. Even in this most optimistic case (i.e. the final issue of 2007) we find very few references to publications in 2005 and 2006 in the ten articles published in this issue. Out of the more than 700 references in this issue, only 20 referred to publications in 2005 and a mere 7 to publications in 2006 (i.e. less than 4% of the total number of citations).

One third of these citations were self-citations. This is not entirely surprising given that of the ten papers in this issue, six were submitted before 2005 (four in 2004, one in 2003, one in 2002). Of the remaining four, two were submitted in January and February 2005 and hence cannot realistically be expected to include references to 2005 papers. The final two papers were submitted in January and May 2006. The fact that we find **any** references to papers published in 2005 and 2006 in these articles is most likely due to these references being included in the review process. As McGarty (2000:14) aptly summarizes:

> *The two year impact factor clearly favors journals which publish work by authors who cite their own forthcoming work and who are geographically situated to make their work readily available in preprint form. The measure punishes journals which publish the work of authors who do not have membership of these invisible colleges and is virtually incapable of detecting genuine impact. It is not just a bad measure, it is an invitation to do bad science.*

In addition to the limitations associated with a 2-year window, there are several technical or statistical problems with the way the JIF is calculated. First, whilst the denominator in the JIF (the number of articles published) only includes normal articles (so called source items), the numerator includes citations to all publications in the journal in question, including editorials, letters, and book reviews (Cameron, 2005). This means that citations in these latter publications are basically "free" as the increase in the numerator is not matched by an increase in the denominator. As a result, journals with a lively letters to the editor/correspondence section (such as for instance *Nature*) will show inflated JIFs.

This problem is compounded by the fact that many journals have increased the proportion of non-source items over time. Gowrishankar & Divakar (1999) indicate the proportion of source items to non-source items in Nature declined from 3.5 to 1.6 between 1977 and 1997. This particular JIF feature also enables manipulation of the JIF by unscrupulous editors who can inflate their JIF by referring frequently to journal articles or even to other editorials in their editorials (Whitehouse, 2002). Bayliss, Gravenor & Kao (1999) argue that even a single research institute could increase the JIF of a journal that publishes few papers from 1 to 6 by asking each of its researchers to cite two papers in that journal.

The second calculation problem is statistical in nature: the JIF calculates the mean number of citations to an article in the journal in question. However, many authors have found that citation distributions are extremely skewed. Seglen (1997) for instance found the most cited 15% of papers to account for 50% of citations and the most cited 50% for 90% of the citations. Hence on average the most cited half of papers are cited nine times as much as the least cited half. Especially for journals publishing a relatively small number of papers, individual highly cited papers have a very strong influence on the mean JIF.

1.4.2   H-INDEX

The h-index was proposed by Hirsch (2005). It is defined as follows:

> A scientist has index h if h of his/her Np papers have at least h citations each, and the other (Np-h) papers have no more than h citations each.

It aims to measure the cumulative impact of a researcher's output by looking at the amount of citations his/her work has received. The properties of the h-index have been analyzed in various papers; see for example Egghe & Rousseau (2006).

Since Hirsch's first publication of the h-index in 2005, this new measure of academic impact has generated a very widespread interest. At the time of writing (July 2010) Google Scholar lists 1180 citations to this paper and the subsequent publication in the Proceedings of the National Academy of Sciences.

Hirsch argues that the h-index is preferable to other single-number criteria, such the total number of papers, the total number of citations and citations per paper. However, Hirsch provides a strong caveat:

> Obviously a single number can never give more than a rough approximation to an individual's multifaceted profile, and many other factors should be considered in combination in evaluating an individual. This and the fact that there can always be exceptions to rules should be kept in mind especially in life-changing decision such as the granting or denying of tenure.

The advantage of the h-index is that it combines an assessment of both quantity (number of papers) and quality (impact, or citations to these papers) (Glänzel, 2006). An academic cannot have a high h-index without publishing a substantial number of papers. However, these papers need to be cited by other academics in order to count for the h-index.

As such the h-index is said to be preferable over the total number of citations as it corrects for "one hit wonders", i.e. academics who might have authored (or co-authored, maybe even as 5th or later author) one or a limited number of highly-cited papers, but have not shown a sustained and durable academic performance. It is also preferable over the number of papers as it corrects for papers that are not cited. Hence the h-index favours academics that publish a continuous stream of papers with lasting and above-average impact. (Bornmann & Daniel, 2007).

VALIDATON AND RECEPTION OF THE H-INDEX

The h-index has been found to have considerable face validity. Hirsch calculated the h-index of Nobel prize winners and found 84% of them to have an h-index of at least 30. Newly elected members in the National Academy of Sciences in Physics and Astronomy in 2005 had a median h-index of 46.

Bornmann & Daniel (2005) found that on average the h-index for successful applications for postdoctoral research fellowships was consistently higher than for non-successful applicants. Cronin & Meho (2006) found that faculty rankings in information sciences based on raw citation counts and on the h-index showed a strong positive correlation, but claim that the h-index provides additional discriminatory power.

Van Raan (2006) calculated the h-index for 147 chemistry research groups in the Netherlands and found a correlation of 0.89 between the h-index and the total number of citations. Both the h-index and more traditional bibliometric indices also related in a quite comparable way with peer judgments.

The h-index has resulted in a flurry of commentaries and articles published in journals such as *Scientometrics* and *Journal of the American Society for Information Science and Technology*, including several articles proposing further refinements and alternatives (see the sections on the contemporary an individual h-index below) and in spite of strong criticism by some bibliometricians, it has generally received a positive reception.

Perhaps the strongest indication that the h-index is becoming a generally accepted measure of academic achievement is that ISI Thomson has now included it as part of its new citation report feature in the Web of Science.

DISADVANTAGES OF THE H-INDEX

A disadvantage of the h-index is that it ignores the number of citations to each individual article over and above what is needed to achieve a certain h-index. Once a paper belongs to the top h papers, its subsequent citations no longer count. Hence, in order to give more weight to highly-cited articles Leo Egghe (2006) proposed the g-index (see Section 1.4.6 below for more details).

The h-index (and any citation-based measures) is a less appropriate measure of academic achievement for junior academics, as their papers have not yet had the time to accumulate citations. Especially in the Social Sciences & Humanities it might take five to ten years before a paper acquires a significant number of citations. For junior academics, the impact factor of the journal they publish in might therefore be a more realistic measure of eventual impact.

However, the h-index should provide a more realistic assessment of the academic achievement of academics that have started publishing at least 10 years ago. I would argue that for more senior academics, assessing the impact of their **own** publications is preferable to assessing the journal impact factor of the journals they publish in. The latter is only a measure of how of the average article in the journal is cited.

1.4.3   M-QUOTIENT

One way to facilitate comparisons between academics with different lengths of academic careers is to divide the h-index by the number of years the academic has been active (measured as the number of years since the first published paper). Hirsch (2005) proposed this measure and called it m.

However, we should note that m generally does not stabilise until later in one's career and that for junior researchers (with low h-indices) small changes in the h-index can lead to large changes in m. In addition, as Hirsch indicates, the first paper may not always be the appropriate starting point, especially if it was a minor contribution that was published well before the academic realised a sustained productivity. Moreover, m discriminates against academics that work part-time or have had career interruptions. However, in some cases m might be a useful additional metric to evaluate an academic's achievement.

1.4.4   CONTEMPORARY H-INDEX

A disadvantage of the h-index is that it cannot decline. That means that academics who "retire" after 10-20 active years of publishing maintain their high h-index even if they never publish another paper. In order to address this issue, Sidiropoulos, Katsaros & Manolopoulos (2006) proposed the contemporary h-index.

It adds an age-related weighting to each cited article, giving (by default; this depends on the parameterization) less weight to older articles. The weighting is parameterized; the PoP implementation uses *gamma*=4 and *delta*=1, like the authors did for their experiments. This means that for an article published during the current year, its citations account four times. For an article published 4 years ago, its citations account only one time. For an article published 6 years ago, its citations account 4/6 times, and so on.

For junior academics the contemporary h-index is generally close to their regular h-index as most of the papers included in their h-index will be recent. For more established academics there can be a substantial difference between the two indices, indicating that most of the papers included in their h-index have been published some time ago. As such the contemporary h-index often provides a fairer comparison between junior and senior academics than the regular h-index.

1.4.5   INDIVIDUAL H-INDEX (3 VARIATIONS)

Hirsch (2005) indicates that there will be large differences in typical h-values in different fields. Academic disciplines differ in the average number of references per paper and the average number of papers published by each academic. As a general rule of thumb h-indices are much higher in the Natural Sciences than in the Social Sciences and Humanities, although there is a large variability even within these fields.

Podlubny (Podlubny, 2005 and Podlubny and Kassayova, 2006) showed that for nine broadly defined disciplines the average ratio of total citations to the number of citations in mathematics varied considerably (Mathematics: 1, Engineering/technology: 5, Biology: 8, Earth/space sciences: 9, Social/behavioral sciences: 13, Chemistry: 15, Physics: 19, Biomedical Research: 78, Clinical Medicine: 78).

Similarly, Iglesias & Pecharroman (2006) calculated the average number of citations/paper in the 21 different ISI fields and used this to design a normalization factor. Unfortunately, the discipline areas used in neither studies map closely enough onto the categories used by Google Scholar to use these normalization factors in Publish or Perish. However, they do show that comparisons of bibliometric data across fields are generally inappropriate.

Part of the differences between disciplines are caused by the fact that academics in the Natural Sciences typically publish more (and often shorter) articles and also publish with a large number of co-authors, while academics in the Social Sciences and Humanities typically published fewer (and longer) articles (or books) and publish with fewer co-authors.

However, differences in the number of co-authors also seem apparent **within** the same discipline. For instance, North American academics tend to publish articles with a larger number of co-authors than European academics. Since 1990, papers in the North-American *Academy of Management Journal* on average have 2.24 authors, papers in the *British Journal of Management* 2.01 authors, and papers in the *European Management Journal* 1.84 authors.

THREE IMPLEMENTATIONS OF THE INDIVIDUAL H-INDEX

Hirsch (2005) suggested that in the case of large differences in the number of co-authors, it might be useful to normalize the h-index by a factor that reflects the average number of co-authors. Here I discuss three different implementations.

The first version of the Individual h-index was proposed by Batista, Campiteli, Kinouchi & (2006). It divides the standard h-index by the average number of authors in the articles that contribute to the h-index, in order to reduce the effects of co-authorship; the resulting index is called h_I.

PoP also implements an alternative individual h-index, $h_{I,norm}$, that takes a different approach: instead of dividing the total h-index, it first normalizes the number of citations for each paper by dividing the number of citations by the number of authors for that paper, then calculates $h_{I,norm}$ as the h-index of the *normalized* citation counts. This approach is much more fine-grained than both Batista et al.'s and Schreiber's; we believe that it more accurately accounts for any co-authorship effects that might be present and that it is a better approximation of the per-author impact, which is what the original h-index set out to provide.

The third variation is due to Michael Schreiber (Schreiber, 2008). Schreiber's method uses fractional paper counts instead of reduced citation counts to account for shared authorship of papers, and then determines the multi-authored h_m index based on the resulting effective rank of the papers using undiluted citation counts.

The three different metrics are very similar for authors with a small number of co-authors. However, both Batista and Schreiber penalize authors who publish with a lot of co-authors. Which of the three implementations is preferable depends on the importance one attaches to single authorships.

1.4.6   G-INDEX

The g-index was proposed by Leo Egghe (2006). It aims to improve on the h-index by giving more weight to highly-cited articles. The h-index ignores the number of citations to each individual article beyond what is needed to achieve a certain h-index. Hence an academic with an h-index of 5 could theoretically have a total of 25 citations (5 for each paper), but could also have more than a 1000 citations (4 papers with 250 citations each and one paper with 5 citations).

In reality these extremes will be unlikely. However, once a paper belongs to the top h papers, its subsequent citations no longer "count". Such a paper can double or triple its citations without influencing the h-index. Hence, in order to give more weight to highly-cited articles Leo Egghe (2006) proposed the g-index. The g-index is defined as follows:

> *[Given a set of articles] ranked in decreasing order of the number of citations that they received, the g-index is the (unique) largest number such that the top g articles received (together) at least g2 citations.*

For instance, an academic has a g-index of 30 if the top 30 most cited of his/her papers combined have at least 900 citations. It aims to improve on the h-index by giving more weight to highly-cited articles. The g-index cannot be larger than the number of articles and academic has published.

Although the g-index has not yet attracted much attention or empirical verification, it would seem to be a very useful complement to the h-index.

1.5   OVERVIEW OF THE BOOK

After this introductory chapter, this book is made up of three parts that together provide a comprehensive, but accessible introduction to all aspects of citation analysis. Throughout the chapters examples and screenshots will be used to illustrate the issues.

Giving meaningful examples requires detailed knowledge of the person or field in question. Therefore, many of the examples will involve my own work as well as the broader field of Business and Management. However, wherever possible I have attempted to draw from a broader discipline base.

1.5.1   PART 1: HOW TO USE PUBLISH OR PERISH MORE EFFECTIVELY

The first part provides step-by-step instructions on how to use Publish or Perish more effectively. An introduction to the main features of the software is first provided in Chapter 2. Chapters 3 and 4 subsequently provide detailed instructions on how to conduct effect Author and Journal Queries. Chapter 5 is devoted to the broader applications of the General Citation search that can be used to find particular papers, conduct advanced author and journal queries, compare institutional performance and conduct a literature review. Finally, Chapter 6 discusses how the Multi-query Center can be used to effectively store and manage queries for future use.

In Part 2, I present the most common day-to-day uses of the Publish or Perish software. Chapter 7 provides tips and tricks for academics that need to make their case for tenure or promotion. I discuss the importance of reference groups as well as several ways to show your citation record to its best advantage.

In Chapter 8, I discuss how to evaluate other academics. The examples in this chapter vary from a 5-minute preparation before meeting someone you don't know, to evaluating editorial board members or prospective PhD supervisors, from writing up tributes (or laudations) and eulogies to deciding on publication awards and preparing for a job interview.

Chapter 9 turns the tables and looks at citation analysis for Deans and other academic administrators. It includes four topics: the need to accept Google Scholar as an alternative data source, the myths about self-citation, the inappropriateness of citation analysis at early career stages, and the differences in citation impact across disciplines.

In Chapter 10, I show how Publish or Perish can be used to assist you when you are uncertain which journal to submit your work to. PoP can be used to get ideas of the types of journals that publish articles on the topic you are writing on, and to compare a set of journals in terms of their citation impact. Finally, once you have decided on the target journal, it can also help you to double-check that you haven't missed any prior work from the journal in question.

Chapter 11 shows you how Publish or Perish can be used to do a quick literature review to identify the most cited articles and/or scholars in a particular field. It can also be employed to identify whether any research has been done in a particular area at all (useful for grant applications). Other applications are to evaluate the development of the literature in a particular topic over time.

Finally, Chapter 12 discusses how to use Publish or Perish when doing bibliometric research. Bibliometric research refers to the quantitative analysis of bodies of literature and their references: citations. These bodies of literature can be grouped in many different ways, but in this chapter, I will focus on the grouping by author or journal and discuss some tips and tricks in doing bibliometric research on authors and journals.

1.5.3   PART 3: ADVANCED TOPICS: DELVING DEEPER INTO THE WORLD OF CITATION ANALYSIS

Part 3 of this book deals with more specialized topics. In Chapters 13 and 14, it first provides a detailed evaluation of the two main data sources for citation analysis: Google Scholar and Thomson ISI's Web of Science. I show that Google Scholar's advantages mainly lie in being a free, easy-to-use, quick and comprehensive source of citation analysis, with its disadvantages related to not being a structured bibliographic database.

ISI's main advantages lie in the fact that, as a traditional bibliographic database, it allows more complex and focused search options, the option to filter and refine queries, and further analyze results. ISI's most important disadvantage lies in its lack of comprehensive coverage, resulting in an often serious underestimation of citation impact. In addition, ISI has a number of idiosyncrasies: difficulty in reliably establishing self-citations, poor handling of stray citations, and frequent misclassification of original research articles as review articles and proceedings articles.

Chapter 15 proposes an alternative to the traditionally used ISI Journal Impact Factor (JIF) to evaluate journals. It proposes both an alternative metric – Hirsch's h-index – and data source – Google Scholar – to assess journal impact. Using a comparison between the Google Scholar h-index and the ISI JIF for a sample of 838 journals in Economics & Business, I argue that the former provides a more accurate and comprehensive measure of journal impact.

Finally, Chapter 16 shows how different data sources and citation metrics impact on comparisons of academics between disciplines. This chapter analyses the citation records of ten full professors in a variety of disciplines to illustrate how different data sources and different citations metrics might lead to very different conclusions.

1.5.4 APPENDICES

At the end of the book I provide a set of appendices that include the license agreement for Publish or Perish, a command reference, the pop-menu for the results page, export formats, a complete message reference and the pop-up menu for the multi-query center list view.

1.6 REFERENCES

- Batista, P.D.; Campiteli, M.G.; Konouchi, O.; Martinez, A.S. (2006) **Is it possible to compare researchers with different scientific interests?** *Scientometrics*, 68(1): 179-189.
- Baylis, M., Gravenor, M .& Kao, R. (1999). **Sprucing up one's impact factor**. *Nature*, 401, 322.
- Bornmann, L.; Daniel, H-D. (2005) **Does the h-index for ranking of scientists really work?** *Scientometrics*, 65(3): 391-392.
- Bornmann, L.; Daniel, H-D. (2007) **What do we know about the h index?** *Journal of the American Society for Information Science and Technology*, 58(9): 1181-1185.
- Cameron, B.D. (2005). **Trends in the Usage of ISI Bibliometric Data, Uses, Abuses, and Implication**. *Portal: Libraries and the Academy*. 5: 105-125.
- Cronin, B.; Meho, L. (2006) **Using the h-Index to Rank Influential Information Scientists**, *Journal of the American Association for Information Science and Technology*, 57(9): 1275-1278.
- Egghe, L.; Rousseau R. (2006) **An informetric model for the Hirsch-index**, *Scientometrics*, 69(1): 121-129.
- Egghe, L. (2006) **Theory and practice of the g-index**, *Scientometrics*, 69(1): 131-152.
- Glänzel, W. (2006) **On the opportunities and limitations of the H-index**, *Science Focus*, vol. 1 (1): 10-11.
- Gowrishankar J. & Divakar, P. (1999). **Sprucing up one's impact factor**. *Nature,* 401, 321-322.
- Harzing, A.W.K. & Wal, R. van der (2008). **Google Scholar as a new source for citation analysis?**, *Ethics in Science and Environmental Politics*, 8(1): 62-71, published online January 8, http://www.int-res.com/articles/esep2008/8/e008pp5.pdf.
- Hirsch, J.E. (2005) **An index to quantify an individual's scientific research output**, *arXiv:physics/0508025* v5 29 Sep 2006.

- Iglesias, J.E, Pecharromán, C. (2006) **Scaling the h-Index for Different Scientific ISI Fields**, arXiv:physics/0607224
- Leydesdorff, L. (2008) **Caveats for the use of citation indicators in research and journal evaluations.** *Journal of the American Society for Information Science and Technology*, 59: 278-287.
- McGarty, C. (2000). **The citation impact factor in social psychology: a bad statistic that encourages bad science.** *Current Research in Social Psychology*, 5: 1-16.
- Podlubny, I. (2005) **Comparison of scientific impact expressed by the number of citations in different fields of science**, *Scientometrics*, 64(1): pp. 95-99.
- Podlubny, I.; Kassayova, K. (2006) **Law of the constant ratio. Towards a better list of citation superstars: compiling a multidisciplinary list of highly cited researchers**, *Research Evaluation*, 15(3): 154-162.
- Raan, A.F.J. van (2006) **Comparison of the Hirsch-index with standard bibliometric indicators and with peer judgement for 147 chemistry research groups**, *Scientometrics*, 67(3): 491-502.
- Schreiber, M. (2008) **To share the fame in a fair way, h_m modifies h for multi-authored manuscripts**, *New Journal of Physics*, 10: 040201-1-8.
- Seglen, P.O. (1997). **Why the impact factor of journals should not be used for evaluating research.** *British Medical Journal*, 314: 497-502.
- Sidiropoulos, A.; Katsaros, C.; Manolopoulos, Y. (2006) **Generalized h-index for disclosing latent facts in citation networks**, *arXiv:cs.DL/0607066* v1 13 Jul 2006.
- Singh, G., Haddad, K. M., & Chow, C. W. 2007. **Are articles in "top" management journals necessarily of higher quality?** *Journal of Management Inquiry*, 16(4): 319–331.
- Tahai, A. & Meyer, M. (1999). **A revealed preference study of management journals' direct influences**, *Strategic Management Journal*, 20: 279-296.
- Van Fleet, D., McWilliams, A., & Siegel, D. 2000. **A theoretical and empirical analysis of journal rankings: The case of formal lists.** *Journal of Management*, 26(5): 839–861.
- Vaughan, L.; Shaw, D. (2008) **A new look at evidence of scholarly citations in citation indexes and from web sources.** *Scientometrics*, 74(2), 317-330.
- Whitehouse, G.H. (2002). **Impact factors: facts and myths.** *European Radiology*, 12: 715-717.

CHAPTER 2:
INTRODUCTION TO PUBLISH OR PERISH

This chapter will provide a basic introduction on how to use Publish or Perish. I first discuss the lay-out and main functions of the software. Subsequently, I explain the citation metrics that are calculated by Publish or Perish and provide illustrative examples on how to use them. Finally, I explain how to export the data and how to trouble-shoot any problems with the software.

2.1 INTRODUCTION TO PUBLISH OR PERISH

Publish or Perish (PoP) is a software program that retrieves and analyzes academic citations. It was first introduced in October 2006 and has been continuously improved and updated since. Its name is a tongue-in-cheek reference to the pressure to publish work constantly to further or sustain a career in academia. However, its main function is to empower individual academics to present their case for research impact to its best advantage.

Publish or Perish uses Google Scholar queries to obtain citation information, which is then analyzed and converted to a number of statistics. To use Publish or Perish, you need a working Internet connection. The results are available on-screen and can also be copied to the Windows clipboard (for pasting into other applications) or saved to a text file (for future reference or further analysis).

Publish or Perish runs on Windows, Macintosh and Linux platforms. For detailed instructions on how to install Publish or Perish for various platforms, see the main Publish or Perish webpage (http//www.harzing.com/pop.htm). The webpage Publish or Perish in the news also provides an overview of the extensive news coverage for Publish or Perish as well as examples of its frequent mentioning on blogs and library websites.

2.1.1 PUBLISH OR PERISH TESTIMONIALS

Section 1.1.1 provides a summary of the many and varied uses of Publish or Perish. A small selection of user feedback below also provides a good insight as to how academics are using Publish or Perish.

> *Many thanks for your generosity and congratulations for your work. If we didn't have your program it would be very complicated to conduct our research, because we are running this project with a shoe-string budget.*

> *I didn't know which papers were the most referenced for my own work, and when discussing with other researchers, in many cases they themselves don't know. Knowledge about these matters is helpful understanding the structure of the research and the social network that surrounds it.*

Publish or Perish has become an essential tool for academics around the world. In my job as an editor of a major international journal, I often need to run a quick check on colleagues, for example, wish to be considered for Board membership. PoP is perfect for such purposes.

PoP has become an academic workhorse for both doing research as well as evaluating researchers and journals (I served as the chair of the "fellows selection committee" of my professional society, where it was an important tool). I also routinely use it to find important papers in an area, or the best people working on a topic (for referees).

As a senior academic in a non-traditional field, I've recommended your web site to a number of my colleagues. I'm always looking for non-ISI options to suggest to junior faculty looking to make the case for tenure. Your efforts are appreciated!

I have been conducting an analysis of highly cited tourism scholars using 'Publish or Perish'. The PoP program is excellent, especially since our field of study is excluded from the Thomson ISI. Google Scholar and your program provide the only valid method of assessing the contribution that individual scholars have made to the field.

2.1.2   MAIN WINDOW

The most important areas in the Publish or Perish main window are shown below.

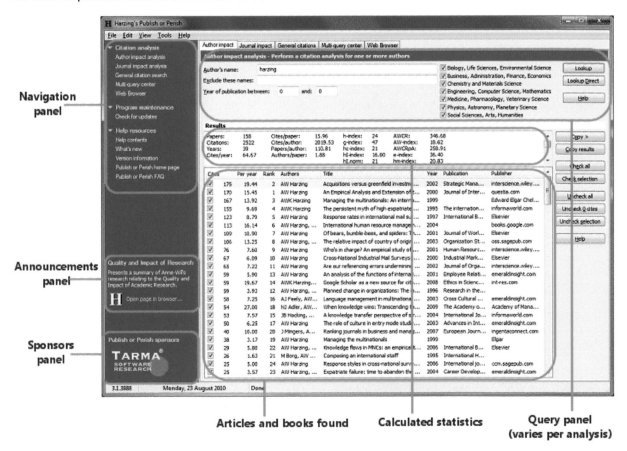

Navigation panel

Announcements panel

Sponsors panel

Articles and books found   Calculated statistics   Query panel (varies per analysis)

NAVIGATION PANEL

This area contains the links to the citation analysis pages and various program resources. Click on a link to go to the indicated page or perform the action. The section headers can be collapsed by clicking on the headers; they can be restored by another click on the same header line.

ANNOUNCEMENTS PANEL

This area displays announcements about the Publish or Perish software or related topics, such as citation analysis. To read more about a specific announcement topic, click on the link.

SPONSORS PANEL

This area displays logos of the sponsors who supported the development of the Publish or Perish software. Click on a logo to visit the sponsor's web site.

ARTICLES AND BOOKS FOUND

This area displays the list of articles and books that matched the search query. Refer to the Results pane section for more information about this area.

CALCULATED STATISTICS

This area displays the statistics that were calculated from the results returned by the search query, subject to the selection status of the items in the lower list. Refer to the Results pane section for more information about this area.

QUERY PANEL

This area contains the entry fields for the search query. The available fields depend on the type of search: author search, journal search or general citation search; see Chapters 3, 4 and 5 for more information about these search types. To manage sets of queries, consult the Chapter 6 which discusses the Multi-query center.

COMMAND REFERENCE

Publish or Perish commands can be reached through the main window (click on the appropriate button) or through the main menu (hit F10, or Alt+*first letter*, or click with the mouse). The full command reference can be found in Appendix 2.

The results pane is part of the Author impact analysis, Journal impact analysis, General citation search, and Multi-query center pages. Although each page has its own copy of the results pane, they operate identically. This pane contains the following fields and options.

(UNNAMED UPPER FIELD)

The upper text field displays the citation metrics for the currently selected query. You can copy the information from this field by right-clicking in the field, then choosing **Select All**, and right-clicking again to choose **Copy**. Alternatively, left-click in the field to give it the keyboard focus, then use Ctrl+A and Ctrl+C to select and copy.

(UNNAMED LOWER LIST)

The lower list displays all results for the currently selected query. By default, the list is sorted by descending number of citations, but you can sort it on any of the columns by clicking on the corresponding column header. Clicking for a second time on the same column header reverses the sort order.

You can exclude individual results by clearing their check box; alternatively, use the **Check all**, **Check selection**, **Uncheck all**, **Uncheck 0 cites**, and **Uncheck selection** buttons to check/uncheck groups of results. When you select/unselect results, citation metrics in the upper field are immediately updated to reflect the remaining results.

If you double-click on an item in the list, Publish or Perish opens your web browser and displays the citing works for the selected item, if any. If an item does not have any citations, a general Google search results page is displayed for the item.

COLUMNS IN THE QUERY RESULTS

The list contains the following columns

Tag	Used for	Notes
Cites	Number of citations	
Per year	Citations per year	Calculated as the total number of citations divided by the age of the article (i.e., the number of years since publication). If the year of publication is not available, this column shows 0.00.
Rank	Google Scholar ranking	The order in which Google Scholar returned the results (1=first, 2=second, etc.). Typically, earlier ranked entries indicate more relevant query results. An irregular rank order when sorted by **Cites** might indicate that the list contains irrelevant results.
Authors	Author names	
Title	Title	

Year	Year of publication	This field might be wrong or missing if the Google Scholar results do not contain a recognizable year.
Publication	Journal name or similar	Not always available; sometimes wrong if the Google Scholar results are mixed up.
Publisher	Publisher	Not always available; sometimes wrong if the Google Scholar results are mixed up.

COPY >

Click this button to open a popup menu with various copy commands.

✅ **Note:** These commands apply to the *currently displayed set of results only*. If you want to copy data from several queries at once, use the popup menu commands from the multi-query center's list view (see Chapter 6). As an alternative, you can also export the data in a variety of formats.

Command	Description
Copy Statistics as Text	Copies the citation metrics (from the upper text field) to the Windows clipboard in plain text format. You can then paste this text into other applications.
Copy Statistics as CSV	Copies the citation metrics (from the upper text field) to the Windows clipboard in CSV (comma-separated value) format. You can then paste this into other applications for further processing.
Copy Statistics as CSV with Header	Does the same as the previous command, but precedes the statistics with an extra line that contains the names of the fields, also in comma-separated format.
Copy Statistics for Excel	Copies the citation metrics (from the upper text field) to the Windows clipboard in tab-separated format. You can then paste this into other applications for further processing, and in particular into spreadsheet applications such as Microsoft Excel, OpenOffice Calc, and SoftMaker's PlanMaker.
Copy Statistics for Excel with Header	Does the same as the previous command, but precedes the statistics with an extra line that contains the names of the fields, also in tab-separated format.
Copy Results as Text	Copies the results (from the lower list) to the Windows clipboard in plain text format. You can then paste this text into other applications.
Copy Results as CSV	Copies the results (from the lower list) to the Windows clipboard in CSV (comma-separated value) format. You can then paste this into other applications for further processing.
Copy Results as CSV with Header	Does the same as the previous command, but precedes the statistics with an extra line that contains the names of the fields, also in comma-separated format.
Copy Results for Excel	Copies the results (from the lower list) to the Windows clipboard in tab-separated format. You can then paste this into other applications for further processing, and in particular into spreadsheet applications such as Microsoft Excel, OpenOffice Calc, and SoftMaker's PlanMaker.

Copy Results for Excel with Header	Does the same as the previous command, but precedes the statistics with an extra line that contains the names of the fields, also in tab-separated format.

COPY RESULTS

Click this button to copy all currently selected results plus the corresponding metrics to the Windows clipboard. You can then paste them into another application. The keyboard shortcut for this command is **Ctrl+Shift+C**.

CHECK ALL

Click this button to check all items in the results list. Alternatively, press Ctrl+A.

CHECK SELECTION

Click this button to check all selected (i.e., highlighted) items in the results list.

UNCHECK ALL

Click this button to uncheck all items in the results list. Alternatively, press Ctrl+U.

UNCHECK 0 CITES

Click this button to uncheck all results that have 0 citations. Alternatively, press Ctrl+0 (that's zero, not Oh).

UNCHECK SELECTION

Click this button to uncheck all selected (i.e., highlighted) items in the results list.

POPUP MENU

If you right-click anywhere in the results list (lower list), a popup menu appears with additional commands that apply to the currently selected results or to the query as a whole. A full description of these commands can be found in appendix 3.

⊘ **Note:** These commands apply to the *currently displayed set of results only*. If you want to copy data from several queries at once, use the popup menu commands from the multi-query center's list view (See Chapter 6). As an alternative, you can also export the data in a variety of formats.

If you think that one or more separate result items really refer to a single article or book, you can merge them in the results list. You do this by dragging one item and dropping it onto another; the resulting item has a small "double document" icon (see screen shot below). An easy way to find duplicates is by sorting the publications by title, publication, author or year.

This process can be repeated as often as you like. However, you cannot merge a merged title with another merged title. Hence, you will first need to establish which title you will use as a master record and merge all "stray" citations into that master record.

In all cases, the following apply:

- The merged information uses the title, authors, etc. information from the target item (the one onto which the other items are dropped).

- The merged item's total citations are the sum of all constituent items. The citation metrics are updated accordingly.

- The merge persists until you perform the **Lookup [Direct]** command on the parent query.

- You can un-merge the item by right-clicking on the item and choosing **Split Citations** from the popup menu.

Results

Papers:	143	Cites/paper:	15.72	h-index:	22	AWCR:	297.24
Citations:	2248	Cites/author:	1829.09	g-index:	45	AW-index:	17.24
Years:	17	Papers/author:	99.92	hc-index:	19	AWCRpA:	220.46
Cites/year:	132.24	Authors/paper:	1.89	hI-index:	14.67	e-index:	34.90
				hI,norm:	20	hm-index:	19.83

Cites	Per year	Rank	Authors	Title
☑ 163	14.82	1	AW Harzing	An Empirical Analysis and Extension of the Bartle
☑ 159	17.67	2	AW Harzing	Acquisitions versus greenfield investments: Inter
☑ 154	12.83	3	AW Harzing	Managing the multinationals: An international stu
☑ 162	10.13	4	AWK Harzing	The persistent myth of high expatriate failure rai
☑ 114	8.14	5	AW Harzing	Response rates in international mail surveys: res
☑ 106	15.14	6	AW Harzing, J Van Ruysseveldt	International human resource management
☑ **Indicates a merged item**			AW Harzing	Of bears, bumble-bees, and spiders: The role of
☑ 95	11.88	8	AW Harzing, A Sorge	The relative impact of country of origin and unive
☑ 70	7.00	9	AW Harzing	Who's in charge? An empirical study of executive

2.2   CITATION METRICS

Publish or Perish calculates the following citation metrics.
- Total number of papers
- Total number of citations
- Years active
- Average number of citations per year
- Average number of citations per paper

- Average number of citations per author
- Average number of papers per author
- Average number of authors per paper
- Hirsch's h-index and related parameters, shown as **h-index** and **Hirsch a=*y.yy*, m=*z.zz*** in the output. [a and m are shown below the fold]
- Egghe's g-index, shown as **g-index** in the output
- The contemporary h-index, shown as **hc-index** and **ac=*y.yy*** in the output
- Three variations of the individual h-index, shown as **hI-index**, **hI,norm**, and **hm-index** in the output
- The age-weighted citation rate and related metrics
- Zhang's **e-index**.

Calculation of these metrics is explained below roughly in the order in which they appear in the screenshot below. Several less frequently used metrics, such as Hirsch's a and m, are shown "below the fold" and can be accessed by using the scroll bar on the right.

Results

Papers:	73	Cites/paper:	31.97	h-index:	25	AWCR:	328.07
Citations:	2334	Cites/author:	1883.00	g-index:	47	AW-index:	18.11
Years:	16	Papers/author:	52.17	hc-index:	21	AWCRpA:	237.12
Cites/year:	145.88	Authors/paper:	1.67	hI-index:	16.89	e-index:	37.16
				hI,norm:	21	hm-index:	20.83

The various basic statistics (number of papers, number of citations, citations per paper/year and citations/papers per author) in the two most left-hand columns are mostly self-explanatory and will be discussed only very briefly below.

I also provide a brief introduction of the more complex metrics. For a more extensive explanation of these metrics as well as an evaluation of their advantages and disadvantages, see Section 1.4 Citation Metrics.

2.2.1   BASIC METRICS BASED ON PAPERS AND CITATIONS

NUMBER OF PAPERS

Publish or Perish first shows the total number of papers found in Google Scholar. Please note that this is nearly always an overestimation of the total number of papers published by the academic/journal or university in question, as many papers are in fact duplicates, caused by inaccurate referencing.

Hence, the number of papers statistic and any statistics relating to it need to be interpreted with caution, unless you have carefully merged all stray citations into a master record and have unchecked all irrelevant publications.

NUMBER OF CITATIONS

Publish or Perish shows the total number of citations to papers listed for the author, journal, topic or university you search for.

The total number of citations is usually fairly accurate as it is not influenced by duplicates of the same paper. Duplicates increase the number of papers, but not the number of citations.

YEARS (ACTIVE)

"Years" shows the number of years since the author's or journal's first article was published. This is calculated as follows: current year − (first year of publication -1). Hence if someone published his or her first article in 1995 and the current year is 2010, Years is 16. This reflects the number of years in which articles could have been published.

Note that on if the search was conducted early in 2010 or if the first article was published late in 1995, this might lead to a slight overestimation of the number of years the author had been active. Hence Publish or Perish provides a conservative estimate. This does not make much of a difference for established researchers. However, for junior researchers it might mean their citations per year values are not absolutely accurate.

It is advisable to check the "Years" value to see whether it reflects common sense. Obviously, if the value is > 100 for an author, something went wrong with Google Scholar's parsing of the data. However, even finding values of > 40 for authors should lead you to be suspicious, unless the academic is close to retirement. A very easy way to check for offending publications is to sort the data by year. For a detailed example, see Section 3.3.5.

AVERAGE NUMBER OF CITATIONS PER PAPER

The average number of citations per paper is calculated by dividing the total number of citations by the total number of papers.

This can be a very useful metric to assess the average impact for a journal or author. However, it is only correct if you have carefully merged all stray citations into a master record and have unchecked all irrelevant publications.

AVERAGE NUMBER OF CITATIONS PER YEAR

The average number of citations per year is calculated by dividing the total number of citations by the number of years the author or journal has been publishing papers. This can be a very useful metric to assess the yearly impact for a journal or author. It compensates for the time an academic/journal has been active, which provides a fairer comparison for junior academics. As such, it can be used as an alternative to the contemporary h-index.

The unnamed lower list of the results panel also includes the number of citations per year for each individual paper of the author or journal in question. This allows one to assess the impact of each paper when corrected for its age. Sorting on the citation per year column allows one to assess an author's or journal's most influential publications (see screenshot).

Per year	Authors	Title	Year
27.00	NJ Adler, AW Harzing	When knowledge wins: Transcending the sense and nonsense of acad...	2009
23.33	AWK Harzing, R van der...	Google Scholar as a new source for citation analysis	2008
21.22	AW Harzing	Acquisitions versus greenfield investments: International strategy and ...	2002
20.82	AW Harzing	An Empirical Analysis and Extension of the Bartlett and Ghoshal Typolo...	2000
18.71	AW Harzing, J Van Ruys...	International human resource management	2004
17.25	AWK Harzing	Managing the multinationals: An international study of control mechani...	1999
16.50	AW Harzing, R van der ...	A Google Scholar h-index for journals: An alternative metric to measur...	2009
13.25	AW Harzing, A Sorge	The relative impact of country of origin and universal contingencies on i...	2003
10.90	AW Harzing	Of bears, bumble-bees, and spiders: The role of expatriates in controlli...	2001
10.81	AWK Harzing	The persistent myth of high expatriate failure rates	1995
10.00	J Mingers, AW Harzing	Ranking journals in business and management: a statistical analysis of ...	2007
9.20	AW Harzing	Response styles in cross-national survey research	2006
9.14	AW Harzing	Response rates in international mail surveys: results of a 22-country st...	1997
7.67	AW Harzing, AJ Feely	The language barrier and its implications for HQ-subsidiary relationships	2008

AVERAGE NUMBER OF CITATIONS PER AUTHOR

The average number of citations per author is calculated by first dividing the number of citations for each publication by the number of authors for that publication. The resulting citations are then added up.

The resulting number of citations can be seen as the single-authored equivalent for the author or journal in question. For authors, the average number of citations per author therefore gives a fairly good picture of an academic's individual impact and can be used as an alternative to the individual h-index. Please note though that the h-index incorporates both impact and productivity.

AVERAGE NUMBER OF PAPERS PER AUTHOR

The average number of papers per author is calculated by first dividing each publication by the number of authors, resulting in a number between 0 and 1 (sole authorship). Subsequently, these fractional author counts are added up.

The resulting number of papers can be seen as the single-authored equivalent for the author or journal in question. For authors, the average number of papers per author therefore gives a fairly good picture of an academic's individual productivity and can be used as an alternative to the individual h-index. Please note though that the h-index incorporates both impact and productivity.

AVERAGE NUMBER OF AUTHORS PER PAPER

The average number of authors per paper is calculated by adding up the total number of authors involved in the result set for the author or journal in question and dividing this by the number of papers. It gives an indication of the extent to which an author or journal publishes sole authored or co-authored articles. However, as single publications with a large number of authors can increase this metric substantially, it is not as good a reflection of an author's individual productivity as the average number of papers per author.

At the bottom of the unnamed upper-field of the results panel (use the scroll bar to make this part visible), you will also find the median and mode for the number of authors per paper (see screenshot). Although the median does not usually provide much additional information, especially for authors/journals with a relatively low number of co-authors, the mode provides a good assessment of the author's tendency for co-authorship.

Results

Authors/paper 1.67/2.0/1 (mean/median/mode)

35 paper(s) with 1 author(s)
27 paper(s) with 2 author(s)
11 paper(s) with 3 author(s)

Finally, an analysis is shown of the number of papers with a certain number of authors. The screenshot above, which shows my own publication statistics, indicates clearly that I most frequently tend to publish alone or with one co-author.

WORKED EXAMPLE: WHAT CAN ONE CONCLUDE FROM SIMPLE METRICS?

Although most bibliometric analyses tend to focus on complex metrics such as the h-index and its variations, there is a lot one can learn from comparing relatively simple metrics.

Results

Papers:	73	Cites/paper:	31.97
Citations:	2334	Cites/author:	1883.00
Years:	16	Papers/author:	52.17
Cites/year:	145.88	Authors/paper:	1.67

Results

Papers:	23	Cites/paper:	96.48
Citations:	2219	Cites/author:	747.50
Years:	14	Papers/author:	8.42
Cites/year:	158.50	Authors/paper:	3.00

The screenshot above compares my own publication record (left) with that of a colleague (right), chosen because her total number of citations and time since first publication are very similar to mine. As a result, our number of citations per year is fairly similar.

However, it is clear that we have followed different publication strategies. I have published almost three times as many papers as my colleague. An important reason is that she has focused mainly on publications in top US journals, whilst I have published in a wider range of journals. I have also published books and book chapters as well as white papers that attract citations. As a result the number of citations per paper is much higher for my former colleague than for me. This could be seen as evidence of publishing higher quality papers.

However, she has also published with a larger number of co-authors. As a result, my number of "single-authored" citations (cites/author) is 2.5 times as high as hers. The difference in the number of single-authored equivalent papers is even larger, with my record showing 6 times as many single-authored equivalents. This is also reflected in the average number of authors per paper. For my colleague the mean, median and mode are all 3.00.

Neither of these strategies is inherently better than the other. They just reflect different approaches to publishing, which might be shaped by factors such as type and country of doctoral training, country of employment and personal temperaments.

The variety of metrics provided by Publish or Perish allows one to select the metrics most appropriate to one's purpose. However, there are metrics that are designed to combine both productivity (number of papers) and impact (number of citations). The h-index, which will be discussed below, is the most important of these metrics.

2.2.2   METRICS BASED ON MORE COMPLEX CALCULATIONS

Here I only provide the basic calculations of each metric. For a more extensive explanation of these metrics as well as an evaluation of their advantages and disadvantages, see Section 1.4 Citation Metrics.

H-INDEX AND RELATED PARAMETERS

The h-index was proposed by Hirsch (2005). It is defined as follows:

> *A scientist has index h if h of his/her Np papers have at least h citations each, and the other (Np-h) papers have no more than h citations each.*

For instance, an academic has a h-index of 20 if 20 of his/her papers have at least 20 citations each and his/her other papers have no more than 20 citations each. The h-index cannot be larger than the number of papers and academic has published.

PoP calculates and displays the h index proper, its associated proportionality constant a (from $N_{c,tot} = ah^2$), and the rate parameter m (from $h \sim mn$, where n is the number of years since the first publication).

These metrics are shown as **h-index**, **Hirsch a=y.yy, m=z.zz**. To see Hirsch a and m, scroll down in the results view.

G-INDEX

The g-index was proposed by Egghe (2006). It is defined as follows:

> *[Given a set of articles] ranked in decreasing order of the number of citations that they received, the g-index is the (unique) largest number such that the top g articles received (together) at least g2 citations.*

For instance, an academic has a g-index of 30 if the top 30 most cited of his/her papers combined have at least 900 citations. It aims to improve on the h-index by giving more weight to highly-cited articles. The g-index cannot be larger than the number of articles and academic has published. This metric is shown as **g-index** in the output.

E-INDEX

Publish or Perish also calculates the e-index as proposed by Zhang (2009). The e-index is the (square root) of the surplus of citations in the h-set beyond h^2, i.e., beyond the theoretical minimum required to obtain an h-index of 'h'.

For instance, if an academic has an h-index of 10, but has a total of 200 citations to the first 10 published articles, his/her e-index would be 10 (the square root of 200 minus the theoretical minimum required to obtain a h-index of 10, i.e. 100).

The aim of the e-index is to differentiate between scientists with similar h-indices but different citation patterns. It is similar in nature to the g-index in that it gives more attention to highly-cited articles. This metric is shown as **e-index** in the output.

CONTEMPORARY H-INDEX

The Contemporary h-index was proposed by Sidiropoulos, Katsaros & Manolopoulos (2006).

It adds an age-related weighting to each cited article, giving (by default; this depends on the parameterization) less weight to older articles. The weighting is parameterized; the Publish or Perish implementation uses gamma=4 and delta=1, as the authors did for their experiments.

This means that for an article published during the current year, its citations account four times. For an article published 4 years ago, its citations account only one time. For an article published 6 years ago, its citations account 4/6 times, and so on.

This metric is shown as **hc-index** and **ac=y.yy** in the output. To see ac, scroll down in the results view.

INDIVIDUAL H-INDEX (3 VARIATIONS)

The Individual h-index was proposed by Batista, Campiteli, Kinouchi & Martinez (2006). It divides the standard h-index by the average number of authors in the articles that contribute to the h-index, in order to reduce the effects of co-authorship; the resulting index is called h_I.

Publish or Perish also implements an alternative individual h-index, $h_{I,norm}$, that takes a different approach: instead of dividing the total h-index, it first normalizes the number of citations for each paper by dividing the number of citations by the number of authors for that paper, then calculates $h_{I,norm}$ as the h-index of the *normalized* citation counts. This approach is much more fine-grained than both Batista et al.'s and Schreiber's (see below); I believe that it more accurately accounts for any co-authorship effects that might be present and that it is a better approximation of the per-author impact, which is what the original h-index set out to provide.

The third variation is due to Michael Schreiber (2006). Schreiber's method uses fractional paper counts instead of reduced citation counts to account for shared authorship of papers, and then determines the multi-authored h_m index based on the resulting effective rank of the papers using undiluted citation counts.

These metrics are shown as **hI-index** (Batista et al.'s), **hI,norm** (PoP's) and **hm-index** (Schreiber's) in the output.

AGE-WEIGHTED CITATION RATE (AWCR, AWCRPA) AND AW-INDEX

The age-weighted citation rate was inspired by Bihui Jin (2007). The AWCR measures the number of citations to an entire body of work, adjusted for the age of each paper. It is an age-weighted citation rate, where the number of citations to a given paper is divided by the age of that paper. Jin defines the AR-index as the square root of the sum of all age-weighted citation counts over all papers that contribute to the h-index.

However, in the Publish or Perish implementation we sum over all papers instead, because we feel that this represents the impact of the total body of work more accurately. (In particular, it allows younger, as yet less cited papers to contribute to the AWCR, even though they may not yet contribute to the h-index.)

The AW-index is defined as the square root of the AWCR to allow comparison with the h-index; it approximates the h-index if the (average) citation rate remains more or less constant over the years. The per-author age-weighted citation rate is similar to the plain AWCR, but is normalized to the number of authors for each paper.

These metrics are shown as **AWCR**, **AWCRpA** and **AW-index** in the output.

WORKED EXAMPLE: WHAT CAN ONE CONCLUDE FROM COMPLEX METRICS?

Here I return the publication records of me and my colleague. We have similar levels of total citations (2334 vs 2219) and have been active for a similar number of years (16 vs 14). This time I show the more complex metrics. What can we conclude from these?

h-index:	25	AWCR:	328.07
g-index:	47	AW-index:	18.11
hc-index:	21	AWCRpA:	237.12
hI-index:	16.89	e-index:	37.16
hI,norm:	21	hm-index:	20.83

h-index:	17	AWCR:	230.57
g-index:	23	AW-index:	15.18
hc-index:	14	AWCRpA:	77.15
hI-index:	5.67	e-index:	43.45
hI,norm:	13	hm-index:	7.50

H-INDEX

First my record shows a higher h-index than that of my colleague. This is not surprising, given that – as we have seen above – she has published far fewer papers and hence it is more difficult for her to achieve a high h-index. In her case, only six of her papers are **not** included in the h-index. In my case, this is true for nearly two-thirds of my papers.

G-INDEX

My g-index is twice as high as that of my colleague. The simple reason is that neither the g-index nor the h-index can be higher than the total number of papers published and my colleague has only published 23 papers so far. Hence, the maximum her g-index can reach is 23. Even if she would publish another paper without **any** citations, her g-index would still increase. This is clearly a limitation of the g-index.

HC-INDEX

Our reduction in hc-index when compared to the regular h-index is very similar (16-18%), reflecting the similarity of our career stage. Our e-index is also fairly similar, indicating that our number of excess citations over and above what would be the minimum necessary to achieve our regular h-index is also similar.

INDIVIDUAL H-INDEX

The three different versions of the individual h-index, however, provide very different results. For the PoP implementation (hI,norm), our reduction in comparison to the regular h-index is again fairly similar (16-24%). For the two other implementations (hI-index and hm-index) my individual h-index is still fairly similar to hI,norm (16.89 and 20.83 versus 21), but for my colleague it is **much** lower (5.57 and 7.50 versus 13).

The reason is that the two other implementations include a far stronger "punishment" for co-authorship. The hI,norm only reduces the number of **citations** for each paper by accounting for the number of co-authors. This means that papers with a large number of citations can still be included in the h-index if their number of citations after co-author correction is high enough. For authors with a high e-index, this will generally be the case for a substantial number of their papers.

On the other hand, the hI-index simply divides the regular h-index by the total number of authors contributing to the h-index. As my colleague has only one single-authored article and many articles with three or four authors, her hI-index is very low when compared to her regular h-index. Although this is not the case for my colleague, theoretically the hI-index could be brought down by modestly cited articles with a large number of co-authors, even though most of the author's highly cited articles are single-authored.

The hm index converts each paper to a fractional paper count, so that a paper with three authors only counts for 0.33 towards the h-index and a paper with four authors for 0.25. Given that my colleague has many papers with three or four authors, her resulting hm index is fairly low. In fact my hm index is nearly three times as high as hers, even though my regular h-index is only 1.5 times as high.

Someone's preference for one of these three individual h-indices depends on the importance one places on single-authored papers. I would argue that the hI,norm is closest to the initial philosophy of the h-index by focusing on **citations**, rather than on papers.

AWCR

Even though our total numbers of citations are fairly similar, my colleague's AWCR – which takes a "total body of work perspective" is a bit lower. The reason for this is the AWCR's correction for the age of papers. Most of my colleague's most highly cited papers are fairly old (around 10 years), whilst in addition to older papers, I also have a number of recent papers that have already accumulated a large number of citations. Finally, my AWCRpA metric is nearly three times as high as that of my colleague. This is caused purely by the fact that she has generally published with a larger number of co-authors.

CONCLUSIONS

Hence, overall the conclusions are not dissimilar from our earlier analysis based on much simpler metrics. My colleague has published a smaller number of papers that – on average – have more impact and has published with a larger number of co-authors. This does show that simple metrics can in fact already go a long way.

Many users want to conduct additional analyses or data processing with the results gathered from Publish or Perish. In order to facilitate this, you can export the citation data from Publish or Perish to the following formats:

- **BibTeX** - a generally used format for bibliographic references, based on the TeX typesetting program and LaTeX macros.
- **CSV** - a comma-separated values format accepted by most databases and spreadsheets.
- **EndNote Import** - a data exchange format for use with the EndNote program from Thomson ResearchSoft.
- **RIS** - a data exchange format used by a variety of reference managers, including Reference Manager.

The general procedure is as follows:

1. In the results pane, check the citation lines that you want to export. By default, all lines are checked and thus exported.
2. If desired, click on the column headers to sort the data in the desired order. The sort is stable, which means that you can sort by multiple columns by clicking them in succession, but in reverse order. (For example, to sort primarily by author, secondary by year, and tertiary by publication, click on **Publication**, then on **Year**, then on **Authors**.)
3. Choose "File > Save As xxx" from the main menu, where 'xxx' is the desired export format.

In Appendix 4 you can find the details of each format as Publish or Perish implements them. This appendix is provided is for reference only; in general you do not need to know these details if you are exchanging the data with other software that recognizes at least one of these formats.

2.3.1   HOW DO I IMPORT POP DATA INTO EXCEL (OR ACCESS, OR CALC)?

First you must export them in the CSV (Comma Separated Value) format. You can do so by using the **File > Save As CSV...** command from the Publish or Perish main menu.

Then you can import the CSV file into Microsoft Excel, Access, OpenOffice Calc, or a similar program by using that program's **File > Open...** or **File > Import Data...** command.

You need to choose the following settings in the receiving program:

- **File type:** *Text CSV*, or *Comma Separated Value*, depending on the receiving program
- **Character set:** *Unicode (UTF-8)*
- **Separated by:** *Comma* (only; uncheck any other separators)
- **Text delimiter:** " (i.e., the straight double quote)

The following screen shot illustrates these settings (details may vary from program to program).

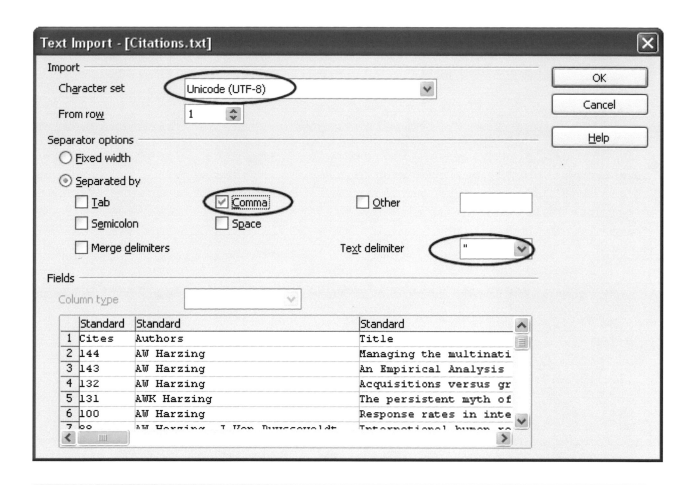

2.4 TROUBLE SHOOTING PROBLEMS

In this section you'll find answers to most of the common questions with regard to the use of Publish or Perish. You may also want to refer to the Message reference in Appendix 5.

2.4.1 PUBLISH OR PERISH DOESN'T FIND ANY OF MY PAPERS!

Assuming that you really have published scholarly papers, there may be several reasons why Publish or Perish doesn't return any results for your name.

- You spelt your name incorrectly. Correct any typos and try again.
- You entered your given names in full instead of as initials. This may find some papers, but many publishers only list the author's initials and a full name search misses those papers. To be on the safe side, try using both full names and initials in a single query, like this (the "quotes" are highly recommended): *"A Harzing" OR "Anne-Wil Harzing"*
- You excluded one or more subject areas. Google Scholar's subject classification is not always perfect: some papers are classified under the wrong subject, others are not classified at all. Select all subject areas and try again.
- Your papers are not available online. If that is the case, then Google Scholar does not know about your papers.

- You published in a language other than English. Google Scholar's coverage is improving, but non-English publications are still underrepresented in the results.

2.4.2 MY PAPER/BOOK DOES NOT APPEAR IN PUBLISH OR PERISH

Publish or Perish uses Google Scholar data to calculate its citation metrics. Google Scholar's processing is automatic (unlike ISI's that involves manual handling and checking, with the associated price tag) and hence occasional errors or omissions do occur.

This may be due to:

- Papers that are not (yet) available online. This includes many older papers.
- The nature of the publication: books and other non-journal publications might not be accessible to Google Scholar.
- Publishing in journals to which Google Scholar has no access because of the publishers' policy.

For more information limitations of Google Scholar, see Chapter 13 which discusses the advantages and disadvantages of the different data sources for citation analyses.

2.4.3 MY PAPER CONTAINS AN INCORRECT TITLE (OR YEAR, AUTHOR NAME OR AUTHOR LIST)

Publish or Perish uses Google Scholar data to calculate its citation metrics. Google Scholar's processing is automatic (unlike ISI's that involves manual handling and checking, with the associated price tag) and hence occasional errors do occur. For more information limitations of Google Scholar, see Chapter 13 which discusses the advantages and disadvantages of the different data sources for citation analyses.

These errors are often due to incorrect or sloppy referencing of your paper by others. Try to find the referencing works to see if this is the case. If these are correct after all, then you can inform Google Scholar of the error (scholar-support@google.com) or lodge an error report here http://www.google.com/support/scholar/bin/request.py?contact_type=general.

Please note though that like Publish or Perish this is a free service and it might take a while before you receive a response. Finally, please note that in some cases your name may be listed incorrectly by the journal publisher itself. In that case of course Google Scholar cannot help.

2.4.4 THE NUMBER OF CITATIONS FOR MY PAPER IS TOO LOW

Publish or Perish uses Google Scholar data to calculate its citation metrics. Google Scholar's processing is automatic (unlike ISI's that involves manual handling and checking, with the associated price tag) and hence occasional errors or omissions do occur.

This may be due to:

- Incorrect or sloppy referencing of your paper by others. Try to find the referencing works to see if this is the case.

- References in older journals or in journals that are not available online. Google Scholar only uses online information; if your paper or the references to it are not online, they will be omitted.
- References in journals to which Google Scholar has no access because of the journals publishers' policy.

For more information limitations of Google Scholar, see Chapter 13 which discusses the advantages and disadvantages of the different data sources for citation analyses.

2.4.5   WHY DOES PUBLISH OR PERISH ALWAYS COUNT YEARS UNTIL THE CURRENT YEAR, AND NOT THE INDICATED PERIOD?

Imagine you have just done a search (any search) with specific start and end years, for example from 2000 to 2005. However, the results do not show "6 years active" as you expected, but "11 years active" (if the search is done in 2010). What's going on?

The simple answer is that the search period (2000 to 2005 in the example) restricts the **original publications**. It does not restrict the **citations**. Regardless of the start and end years in your query, the results will always show the citations until the present day, give or take a few weeks. And because Publish or Perish shows citation statistics, we must count all years from the start year until the present day. Publish or Perish does not have control over this aspect of the results; it's Google Scholar that provides these data.

2.4.6   WHAT IS THIS ERROR 13?

This means that the Google Scholar response to your query contained no recognizable data. Possible causes include:

- The Google Scholar output format has changed.
- Your Internet connection does not work.

While we try to adapt as quickly as possible to changes in the Google Scholar output format, there may be a delay of a few days after Google Scholar introduces a new format.

Furthermore, even after we release a new version of the software, you must update your own copy of Publish or Perish to receive the benefit of the new software version. You can do so through the Publish or Perish web page, or by using the Help > Check for Updates command from the Publish or Perish main menu.

After updating the Publish or Perish software, retry the query using the **Lookup Direct** button (instead of **Lookup**). This retrieves fresh query data from Google Scholar, which might resolve the problem.

If nothing else helps, then please lodge an error report to pop@harzing.com as follows:

1. Repeat the query that failed.
2. Choose the Help > Report Error command from the main menu.

This generates an error report (a plain text file) called *PoPError.txt* that you should attach to your email to the Publish and Perish support address. We need the information in the error report for an accurate diagnosis.

2.4.7 WHAT IS THIS ERROR 1169?

This means that the Google Scholar response to your query contained no entries. Possible causes include:

- A query that did not match any papers. Try changing the query parameters.
- Google Scholar refused access due to an excessive number of prior queries. Retrying the query after an hour or two might resolve the situation.
- Your Internet connection does not work.

If you are unlucky, it could be that your computer is located behind a web proxy that forwards your queries and those of your colleagues to Google Scholar. In that case, all those queries appear to come from a single system as far as Google Scholar is concerned, which may cause it to block further queries from any of you. Contact your local system administrator if you suspect that this might be the case.

2.5 REFERENCES

- Batista, P.D.; Campiteli, M.G.; Konouchi, O.; Martinez, A.S. (2006) **Is it possible to compare researchers with different scientific interests?** *Scientometrics*, 68(1): 179-189.
- Egghe, L. (2006) **Theory and practice of the g-index**, *Scientometrics*, 69(1): 131-152.
- Hirsch, J.E. (2005) **An index to quantify an individual's scientific research output**, *arXiv:physics/0508025* v5 29 Sep 2006.
- Jin B. (2007) **The AR-index: complementing the h-index**, *ISSI Newsletter*, vol. 3(1), p. 6
- Schreiber, M. (2008) **To share the fame in a fair way, h$_m$ modifies h for multi-authored manuscripts**, *New Journal of Physics*, 10: 040201-1-8.
- Sidiropoulos, A.; Katsaros, C.; Manolopoulos, Y. (2006) **Generalized h-index for disclosing latent facts in citation networks**, *arXiv:cs.DL/0607066* v1 13 Jul 2006.
- Zhang, C.-T. (2009) **The e-index, complementing the h-index for excess citations**, *PLoS ONE*, 5(5): e5429.

CHAPTER 3:
AUTHOR SEARCHES

3.1   INTRODUCTION TO AUTHOR SEARCHES

The **Author impact analysis** page allows you to perform a quick analysis of the impact of an author's publications. This page contains a query pane (see Section 3.1.1) with the minimum parameters that are necessary to look up an author's publications on Google Scholar. Publish or Perish uses these parameters to perform an Advanced Scholar Search query, which is then analyzed and converted to a number of statistics.

The results are available on-screen and can also be copied to the Windows clipboard (for pasting in other applications) or saved to a text file (for future reference or further analysis). See General search if you want to perform a search with more parameters than available on the **Author impact analysis** page. For a description of the results pane, see Section 2.1.2.

 Tip: Any queries that you execute on this page are automatically added to the **Recent Queries** folder on the Multi-queries center page.

3.1.1   AUTHOR QUERY PANE

This pane contains the following fields.

AUTHOR(S)

Enter the names of the authors you want to look up. The recommended format is to use one or more initials and to quote each name, for example "A Harzing". Try to use the initials that the author usually publishes under.

EXCLUDE THESE NAMES

Enter any additional names that must not appear in the returned papers. This can be used to narrow down the search for a specific set of papers.

YEAR OF PUBLICATION BETWEEN ... AND ...

Enter the range of years in which the papers must have been published.

SUBJECT AREAS

Check the boxes of the subject areas that you want to search in; clear the others. Clearing all boxes has the same effect as checking them all: the lookup will ignore the subject areas.

Please note that the subject area classification is not always accurate; see "How to perform an effective author impact analysis" for more information

LOOKUP

Click this button to perform the query. If possible, the query is satisfied from the local Publish or Perish cache; this saves time and reduces the load on Google Scholar. If no cache entry for the query exists or the entry is older than the maximum cache age, then the query is forwarded to Google Scholar. After the results are received from Google Scholar, the local cache is automatically refreshed.

Tip: You can change the maximum cache age in the Preferences - Queries dialog box, which is accessible through the File > Preferences command.

LOOKUP DIRECT

Click this button to send the query directly to Google Scholar, bypassing the local Publish or Perish cache. This may be useful if you suspect that Google Scholar may have newer information available than is available through the local cache. When the results are returned from Google Scholar, the local cache is automatically refreshed.

Note: It is not useful to perform multiple direct lookups for the same query shortly after another; this merely increases the load on Google Scholar and increases the chance that your computer may be temporarily denied access by Google Scholar. We recommend that you only use the **Lookup Direct** function as a last resort.

| **3.2** | **HOW TO PERFORM AN EFFECTIVE AUTHOR IMPACT ANALYSIS** |

To perform a basic impact analysis:

1. Enter the author's name in the **Author's name** field;
2. Click **Lookup** or press the **Enter** key.

The program will now contact Google Scholar to obtain the citations, process the list, and calculate the Citation metrics, which are then displayed in the Results pane. The full list of results is also available for inspection or modifications and can be exported in a variety of formats.

Tip: Name matching is case-insensitive; *harzing*, *Harzing*, and *HARZING* all match the same works.

Tip: An author query is **not** the same as a standard Google Scholar search (i.e., from the Google Scholar home page); it is more specific. If you want to duplicate the results from a standard Google Scholar search, then follow the instructions in Section 3.3.1.

3.2.1   REFINING YOUR SEARCH

In many cases, the list of results will contain works of authors that are not the intended author. You can refine the citation search and analysis with one or more of the following methods. If you change any of the fields (except the selections in the **Results** list), you must resubmit the search by clicking **Lookup** again.

INCLUDE AN AUTHOR'S INITIALS

You can use a more detailed author's name, for example by including initials. A search for *Harzing* can be refined by changing it to *"A Harzing"* (or *"Harzing A"*, which has the same effect); likewise, you can use *"CT Kulik"* instead of *"Kulik"* if you know that the author usually publishes with those two initials.

Be careful, though: authors are not always consistent in the initials that they use. Even if they are, references to their articles may use other combinations or formats. It is usually safer to start your search with only one initial.

QUOTING THE AUTHOR'S NAME

By default, Google Scholar matches the name and initials anywhere in the list of authors, so *CT Kulik* would also be matched by *P Kulik, CT Williamson*. To match an author's initials only in combination with her or his own surname, use "quotes" around the author's name: *"CT Kulik"* will **not** match *P Kulik, CT Williamson*, but it will match *CT Kulik, CTM Kulik, NCT Kulik* or any other name that contains both *CT* and *Kulik*.

EXCLUDING CERTAIN AUTHORS

To exclude certain author names, enter them in the **Exclude these names** field. For example, to exclude *CLC Kulik* from the earlier example, enter *"CLC Kulik"* in the **Exclude these names** field. You can enter more than one exclusion in **Exclude these names**: *"CL Kulik" "CLC Kulik"* would exclude both these combinations from the search.

When searching for an author who only publishes with one initial, you can exclude academics with the same last name and first initial through the use of * (see above). For instance Graham Sewell has only published as "G Sewell". One can exclude other academics with the same last name and first initial by using "G* Sewell", "G** Sewell", "G*** Sewell" in the **Exclude these names** field.

This would exclude "GJ Sewell", "GW Sewell", "GWF Sewell" as well as dozens of other combinations in one go. Unfortunately, you can't use "*G Sewell" to exclude "TG Sewell" or "RG Sewell" or "DG Sewell" as this excludes all names including "G Sewell", including our target academic. Hence, these need to be excluded one by one (see screenshot below).

| Author impact | Journal impact | General citations | Multi-query center | Web Browser |

Author impact analysis - Perform a citation analysis for one or more authors

Author's name: "G Sewell"

Exclude these names: "G* sewell" "G** sewell" "G*** Sewell" "WG Sewell" "RG Sewell" "DG Sewell"

Year of publication between: 0   and: 0

Results

Papers:	132	Cites/paper:	10.19	h-index:	12	AWCR:	121.63
Citations:	1345	Cites/author:	903.62	g-index:	35	AW-index:	11.03
Years:	299	Papers/author:	91.00	hc-index:	8	AWCRpA:	78.59
Cites/year:	4.50	Authors/paper:	1.95	hI-index:	6.26	e-index:	31.92
				hI,norm:	9	hm-index:	8.75

Cites		Authors	Title	Year
☑	428	G Sewell, B Wilkinson	Surveillance, discipline and the just-in-time labour process	2001
☑	341	G Sewell	The discipline of teams: the control of team-based industrial work thr...	1998
☑ 🗋	110	P Fleming, G Sewell	Looking for the good soldier, Svejk: Alternative modalities of resistan...	2002

INCLUDING AN AUTHOR'S GIVEN NAME

Another possibility to limit the number of false hits is to include the author's full given name, for instance "Carol Kulik". However, this excludes any publications in which the authors' given names are not spelled out in full. As journals in some fields (e.g. Operations Research) have a tendency use initials only, this might miss many publications.

This strategy is also likely to fail with authors with hyphenated names as these are more likely to be re-produced incorrectly. For instance "Anne-Wil Harzing" only results in 1768 citations, whilst "A Harzing" results in 2346 (all referring to the same academic).

However, a strategy of using "initials + last name" combined with "given name + last name" might be use-ful if an author has mainly published with two or more initials, but has some publications with only one initial. For instance searching for "CT Kulik" or "Carol Kulik" produces results that are identical to the broader search for "C Kulik" with a large number of exclusions (e.g "CC Kulik" "CL Kulik" "CJ Kulik" "JC Ku-lik" "AC KUlik" "JA Kulik" "GC Kulik").

In general though, one should only use the author's given name:
- as a last resort for authors with very common names
- as a very "quick-and-dirty" check to see whether a particular academic has published something.

RESTRICTING THE YEARS OF PUBLICATION

If you know that a certain author only published after (or before) a certain year, you can enter the start or end years in the **Year of publication between ... and ...** fields. You can also use these fields if you want to analyze the author's publications from a given period. Although this strategy is often effective, it has to be used with some care. In some cases Google Scholar's parsing does not include the year of publication in the cited work. This means that if you restrict the years of publication, this work will not show up.

In some isolated cases, differences can be significant. For instance "Estimating and interpreting the instantaneous frequency of a signal. I. Fundamentals" by B. Boashash is incorrectly parsed by Google Scholar which leaves it without a year indication (see below). This means that this author's most cited work (with 580 citations) would be excluded if one restricted the years of publication.

Although Google Scholar is constantly improving these parsing errors, it is safer to re-run the analysis without the year restrictions and check whether there are any highly cited works without a year indication in the results.

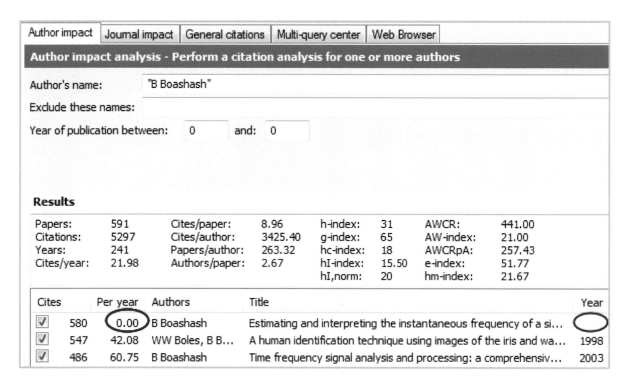

Fortunately, in most cases, this will not impact significantly on the total number of citations and even less so on robust indicators such as the h-index and g-index. For instance searching for "A Harzing" without year limitations results in 2346 citations, whilst including 1995 (the year of my first publication) as a starting year results in 2269 citations. However, the h-index and g-index are not affected.

RESTRICTING THE SUBJECT AREAS

If you know the subject area in which the author usually publishes, you can restrict the search to those areas by checking the corresponding boxes. Please be careful, though: Google's subject classification is not always spot-on. It pays to experiment a little with the **Subject areas** boxes that you check to avoid missing citations. If in doubt, leave all boxes checked; this will return all articles, whether classified or not.

Some examples of misclassifications:

- The following journals are classified under *Social Sciences* rather than *Business*: *Journal of Management*, *The International Journal of Cross-cultural Management*.
- The *J Appl Psychol* (i.e., the *Journal of Applied Psychology*) is sometimes classified under *Business*, sometimes under *Social Sciences*, and sometimes even under *Medicine*.
- Some articles appear not to be classified at all. For instance, a search for the article *Sources of support and expatriate performance* by ML Kraimer et al. succeeds if all **Subject areas** boxes are checked, but fails for any individual subject area.

These errors and omissions appear to occur fairly rarely, so most searches will be reasonably accurate. However, if they do occur, their effect on the citation analysis is that:
- Some articles may be omitted from the results, because they were classified in an unexpected subject area that wasn't included in the search, or weren't classified at all.
- The total number of articles and other statistics may be underestimated for that reason.

INCLUDE OR EXCLUDE INDIVIDUAL WORKS

If the list of results is fairly limited, you can manually include or exclude citations from the analysis by checking or clearing the boxes in the **Results** list.

Here are some shortcuts:

- The **Check all** button places check marks in all boxes;
- The **Uncheck all** button clears all boxes;
- When you use the keyboard to travel up and down in the **Results** list, pressing the space bar toggles the check mark on and off on the selected line.

You can also select a consecutive range of items in the list (left-click on the first item, then hold either Shift key and left-click on the last item) and use the **Check selection/Uncheck selection** buttons to check/uncheck all selected items and recalculate the citation statistics.

Selecting relevant publications can be made easier by first sorting the results by **Cites**, **Authors**, **Title**, **Year**, **Publication**, or **Publisher**. Sorting is done simply by clicking on the corresponding column heading. Click twice to reverse the sort order. Sorting by author is often a very effective way to exclude a range of publications in one go as one can easily identify authors with inappropriate initials or recognize irrelevant co-authors.

 Tip: In contrast to the other refinements, changes in the **Results** list take effect immediately and are reflected in the summary field. You do not have to resubmit your search.

SEARCH FOR MULTIPLE AUTHORS

To search for articles co-written by specific authors, enter all their names in the **Author's name** field: *"C Kulik" "M Ambrose"* will return only articles that have both authors in their author list (see below).

Author impact analysis - Perform a citation analysis for one or more authors

Author's name: "C Kulik" "M Ambrose"

Exclude these names:

Year of publication between: and:

Results

Papers:	15	Cites/paper:	73.53	h-index:	11	AWCR:	66.38
Citations:	1103	Cites/author:	413.80	g-index:	15	AW-index:	8.15
Years:	25	Papers/author:	5.78	hc-index:	7	AWCRpA:	26.39
Cites/year:	44.12	Authors/paper:	2.93	hI-index:	3.78	e-index:	30.95
				hI,norm:	8	hm-index:	5.03

Cites	Authors	Title	Year
☑ 292	ML Ambrose, CT Kulik	Old friends, new faces: Motivation research in ...	1999
☑ 273	EA Lind, CT Kulik, M Ambrose, MV de Vera ...	Individual and corporate dispute resolution: Usi...	1993
☑ 160	CT Kulik, ML Ambrose	Personal and situational determinants of refere...	1992
☑ 97	GR Oldham, CT Kulik, LP Stepina, ML ...	Relations between situational factors and the c...	1986
☑ 89	GR Oldham, CT Kulik, ML Ambrose, LP Ste...	Relations between job facet comparisons and ...	1986
☑ 78	ML Ambrose, LK Harland, CT ...	Influence of social comparisons on perceptions ...	1991

You can also use the logical OR operator in the field to find articles written by either author or by both: *"C Kulik" OR "M Ambrose"* returns articles authored by *C Kulik* and *M Ambrose* separately (although possibly with others), or co-authored by both.

This strategy is also useful if you are searching for an author who has published under different names. The most frequent reason for this is women publishing under their maiden and married name or under different married names. Using the OR operator will allow you to find all publications of the academic in question. Of course the inclusion of multiple names will make it more difficult to disambiguate the academic in question.

✓ **Tip:** Do **not** try to use the AND keyword in an author search. Google Scholar does not recognize this keyword and will treat it as a normal search word. Instead, just enter multiple author names; this will behave as an "and" search by default.

3.2.2   STEP-BY-STEP SEARCH STRATEGY

I have found that the following search strategy is often very effective:

1. Search for the target academic's name with his/her first initial and surname in quotes, e.g. *"A Harzing"*. Please note that Google Scholar matches the surname and initials anywhere in the initials+surname combination, so *"C Kulik"* would be matched by *CT Kulik* (our target academic), *CLC Kulik*, but also by *PC Kulik*.

2. It is generally better to use fewer initials and then exclude the ones you don't want (see next point) instead of using more initials, because many citations (or authors) are sloppy with the in-

itials they use. With too many initials in the **Author's name** field you run the risk of missing a substantial number of relevant articles.

3. To exclude certain names, enter them in the **Exclude these names** field. For example, to exclude *CLC Kulik* from the previous example, enter *"CLC Kulik"* in the **Exclude these names** field (and keep *"C Kulik"* in the **Author's name** field). You can enter more than one exclusion in **Exclude these names**: *"CL Kulik" "CLC Kulik"* would exclude both these combinations from the search.

4. A quicker way to exclude names for academics who have only published with one or two initials is to use *. For instance, any authors with three or more initials could be excluded from the above search by including *"C** Kulik"* in the **Exclude these names** field. This strategy is particularly effective for academics who systematically publish with one initial only.

5. Ensure you have ticked the relevant subject areas, but do not define these too narrow. For academics in Management for instance, it is usually safest to click both **Business** and **Social Sciences**.

6. If the result includes publications not published by the target academic, deselect those publications (remove the tick mark in the first column by clicking on it). If the list is long, it might be easier to deselect all publications first and then only select the relevant publications. Please note that any titles with less than 5 citations usually have very little or no impact on the h-index, but might influence the g-index. Hence, if you are faced with a very long list and are only interested in the h-index, you might consider deselecting all and only reviewing titles with 5 or more citations.

7. Selecting relevant publications can be made easier by first sorting the results by **Cites**, **Authors**, **Title**, **Year**, **Publication**, or **Publisher**. Sorting is done simply by clicking on the corresponding column heading. Click twice to reverse the sort order.

3.3 HOW TO IMPROVE ACCURACY IN AUTHOR SEARCHES

The citation analysis is based on the results returned by Google Scholar. These are not always 100% accurate. Here are some issues to be aware of. Please also note that Google Scholar limits its results to 1000. The results are ranked by number of citations, so the 1000 shown are the most-cited results.

3.3.1 RESULTS THAT DIFFER FROM GOOGLE SCHOLAR

If the Publish or Perish results differ from the ones you get by using Google Scholar directly, this is typically caused by the fact that Publish or Perish uses the Advanced Scholar Search capabilities of Google Scholar, whereas your manual search probably used the standard Google Scholar search.

The latter is equivalent to an **All of the words** search, which matches the search terms anywhere in the searched documents (author, title, source, abstract, references etc.) and usually provides far too many irrelevant results for an effective citation analysis.

If you would for instance search for my family name using the standard Google Scholar search (i.e. all of the words) rather than the author search, you would get nearly 8,000 citations. This search matches "harzing" anywhere in the document, including articles citing my work that appear full-text in Google Scholar.

General citation search - Perform a general citation search

Author(s):	
Publication:	
All of the words:	harzing
Any of the words:	
None of the words:	
The phrase:	
Year of publication between:	0 and: 0

Results

Papers:	1000	Cites/paper:	7.90	h-index:	49	AWCR:	1217.98
Citations:	7902	Cites/author:	5140.43	g-index:	73	AW-index:	34.90
Years:	39	Papers/author:	661.17	hc-index:	35	AWCRpA:	747.76
Cites/year:	202.62	Authors/paper:	1.98	hI-index:	24.75	e-index:	46.58
				hI,norm:	35	hm-index:	36.33

Cites	Authors	Title
☑ 222	RL Tung	American expatriates abroad: From neophytes to cosmopolitans
☑ 183	KD Brouthers, LE Brouthers	Acquisition or greenfield start-up? Institutional, cultural and transactio..
☑ 175	AW Harzing	Acquisitions versus greenfield investments: International strategy an...
☑ 175	KD Brouthers, LE Brouthers	Explaining the national cultural distance paradox
☑ 170	AW Harzing	An Empirical Analysis and Extension of the Bartlett and Ghoshal Typol...
☑ 167	AWK Harzing	Managing the multinationals: An international study of control mechan..
☑ 159	A Ferner, J Quintanilla	Multinationals, national business systems and HRM: the enduring influ...
☑ 157	AWK Harzing	The persistent myth of high expatriate failure rates
☑ 138	CE Lance, MM Butts, LC Michels	The sources of four commonly reported cutoff criteria: What did they ..
☑ 137	G Morgan, PH Kristensen, R ...	The multinational firm: organizing across institutional and national divide:
☑ 123	N Forster	The persistent myth of high expatriate failure rates': a reappraisal
☑ 123	AW Harzing	Response rates in international mail surveys: results of a 22-country s..
☑ 120	FJ Acedo, C Barroso, JL Galan	The resource-based theory: Dissemination and main trends

However, if you do want to get the same results in Publish or Perish as with a standard Google Scholar search, do the following.

1. Go to the General citation search page.
2. Empty all text fields *except* **All of the words**.
3. Enter your query terms in the **All of the words** field.
4. Set the **Year of publication** fields both to 0.
5. Make sure that all subject area boxes are checked.
6. Clear the **Title words only** field.
7. Click on **Lookup**.
8. When the results appear, click on the **Rank** column header to sort the results in the order in which Google Scholar returned them.

3.3.2 INEFFECTIVE QUERIES

Not all queries return the results you would expect. You might have to refine your queries to get the most accurate results. Some tell-tale signs of ineffective queries are:

TOO MANY RESULTS THAT YOU ARE NOT INTERESTED IN

This is typically caused by criteria or search terms that are too broad. Try to refine your search as detailed in Section 3.2.

MISSING WORKS

This may be caused by problems with subject area classification or because you have restricted the year range. See the "Restricting the subject area" and "Restricting the year range" in Section 3.2 for details.

3.3.3 MIXED-UP TITLE AND SOURCE FIELDS

Some references contain mixed-up fields as illustrated in the second reference below:

Cites	Authors	Title	Source	
☑6	AW Harzing	Acquisitions Versus Greenfield I...		▲
☑4	AW Harzing	K., 1999	Managing the Multinationals: an Interna	

This is caused by garbled information returned by Google Scholar, presumably because its sources were inaccurate or difficult to parse automatically by Google's web crawler.

The effect on the citation analysis is similar to having duplicates (see below), because some works end up as separate entries instead of being included with the correct title. Since Version 3.0 of Publish or Perish duplicates can be merged into the master record. See Section 2.1.3 for further details.

3.3.4 AUTHOR OF PUBLICATION LISTED UNDER TITLE

For some references Google Scholar lists the author name as part of the title, rather than including the author's name in the author field, presumably because its sources were inaccurate or difficult to parse automatically by Google's web crawler.

As a result the reference does not show up if you search using the author's name in an author query, as this query only lists results where the name is listed in the author field. For example, the following highly cited paper by *Anbulagan* did not show up when searching for his name in the author field [this particular problem has since been fixed by Google Scholar].

```
[CITATION] Anbulagan. Heuristics based on unit propagation for satisfiabil-
ity problems
CM Li - Proceedings of the International Joint Conference on ..., 1997
Cited by 237
```

If you have reason to believe that certain publications of a particular author are missing, you might want to repeat the search using a general query with the author's name in the **Any of the words** field. This query searches for the author's name in all parts of the database. Whilst it normally provides a large range of irrelevant results (especially if an author's name is also a common noun, e.g. *Robert Wood*), it does allow you to find publications where Google Scholar has accidentally misplaced the author's name.

3.3.5   YEARS VALUE SEEMS IMPOSSIBLE

It is advisable to check the "Years" to see whether it reflects common sense. Obviously, if the value is >100 for an author, something is wrong with the Google Scholar data. However, even finding values of >40 for authors should lead you to be suspicious, unless the academic is close to retirement. A very easy way to do so is to sort the data by year. This will allow you to easily spot the offending publications.

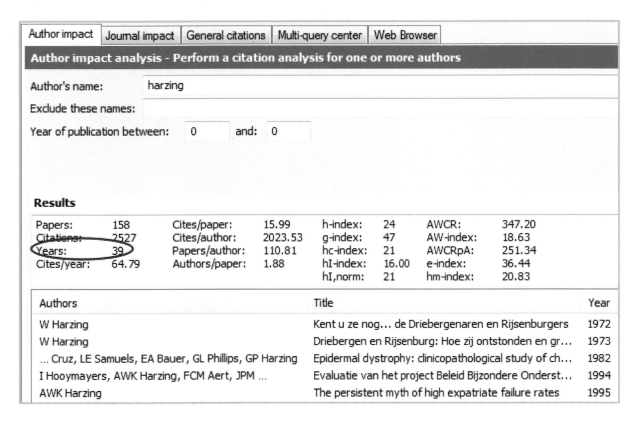

As my last name (Harzing) is fairly unique and there are no other academics with the same last name that publish regularly, I often tend to conduct Publish or Perish searches with my last name only (see screenshot). However, this leads to a Years value of 39, which make me either feel very old or a genius who published at a very young age. Sorting by year easily allows me to spot the offending publications.

The first two publications are historical books by my late grandfather (Wim Harzing) about the city in which he lived. The third publication is the only publication ever by GP Harzing, who seems to have acted as a research assistant on a project on epidermal dystrophy. The fourth publication is a Masters thesis that I supervised. My name and those of the two other supervisors were accidentally added as authors. Hence sorting by year is also a very good way to separate your own publications from those of a name-sake from an earlier generation.

For most authors you will notice duplicate or near-duplicate articles in the **Results** list. These duplicates may be due to one or more of the following:

- Sloppy referencing. Not all references to an author's work are perfectly accurate and small differences in the names of the authors, the article's title, or its sources may cause the same article to appear more than once.
- Other funnies. Google Scholar occasionally appears to return duplicate citations or just different results for the same query. This seems to happen particularly when the name you are looking for appears both as a given name and a surname in the returned results, for example *Martin, Neal, Tania*. If this happens, a second **Lookup** (with the same parameters) may return more accurate results.

The effect on the citation analysis is that:

- The total number of articles may come out higher than the actual number, because duplicates are counted separately.
- The citations per paper may come out lower, for the same reason.
- The h-index and g-index may come out differently, because citations are spread over the duplicates.

Since Version 3.0 of Publish or Perish, duplicates can be merged into the master record, simply by dragging the stray citation onto the master record. An example of a merged record is shown in the screenshot below. See Section 2.1.3 for further details on how to do this.

Results

Papers:	143	Cites/paper:	15.72	h-index:	22	AWCR:	297.24	
Citations:	2248	Cites/author:	1829.09	g-index:	45	AW-index:	17.24	
Years:	17	Papers/author:	99.92	hc-index:	19	AWCRpA:	220.46	
Cites/year:	132.24	Authors/paper:	1.89	hI-index:	14.67	e-index:	34.90	
				hI,norm:	20	hm-index:	19.83	

Cites		Per year	Rank	Authors	Title
☑	163	14.82	1	AW Harzing	An Empirical Analysis and Extension of the Bartle
☑	159	17.67	2	AW Harzing	Acquisitions versus greenfield investments: Inter
☑	154	12.83	3	AW Harzing	Managing the multinationals: An international stu
☑	162	10.13	4	AWK Harzing	The persistent myth of high expatriate failure rat
☑	114	8.14	5	AW Harzing	Response rates in international mail surveys: res
☑	106	15.14	6	AW Harzing, J Van Ruysseveldt	International human resource management
☑	**Indicates a merged item**			AW Harzing	Of bears, bumble-bees, and spiders: The role of
☑	95	11.88	8	AW Harzing, A Sorge	The relative impact of country of origin and unive
☑	70	7.00	9	AW Harzing	Who's in charge? An empirical study of executive

CHAPTER 4:
JOURNAL SEARCHES

4.1   INTRODUCTION TO JOURNAL SEARCHES

The **Journal impact analysis** page allows you to perform a quick analysis of the impact of a journal's publications. This page contains a query pane (see Section 4.1.1) with the minimum parameters that are necessary to look up the journal's publications on Google Scholar. Publish or Perish uses these parameters to perform an Advanced Scholar Search query, which is then analyzed and converted to a number of statistics.

The results are available on-screen and can also be copied to the Windows clipboard (for pasting in other applications) or saved to a text file (for future reference or further analysis). See General search if you want to perform a search with more parameters than available on the **Journal impact analysis** page. For a description of the results pane, see Section 2.1.2.

 Tip: Any queries that you execute on this page are automatically added to the **Recent Queries** folder on the Multi-queries center page.

4.1.1   JOURNAL QUERY PANE

This pane contains the following fields.

JOURNAL TITLE

Enter the name of the journal you want to look up. The recommended format is the full title enclosed in quotes, for example "Journal of International Business". However, you might have to experiment with common abbreviations as well.

EXCLUDE THESE WORDS

Enter any additional words that must not appear in the returned papers. This can be used to narrow down the search for a specific set of papers.

YEAR OF PUBLICATION BETWEEN ... AND ...

Enter the range of years in which the papers must have been published.

SUBJECT AREAS

Check the boxes of the subject areas that you want to search in; clear the others. Clearing all boxes has the same effect as checking them all: the lookup will ignore the subject areas.

Please note that the subject area classification is not always accurate; see "How to perform an effective journal impact analysis" for more information

---

LOOKUP

Click this button to perform the query. If possible, the query is satisfied from the local Publish or Perish cache; this saves time and reduces the load on Google Scholar. If no cache entry for the query exists or the entry is older than the maximum cache age, then the query is forwarded to Google Scholar. After the results are received from Google Scholar, the local cache is automatically refreshed.

✅ **Tip:** You can change the maximum cache age in the Preferences - Queries dialog box, which is accessible through the File > Preferences command.

LOOKUP DIRECT

Click this button to send the query directly to Google Scholar, bypassing the local Publish or Perish cache. This may be useful if you suspect that Google Scholar may have newer information available than is available through the local cache. When the results are returned from Google Scholar, the local cache is automatically refreshed.

Note: It is not useful to perform multiple direct lookups for the same query shortly after another; this merely increases the load on Google Scholar and increases the chance that your computer may be temporarily denied access by Google Scholar. We recommend that you only use the **Lookup Direct** function as a last resort.

4.2   HOW TO PERFORM AN JOURNAL IMPACT ANALYSIS

To perform a basic impact analysis:

1. Enter the journal title in the **Journal title** field;
2. Click **Lookup** or press the **Enter** key.

The program will now contact Google Scholar to obtain the citations, process the list, and calculate the Citation metrics, which are then displayed in the Results pane. The full list of results is also available for inspection or modifications and can be exported in a variety of formats.

✅ **Tip:** A journal query is **not** the same as a standard Google Scholar search (i.e., from the Google Scholar home page); it is more specific. If you want to duplicate the results from a standard Google Scholar search, then follow the instructions in Section 4.3.1.

4.2.1   REFINING YOUR ANALYSIS

In many cases, the results will contain works of journals that are not the intended journal. You can refine the citation search and analysis with one or more of the following methods.

✅ Tip: Title matching is case-insensitive; *Journal, journal,* and *JOURNAL* all match the same publications.

✅ Tip: If you change the any of the fields (except the selections in the **Results** list), you must resubmit the search by clicking **Lookup** again.

QUOTING THE JOURNAL'S TITLE

Google Scholar is not sensitive to the word order in the journal title field. *Journal of Management* will not only match *Journal of Management Studies* and *British Journal of Management*, it will also match *Strategic Management Journal* or *Academy of Management Journal*.

In order to avoid this put "quotes" around the journal title: "*Journal of Management*" will only be matched by journal with the words in that order. However, it will still be matched by *Journal of Management Studies* or *"British Journal of Management"*.

Google Scholar will also provide results where the search term matches the **publisher** rather than the source title, i.e., a working paper published by a *Department of Accounting and Finance* might also match a search for *"Accounting and Finance"*.

The easiest way to exclude unwanted results is to sort the results by journal title, select all unwanted journals and click the button "Uncheck selection". For further details see "How to Improve Accuracy in Journal Searches" below.

| Author impact | Journal impact | General citations | Multi-query center | Web Browser |

Journal impact analysis - Perform a citation analysis for one or more journals

Journal title: "Academy of Management Journal"

Exclude these words:

Year of publication between: 0   and: 0

Results

Papers:	1000	Cites/paper:	242.17	h-index:	277	AWCR:	15522.62
Citations:	242170	Cites/author:	145453.52	g-index:	428	AW-index:	124.59
Years:	46	Papers/author:	580.73	hc-index:	121	AWCRpA:	8965.47
Cites/year:	5264.57	Authors/paper:	2.10	hI-index:	134.14	e-index:	267.77
				hI,norm:	199	hm-index:	219.10

	Cites	Authors	Title	Year	Publication
☑	3504	MA Huselid	The impact of human resource management...	1995	Academy of management journal
☑	2392	R Gulati	Does familiarity breed trust? The implication...	1995	Academy of management journal
☑	2062	DJ McAllister	Affect-and cognition-based trust as foundat...	1995	Academy of management journal
☑	1693	KM Eisenhardt	Making fast strategic decisions in high-veloci...	1989	Academy of Management Journal
☑	1621	JB Arthur	Effects of human resource systems on man...	1994	Academy of Management journal

The screenshot above shows a search for the *Academy of Management Journal*, one of the top journals in the field of Business without any year limitations. It is apparent that some articles are cited very frequently, but many of these are 15-20 years old. In order to get a better feel for the impact of articles from a specific period of time one can restrict the years of publication (see below).

EXCLUDING CERTAIN JOURNALS

To exclude certain journal titles, enter them in the **Exclude these words** field. For example, to exclude journals with the word *Strategic* in their title from the earlier example, enter *Strategic* in the **Exclude these words** field. You can enter more than one exclusion in **Exclude these words**: *Strategic Academy* would exclude all journals whose titles contained either or both these words (see below).

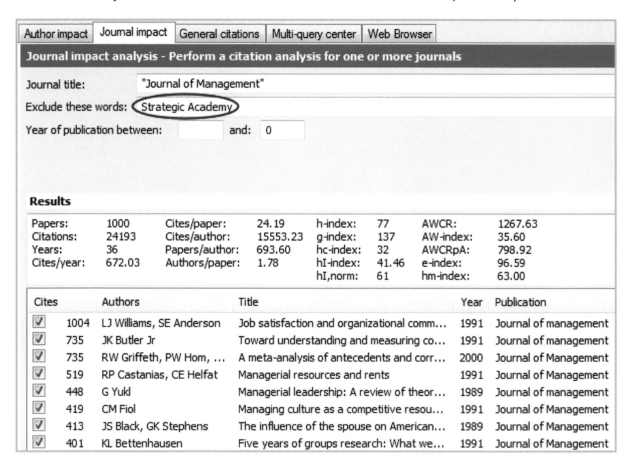

This strategy needs to be applied with extreme care, however, as Google Scholar matches "exclude these words" anywhere in the papers (i.e. including the list of references for those publications that have full-text online access).

RESTRICTING THE YEARS OF PUBLICATION

If you know that a certain journal only existed after (or before) a certain year, you can enter the start or end years in the **Year of publication between ... and ...** fields. You can also use these fields if you want to analyse the journal's publications from a given period.

In the above example for the *Academy of Management Journal*, we saw that some articles were cited more than 1500 times. However, if we limit the search to a specific year range, we get a better feel for average impact for articles published in that period (see below).

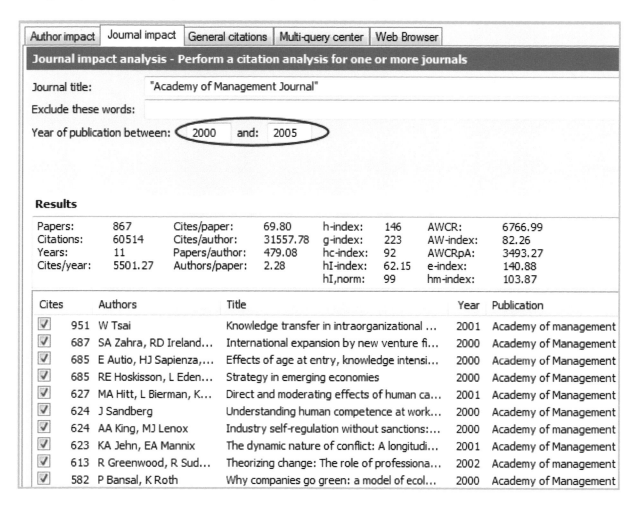

RESTRICTING THE SUBJECT AREAS

If you know the subject area in which the journal is usually classified, you can restrict the search to those areas by checking the corresponding boxes. Please be careful, though: Google's subject classification is not always spot-on. For example, the following journals are classified under *Social Sciences* rather than *Business*: *Administrative Science Quarterly*, *Journal of Management*, and *The International Journal of Cross-cultural Management*.

If the list of results is fairly limited, you can manually include or exclude citations from the analysis by checking or clearing the boxes in the **Results** list.

⊘ **Tip:** In contrast to the other refinements, changes in the **Results** list take effect immediately and are reflected in the summary field. You do not have to resubmit your search.

Here are some shortcuts:
- The **Check all** button places check marks in all boxes;
- The **Uncheck all** button clears all boxes;
- When you use the keyboard to travel up and down in the **Results** list, pressing the space bar toggles the check mark on and off on the selected line.

You can also select a consecutive range of items in the list (left-click on the first item, then hold either Shift key and left-click on the last item) and use the **Check selection/Uncheck selection** buttons to check/uncheck all selected items and recalculate the citation statistics.

4.2.2   SEARCHING FOR CITATIONS OF CHAPTERS IN AN EDITED VOLUME

Although journals are the most common sources of publications, the Journal Impact search can also be used to search for publications in other sources. Edited book volumes are a common source in the Social Sciences and Humanities.

Typically a lot of authors will refer to individual chapters within an edited book. Hence, in order to assess the overall impact of this book, one would need to search for citations to individual chapters as well as citations to the book as a whole.

The easiest way to search for citations to the book as a whole is to search for the editor of the book. To find citations of chapters that appear in an edited volume, use the following parameters:

- **Journal title**: enter the title of the edited volume, preferably within quotes.
- **Year of publication between ... and ...**: enter the copyright year of the volume in both fields.
- Depending on the number of matches that you find, you may want to use the **Exclude these words** field to restrict the search.

WORKED EXAMPLE: HANDBOOK OR ORGANIZATION STUDIES

In 1996 Cynthia Hardy, Stewart Clegg and Walter Nord published the *Handbook of Organization Studies*. If we want to establish the impact that this handbook has had on the field, we need to be able to accumulate citations to all chapters in this handbook.

When searching for the editors, I found a total of 397 citations to the Handbook as such. As described in Section 3.1.1, this can be done easily by including the three family names in the author's name field. Google Scholar then only provides publications co-written by these three authors.

In addition, searching for the editors displayed another 327 citations – spread of 22 separate entries – for individual chapters in the handbook (see screenshot below). In these cases, the editors had accidentally been interpreted as chapter co-authors authors by the Google Scholar parsing.

However, the combined number of 724 citations still substantially underestimates the total impact of this book. To see why this is the case, one needs to conduct a systematic search for citations to chapters within the edited volume.

| Author impact | Journal impact | General citations | Multi-query center | Web Browser |

Author impact analysis - Perform a citation analysis for one or more authors

Author's name: Hardy Clegg Nord

Exclude these names:

Year of publication between: 1996 and: 1996

Results

Papers:	23	Cites/paper:	31.48	h-index:	11	AWCR:	48.27
Citations:	724	Cites/author:	203.65	g-index:	23	AW-index:	6.95
Years:	15	Papers/author:	5.35	hc-index:	6	AWCRpA:	13.58
Cites/year:	48.27	Authors/paper:	4.43	hI-index:	2.33	e-index:	22.91
				hI,norm:	5	hm-index:	4.27

Cites	Authors	Title	Year
☑ 397	SR Clegg, C Hardy, WR Nord	Handbook of organization studies	1996
☑ 54	JAC Baum, SR Clegg, C Hardy, WR Nord	Handbook of organization studies	1996
☑ 43	PS Tolbert, LG Zucker, S Clegg, C Hardy, WR Nord	Handbook of organization studies	1996
☑ 30	KE Weick, F Westley, SR Clegg, C Hardy, WR Nord	Handbook of organization studies	1996
☑ 27	MB Calás, L Smircich, S Clegg, C Hardy, W Nord	Handbook of organization studies	1996
☑ 24	M Alvesson, S Deetz, SR Clegg, C Hardy, WR Nord	Handbook of organization studies	1996
☑ 19	C Eden, C Huxham, S Clegg, C Hardy, W Nord	Handbook of organization studies	1996
☑ 16	... , N Phillips, P Chapman, SR Clegg, C Hardy, WR Nord	Handbook of organization studies	1996
☑ 12	A Bryman, S Clegg, C Hardy, WR Nord	Handbook of organization studies	1996
☑ 12	JB Barney, W Hesterly, SR Clegg, C Hardy, WR Nord	Handbook of organization studies	1996
☑ 12	SM Nkomo, T Cox, SR Clegg, C Hardy, WR Nord	Handbook of organization studies	1996
☑ ⧉ 11	D Dougherty, SR Clegg, C Hardy, WR Nord	Handbook of organization studies	1996
☑ 11	R Whipp, SR Clegg, C Hardy, W Nord	Handbook of organization studies	1996
☑ 10	... , DJ Hickson, DC Wilson, S Clegg, C Hardy, W NORD	Handbook of organization studies	1996
☑ 8	M Reed, SR Clegg, C Hardy, WR Nord	Handbook of organization studies	1996
☑ 7	L Donaldson, S Clegg, C Hardy, R Nord	Handbook of Organization Studies	1996
☑ 7	S Fineman, SR Clegg, C Hardy, WR Nord	Handbook of organization studies	1996
☑ 5	J Martin, P Frost, SR Clegg, C Hardy, WR Nord	Handbook of organization studies	1996
☑ 5	R Stablein, SR Clegg, C Hardy, WR Nord	Handbook of organization studies	1996
☑ 4	G Burrell, SR Clegg, C Hardy, W Nord	Handbook of organization studies	1996
☑ 4	P Gagliardi, S Clegg, C Hardy, WR Nord	Handbook of Organization Studies	1996
☑ 4	RC Stewart, C Hardy, RW Nord	Handbook of Organization Studies	1996
☑ 2	B Parker, SR Clegg, C Hardy, W NORD	Handbook of organization studies	1996

The screenshot below shows that another 2183 citations can be found when search for citations to individual chapters within the handbook when searching through the procedure described above. Hence, less than 14% of the total number of citations to the Handbook was to the handbook as a whole.

It is needless to say that the editors of the Handbook could make a much stronger case for the impact of the Handbook if they conducted a comprehensive citation search as described above. As edited volumes are an important way to publish state-of-the art research in some disciplines, it is very important to be able to conduct a comprehensive citation search for all references to the edited volume.

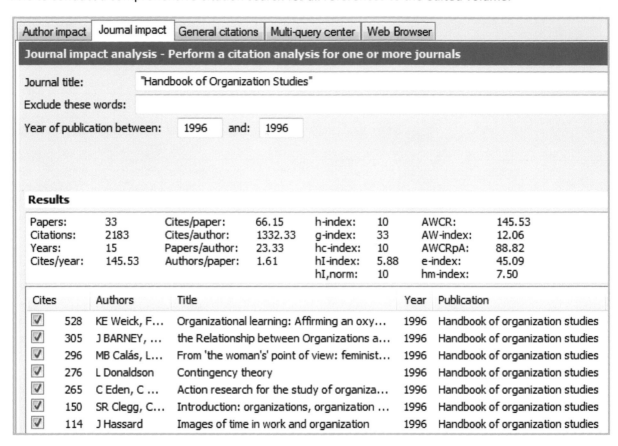

4.3.1   RESULTS THAT DIFFER FROM GOOGLE SCHOLAR

If the Publish or Perish results differ from the ones you get by using Google Scholar directly, this is typically caused by the fact that Publish or Perish uses the Advanced Scholar Search capabilities of Google Scholar, whereas your manual search probably used the standard Google Scholar search.

The latter is equivalent to an **All of the words** search, which matches the search terms anywhere in the searched documents (author, title, source, abstract, references etc.) and usually provides too many irrelevant results for an effective citation analysis.

If you would for instance search for *Journal of International Business Studies* using the standard Google Scholar search (i.e. all of the words) rather than the **journal** search, many of your highly cited results would not refer to this journal (see screenshot). This search matches "Journal of International Business Studies" anywhere in the document, including articles published in other journals that cite articles in Journal of International Business Studies.

| Author impact | Journal impact | General citations | Multi-query center | Web Browser |

General citation search - Perform a general citation search

Author(s):	
Publication:	
All of the words:	"Journal of International Business Studies"
Any of the words:	
None of the words:	
The phrase:	
Year of publication between:	0 and: 0

Results

Papers:	1000	Cites/paper:	232.33	h-index:	218	AWCR:	13992.13
Citations:	232328	Cites/author:	162712.03	g-index:	457	AW-index:	118.29
Years:	53	Papers/author:	647.45	hc-index:	110	AWCRpA:	8990.22
Cites/year:	4383.55	Authors/paper:	1.91	hI-index:	121.23	e-index:	356.07
				hI,norm:	172	hm-index:	174.17

Cites	Rank	Authors	Title	Publication
☑ 15086	790	RH Coase	The problem of social cost	The journal of Law and Economics
☑ 6550	591	OE Williamson	Transaction-cost economics: t…	The journal of Law and Economics
☑ 5691	552	P Krugman	Increasing returns and econo…	Journal of political economy
☑ 4787	740	EF Fama, JD Mac…	Risk, return, and equilibrium: …	Journal of political economy
☑ 4247	684	MT Hannan, J Fre…	The population ecology of org…	ajs
☑ 3712	①	J Johanson, JE Va…	The internationalization proce…	Journal of international business st…
☑ 3601	668	A Shleifer, RW Vis…	Large shareholders and corpo…	The Journal of Political Economy
☑ 3423	667	MC Jensen, KJ Mu…	Performance pay and top-ma…	Journal of political economy
☑ 3268	478	O Hart, J Moore	Property Rights and the Natu…	Journal of political economy
☑ 2353	541	OE Williamson	The economics of organizatio…	ajs
☑ 2348	728	B Kogut	Joint ventures: Theoretical an…	Strategic management journal
☑ 2315	469	MH Miller, F Modig…	Dividend policy, growth, and t…	Journal of business
☑ 2200	610	HS Becker	Notes on the concept of com…	ajs
☑ 2031	④	B Kogut, H Singh	The effect of national culture …	Journal of international business st…
☑ 1970	767	JL Zaichkowsky	Measuring the involvement co…	Journal of consumer research

As a result you will get many highly cited articles referring to articles in Journal of International Business Studies, rather than **published** in Journal of International Business Studies. This is also illustrated by the difference in citation rank and Google Scholar rank. These articles are highly cited (hence highly ranked on citations), but not very relevant to the search (hence low-ranked on the Google Scholar rank).

However, if you do want to get the same results in Publish or Perish as with a standard Google Scholar search, do the following.

1. Go to the General citation search page.
2. Empty all text fields *except* **All of the words**.
3. Enter your query terms in the **All of the words** field.
4. Set the **Year of publication** fields both to 0.
5. Make sure that all subject area boxes are checked.
6. Clear the **Title words only** field.
7. Click on **Lookup**.
8. When the results appear, click on the **Rank** column header to sort the results in the order in which Google Scholar returned them.

4.3.2   DUPLICATE RESULTS

Occasionally you might notice duplicate or near-duplicate articles in the **Results** list. These duplicates may be due to one or more of the following:

- Sloppy referencing. Not all references to an author's work are perfectly accurate and small differences in the names of the authors, the article's title, or its sources may cause the same article to appear more than once.
- Other funnies. Google Scholar occasionally appears to return duplicate citations or just different results for the same query. This seems to happen particularly when the name you are looking for appears both as a given name and a surname in the returned results, for example *Martin, Neal, Tania*. If this happens, a second **Lookup** (with the same parameters) may return more accurate results.

The effect on the citation analysis is that:

- The total number of articles may come out higher than the actual number, because duplicates are counted separately.
- The citations per paper may come out lower, for the same reason.
- The h-index and g-index may come out differently, because citations are spread over the duplicates.

Since Version 3.0 of Publish or Perish, duplicates can be merged into the master record, simply by dragging the stray citation onto the master record. An example of a merged record is shown in the screenshot below. See Section 2.1 for further details on how to do this.

4.3.3   SEARCHING FOR JOURNALS USING ISSNS

It is possible to conduct a journal impact analysis using ISSNs instead of journal titles. In order to do so use the General citation search tab and include the ISSN in the field **The phrase**. For more information on the General Search Queries see Chapter 5.

Considerable caution is necessary in using this approach, because Google Scholar results do not seem to be identical when using the ISSN instead of journal title. For many journals the differences are only small, with the h-index generally being 1-4% lower when using ISSN searches.

However, for some journals differences are much larger: *Journal of Applied Psychology* for instance registers a 15% lower h-index when searching with its ISSN. Finally, for some journals (e.g. *Australian Journal of Management*) Google Scholar provides virtually no hits when searching with their ISSN. I would therefore not recommend using ISSNs except to exclude false hits when searching for journal titles that include common words (see next section).

4.3.4   SEARCHING FOR JOURNAL TITLES THAT INCLUDE COMMON WORDS

Although Google Scholar provides good results for most journal titles, journal titles that include common words provide some difficulties.

The journal impact analysis uses the Google Scholar Advanced query "return articles published in". Google Scholar interprets this query broadly and returns matches for both the publication and the publisher.

This means that a search for a relatively generic journal title such as *Information Systems Research* might get additional matches in the publisher field, such as *Center for Information Systems Research,* or even the eventual co-sponsor/co-publisher of *MIS Quarterly* (*Management Information Systems Research Center*, University of Minnesota), even though this is not directly visible in the Google Scholar output.

As a result most hits for a citation analysis for the journal *Information Systems Research* would be papers published in *MIS Quarterly*, which on average tend to be more highly cited than papers in *Information Systems Research*. Including *MIS Quarterly* in the **Exclude these words** field is not an option, because Google Scholar matches the exclusion words anywhere in the paper and would therefore also exclude any papers in *Information Systems Research* that merely refer to papers published in *MIS Quarterly* (which is likely to be the case for a very substantial number of papers).

One of the two following strategies is recommended to calculate the citation impact in this and similar cases:

1. Search for *Information Systems Research* without any exclusions.
2. Sort the results by **Publication**.
3. Unselect all papers.
4. Manually selected all papers published in *Information Systems Research* and click **Check selection**.

This is probably the fastest option, but might not provide completely accurate results in cases where there are a lot of false hits. Since Google Scholar limits the total number of results to 1000, the false hits might suppress some papers of the journal of interest that are not as highly cited.

This is most likely to be a problem in disciplines where papers are generally highly cited (e.g. medicine), but it might make a difference for other fields as well. Citations metrics such as the total number of citations and citations per paper are more sensitive to different search strategies than citation metrics such as the h-index, which will generally not be influenced by this.

The second strategy safely eliminates false hits and hence provides a more accurate result:

1. Search for *Information Systems Research*, but include the ISSN of *MIS Quarterly* (0276-7783) in the **Exclude these words** field. This prevents Google Scholar from excluding all ISR papers that include a MISQ reference in their list of references, but still excludes the many MIS Quarterly hits. Additional exclusions are possible, as long as they are unique enough to not be likely to appear anywhere in papers published in ISR.
2. Sort the results by **Publication**.
3. Unselect all papers.
4. Manually selected all papers published in *Information Systems Research* and click **Check selection**.

CHAPTER 5:
GENERAL CITATION SEARCH QUERIES

The **General citation search** page allows you to perform an Advanced Scholar Search query and analyze its results. This page contains a query pane (see 5.1.1) with **all** parameters accepted by Google Scholar.

If you mainly interested in citation data for particular authors or journals, you might find the **Author Impact search** page (see Chapter 3) or the **Journal Impact search page** (see Chapter 4) more useful. These pages are tailored to provide only what is needed for an author or journal impact search.

The results of a general citation search are available on-screen and can also be copied to the Windows clipboard (for pasting in other applications) or saved to a text file (for future reference or further analysis). For a description of the results pane, see Section 2.1.2.

⊘ **Tip:** Any queries that you execute on this page are automatically added to the **Recent Queries** folder on the Multi-queries center page.

5.1.1   GENERAL QUERY PANE

This pane contains the following fields.

AUTHOR(S)

Enter the names of the authors you want to look up. The recommended format is to use one or more initials and to quote each name, for example *"A Harzing"*. Try to use the initials that the author usually publishes under. You can enter more than one name; this behaves as an AND clause, for example *"A Harzing" "NG Noorderhaven"*. To perform an OR query (individual papers AND co-authored ones), include OR in the query: *"A Harzing" OR "NG Noorderhaven"*

PUBLICATION

Enter the name of the publication you want to look up. The recommended format is the full title enclosed in quotes, for example "Journal of International Business". However, you might have to experiment with common abbreviations as well.

ALL OF THE WORDS

Enter any words that must all appear in the returned papers. This can be used to narrow down the search for a specific set of papers. If you use quotes around the words, this provides you with the same results as using "The phrase" field. If you include the search terms without quotes, it will provide many more matches as it matches the words in any order. Therefore, if the words are very generic there will be lots of publications that include them.

Please note that the standard Google Scholar search uses "All of the words". As discussed in Section 3.3.1 and 4.3.1 a standard Google Scholar search often gives meaningless results if you are interested in author or journal impact.

ANY OF THE WORDS

Enter any words that must appear alone or in combination in the returned papers. This can be used to narrow down the search for a specific set of papers. Unless the terms are very specific, it is usually not very effective to use this field without completing any of the other fields as you might get a lot of irrelevant results.

NONE OF THE WORDS

Enter any words that must **not** appear in the returned papers. This can be used to narrow down the search for a specific set of papers.

THE PHRASE

Enter a phrase (i.e., a specific **sequence** of words) that must all appear in the returned papers. This can be used to narrow down the search for a specific set of papers.

YEAR OF PUBLICATION BETWEEN ... AND ...

Enter the range of years in which the papers must have been published.

SUBJECT AREAS

Check the boxes of the subject areas that you want to search in; clear the others. Clearing all boxes has the same effect as checking them all: the lookup will ignore the subject areas.

Note: Please note that the subject area classification is not always accurate; see "How to perform an effective author/journal impact analysis" for more information

TITLE WORDS ONLY

Check this box to restrict the additional word matches (i.e., **All of the words**, **Any of the words**, **None of the words**, **The phrase**) to the titles of the returned papers; clear the box to match them anywhere in the papers.

LOOKUP

Click this button to perform the query. If possible, the query is satisfied from the local PoP cache; this saves time and reduces the load on Google Scholar. If no cache entry for the query exists or the entry is older than the maximum cache age, then the query is forwarded to Google Scholar. After the results are received from Google Scholar, the local cache is automatically refreshed.

Click this button to send the query directly to Google Scholar, bypassing the local Publish or Perish cache. This may be useful if you suspect that Google Scholar may have newer information available than is available through the local cache. When the results are returned from Google Scholar, the local cache is automatically refreshed.

Note: It is not useful to perform multiple direct lookups for the same query shortly after another; this merely increases the load on Google Scholar and increases the chance that your computer may be temporarily denied access by Google Scholar. I recommend that you only use the **Lookup Direct** function as a last resort.

5.2   HOW TO PERFORM A GENERAL CITATION SEARCH

To perform a general citation analysis:

1. Enter the relevant parameters in the various fields (see General query pane for an explanation of each parameter);
2. Click **Lookup** or press the **Enter** key.

The program will now contact Google Scholar to obtain the citations, process the list, and calculate the metrics, which are then displayed in the Results pane. The full list of results is also available for inspection or modifications and can be exported in a variety of formats.

5.2.1   IMPORTANT NOTE

A general citation query gives access to all the query fields of an Advanced Scholar Search, accessible through a separate link on the Google Scholar home page. This is **not** the same as a standard Google Scholar search (i.e., from the Google Scholar home page).

A standard Google Scholar search is equivalent to performing an **All of the words** query, which matches the search terms anywhere in the searched documents (author, title, source, abstract, references etc.) and usually provides too many irrelevant results for an effective citation analysis. Hence it is normally recommended to use a more specific query; see Author impact analysis, Journal impact analysis, and the section **Refining the search** below.

However, if you do want to get the same results in Publish or Perish as with a standard Google Scholar search, do the following.

1. Empty all text fields except **All of the words**.
2. Enter your query terms in the **All of the words** field.
3. Set the **Year of publication** fields both to 0.
4. Make sure that all subject area boxes are checked.
5. Clear the **Title words only** field.
6. Click on **Lookup**.
7. When the results appear, click on the **Rank** column header to sort the results in the order in which Google Scholar returned them.

All of the strategies described in detail in the Author Searches (Chapter 3) and Journal Searches chapter (Chapter 4) can be used to refine your general citation search and/or improve its accuracy.

5.3   APPLICATIONS FOR THE GENERAL CITATION SEARCH

In many cases you will find that the Author Impact Search or the Journal Impact Search provides you with all the information you need. However, there are some situations in which a General Citation Search might be helpful. The General Citation Search can be used to find particular papers, conduct advanced author and journal queries, compare institutional performance and conduct a literature review. I will discuss each of these applications in turn.

5.3.1   FINDING A SPECIFIC PAPER

The General Citation Search can be used to find specific papers. Does this scenario sound familiar? Someone mentioned a recent journal article that you should read, but you forgot both the author and the journal the paper was published in. All you remember is some words in the title: Google Scholar and h-index. Of course you could search for the article in Google, but this is likely to provide you with many false hits.

Author impact	Journal impact	General citations	Multi-query center	Web Browser

General citation search - Perform a general citation search

Author(s):		☑ Biology, Life Sciences, Environmental Science
Publication:		☑ Business, Administration, Finance, Economics
		☑ Chemistry and Materials Science
All of the words:	"Google Scholar" h-index	☑ Engineering, Computer Science, Mathematics
Any of the words:		☑ Medicine, Pharmacology, Veterinary Science
None of the words:		☑ Physics, Astronomy, Planetary Science
The phrase:		☑ Social Sciences, Arts, Humanities
Year of publication between:	0 and: 0	☑ Title words only

Results

Papers:	8	Cites/paper:	18.63	h-index:	6	AWCR:	53.33
Citations:	149	Cites/author:	129.00	g-index:	8	AW-index:	7.30
Years:	3	Papers/author:	6.50	hc-index:	6	AWCRpA:	44.83
Cites/year:	49.67	Authors/paper:	1.38	hI-index:	4.00	e-index:	10.63
				hI,norm:	5	hm-index:	4.50

Cites		Authors	Title	Year	Publication
☑ 🗋	75	J Bar-Ilan	Which h-index?—A comparison of WoS, Scopus and G...	2008	Scientometrics
☑ 🗋	22	AW Harzing...	A Google Scholar h-index for journals: An alternative ...	2009	Journal of the American ...
☑ 🗋	21	P Jacso	Testing the calculation of a realistic h-index in Google ...	2008	Library Trends
☑ 🗋	13	P Jacso	The pros and cons of computing the h-index using Go...	2008	Online information review
☑ 🗋	12	AW Harzing...	'A Google Scholar H-Index for journals: a better metri...	2008	Proceedings of the Aca...
☑	6	A Harzing, ...	Comparing the Google Scholar h-index with the ISI jou...	2008	Harzing. com white paper
☑	0	P Jacso	Calculating the h-index and other bibliometric and scie...	2009	Online Information Review

Using Google Scholar through Publish or Perish can – within seconds – provide you with a list of likely candidates. The screenshot above shows the search in question. As we can immediately see there are only a couple of publications in the list, all recent. Although it was the most-cited article by Bar-Ilan you were interested in, you now also have a list of related articles that might of interest to you.

This strategy can work even if you remember only one word in the title, provided that it is not a very common word. For instance someone mentions a paper to you about serendipity. You are not sure of any other words in the title and searching for the word anywhere in the document will give too many results.

However, as your counterpart was an academic working in the field of Business, you are fairly certain that the paper you are looking was published in a journal in that area. Hence you search for serendipity in the subject area of Business, Administration, Finance & Economics. After removing duplicates, this leaves you with less than 100 results (see below), hence it would not take a long time to review them.

Author impact	Journal impact	General citations	Multi-query center	Web Browser

General citation search - Perform a general citation search

Author(s):		☐ Biology, Life Sciences, Environmental Science
Publication:		☑ Business, Administration, Finance, Economics
All of the words:	serendipity	☐ Chemistry and Materials Science
Any of the words:		☐ Engineering, Computer Science, Mathematics
None of the words:		☐ Medicine, Pharmacology, Veterinary Science
The phrase:		☐ Physics, Astronomy, Planetary Science
		☐ Social Sciences, Arts, Humanities
Year of publication between: 0 and: 0		☑ Title words only

Results

Papers:	100	Cites/paper:	5.27	h-index:	10	AWCR:	61.34
Citations:	527	Cites/author:	402.00	g-index:	21	AW-index:	7.83
Years:	50	Papers/author:	86.95	hc-index:	7	AWCRpA:	46.88
Cites/year:	10.54	Authors/paper:	1.37	hI-index:	6.25	e-index:	16.43
				hI,norm:	9	hm-index:	8.33

Cites	Authors	Title	Year	Publication
☑ ☐ 98	ME Graebner	Momentum and serendipity: How acquired lead...	2004	Strategic Management ...
☑ 97	A Foster, N Ford	Serendipity and information seeking: an empiri...	2003	Journal of Documentation
☑ 52	K Meyer, A Skak	Networks, serendipity and SME entry into East...	2002	European Management ...
☑ 24	P Michel, P Pesti...	Population growth and optimality: when does s...	1993	Journal of Population Ec...
☑ ☐ 23	B Merrilees, D M...	Serendipity, leverage and the process of entre...	1998	Small Enterprise Research

5.3.2 FINDING A SPECIFIC ACADEMIC

The General Citation Search can be used to find specific academics. Does this scenario sound familiar? You have attended your field's major academic conference and had a good conversation with someone you really want to follow up with. However, you did not get their business card and forgot their name. The only two things you remember is that they were working at the University of Melbourne and published in the Academy of Management of Learning & Education, which is the journal you were talking about.

You could go to the University of Melbourne website and review their staff list, but that might be a tedious process. You could go through the table of content of the Academy of Management Learning & Education hoping you remember their name. However, what would be much simpler is to conduct the search below. This would allow you to refresh your memory in seconds and realize that you had been talking to me ☺ This search strategy will not always lead to such a quick result, but it is worth a try.

| Author impact | Journal impact | General citations | Multi-query center | Web Browser |

General citation search - Perform a general citation search

Author(s):		☑ Biology, Life Sciences, Environmental Scie
Publication:	Academy of Management Learning and Education	☑ Business, Administration, Finance, Econor
All of the words:	"University of Melbourne"	☑ Chemistry and Materials Science
Any of the words:		☑ Engineering, Computer Science, Mathema
None of the words:		☑ Medicine, Pharmacology, Veterinary Scien
The phrase:		☑ Physics, Astronomy, Planetary Science
Year of publication between: 0 and: 0		☑ Social Sciences, Arts, Humanities
		☐ Title words only

Results

Papers:	4	Cites/paper:	16.00	h-index:	3	AWCR:	31.00
Citations:	64	Cites/author:	35.00	g-index:	4	AW-index:	5.57
Years:	3	Papers/author:	3.00	hc-index:	3	AWCRpA:	16.50
Cites/year:	21.33	Authors/paper:	1.50	hI-index:	1.80	e-index:	7.35
				hI,norm:	2	hm-index:	2.00

Cites		Authors	Title	Year
☑	54	NJ Adler, AW Harzing	When knowledge wins: Transcending the sense and nonsense of acade...	2009
☑	5	RF Zammuto	Accreditation and the globalization of business	2008
☑	4	I Metz, AW Harzing	Gender diversity in editorial boards of management journals	2009
☑	1	NM Ashkanasy	Introduction: Is accreditation good for business (schools)?	2008

Please note that this search is not flawless. Google Scholar does not have an "affiliation" field, hence the name of the university will be matched anywhere in the document. The results of our search contain four articles, two by myself, one by a (former) colleague Ray Zammuto and one by Neal Ashkanasy (University of Queensland). In his article though, Neal refers to Ray Zammuto's paper and Melbourne affiliation.

5.3.3   ADVANCED AUTHOR QUERIES

The General Citation Search can be used for advanced author queries. In the search described above, you noticed that two author names (Harzing and Jacsó) occur several times. You therefore wonder whether these authors have published additional work on Google Scholar. To find out you can run an advanced author query by combining an author name with the words Google Scholar in the "All of the words" or "The phrase" field. As the search is already fairly refined by including the author names, it is better to not tick the title-words only box. This allows you to find not only articles with Google Scholar in the title, but also articles referring in some way to Google Scholar. In the screenshot, you will find some articles that explicitly discuss advantages and disadvantages of Google Scholar and its use for citation analysis. However, you also find papers reflecting on the nature of evaluating academic research and impact in a broader sense.

General citation search - Perform a general citation search

Author(s):	"P Jacso" OR "A Harzing"	☑ Biology, Life Sciences, Environmental Sc
Publication:		☑ Business, Administration, Finance, Econ
		☑ Chemistry and Materials Science
All of the words:	"Google Scholar"	☑ Engineering, Computer Science, Mather
Any of the words:		☑ Medicine, Pharmacology, Veterinary Sci
None of the words:		☑ Physics, Astronomy, Planetary Science
The phrase:		☑ Social Sciences, Arts, Humanities
Year of publication between:	0 and: 0	☐ Title words only

Results

Papers:	55	Cites/paper:	13.95	h-index:	13	AWCR:	201.53
Citations:	767	Cites/author:	678.67	g-index:	26	AW-index:	14.20
Years:	13	Papers/author:	50.50	hc-index:	13	AWCRpA:	166.02
Cites/year:	59.00	Authors/paper:	1.20	hI-index:	10.56	e-index:	20.64
				hI,norm:	13	hm-index:	11.50

Cites		Authors	Title	Year	Publication
☑	132	P Jacso	As we may search–comparison of major features ...	2005	Current science
☑	119	P Jacsó	Google Scholar: the pros and the cons	2005	Online Information Review
☑ ▢	76	AWK Harzing, ...	Google Scholar as a new source for citation analysis	2008	Ethics in Science and En...
☑	54	NJ Adler, AW ...	When knowledge wins: Transcending the sense a...	2009	The Academy of Manag...
☑	49	P Jacso	Deflated, inflated and phantom citation counts	2006	Online information review
☑	27	P Jacsó	Google Scholar revisited	2008	Online Information Review
☑ ▢	25	AW Harzing, R...	A Google Scholar h-index for journals: An alterna...	2009	Journal of the American ...
☑ ▢	24	P Jacso	Google Scholar Beta	2004	Peter's Digital Referenc...

5.3.4   ADVANCED JOURNAL QUERIES

The General Citation Search can be used for advanced journal queries to find out whether a particular journal has published on a particular topic. In the search for publications on Google Scholar that I described above, we saw that many of the publications on Google Scholar by Peter Jacsó appeared in Online Information Review.

Therefore, I want to try to establish whether the journal has published any further papers about this topic. The screenshot below shows the search I would conduct and the results I would receive. Please note that if we do not want to get all the articles by Peter Jacsó again, we can exclude them by putting "P Jacso" in the "All of the words" field.

It is important to use this exact combination. If instead I would use "Peter Jacso" I would also exclude articles that talk about Peter Jacsó, which they would normally do as Jacsó or Peter Jacsó. If I did not put quotes around P Jacso, it would also match Jacso, P. As most referencing standards prescribe the use Last Name, Initial(s) in the list of references, this would exclude any article that referred to an article by Jacsó in the list of references. As many of the academics writing about Google Scholar include a reference to an article by Jacsó, this would leave us with very few results.

| Author impact | Journal impact | General citations | Multi-query center | Web Browser |

General citation search - Perform a general citation search

Author(s):
Publication: "Online Information Review"
All of the words: Google Scholar
Any of the words:
None of the words: "P Jacso"
The phrase:
Year of publication between: 0 and: 0
☐ Title words only

☑ Biology, Life Sciences, Environmental Science
☑ Business, Administration, Finance, Economics
☑ Chemistry and Materials Science
☑ Engineering, Computer Science, Mathematics
☑ Medicine, Pharmacology, Veterinary Science
☑ Physics, Astronomy, Planetary Science
☑ Social Sciences, Arts, Humanities

Results

Papers:	30	Cites/paper:	4.07	h-index:	7	AWCR:	28.87
Citations:	122	Cites/author:	84.83	g-index:	10	AW-index:	5.37
Years:	9	Papers/author:	20.33	hc-index:	7	AWCRpA:	18.60
Cites/year:	13.56	Authors/paper:	1.80	hI-index:	4.08	e-index:	7.14
				hI,norm:	6	hm-index:	5.17

Cites		Authors	Title	Year	Publication
☑	21	P Mayr, ...	An exploratory study of Google Scholar	2007	Online Information Review
☑	16	X Chen	MetaLib, WebFeat, and Google	2006	Online Information Review
☑	16	Y Gavel, ...	Web of Science and Scopus: a journal title ...	2008	Online Information Review
☑	15	GE Gorman	Giving way to Google	2006	Online Information Review

Analogous to advanced author queries, you can use this search strategy whenever you want to know what a journal has published about a particular topic. If you want to know what *Science* has published about HIV, an advanced journal query like the one below will give you the answer in less than a minute.

| Author impact | Journal impact | General citations | Multi-query center | Web Browser |

General citation search - Perform a general citation search

Author(s):
Publication: Science
All of the words: HIV
Any of the words:
None of the words:
The phrase:
Year of publication between: 0 and: 0
☑ Title words only

☑ Biology, Life Sciences, Environmental Science
☑ Business, Administration, Finance, Economics
☑ Chemistry and Materials Science
☑ Engineering, Computer Science, Mathematics
☑ Medicine, Pharmacology, Veterinary Science
☑ Physics, Astronomy, Planetary Science
☑ Social Sciences, Arts, Humanities

Results

Papers:	1000	Cites/paper:	94.67	h-index:	162	AWCR:	7022.17
Citations:	94668	Cites/author:	26905.78	g-index:	298	AW-index:	83.80
Years:	259	Papers/author:	470.44	hc-index:	90	AWCRpA:	2040.25
Cites/year:	365.51	Authors/paper:	3.32	hI-index:	36.81	e-index:	221.62
				hI,norm:	86	hm-index:	76.43

Cites		Authors	Title	Year	Publication
☑	2072	G Alkhatib, ...	CC CKR5: a RANTES, MIP-1alpha, MIP-1beta receptor as a f...	1996	Science
☑	1968	JW Mellors,...	Prognosis in HIV-1 infection predicted by the quantity of viru...	1996	Science
☑	1938	AS Perelson...	HIV-1 dynamics in vivo: virion clearance rate, infected cell lif...	1996	Science
☑	1918	F Cocchi, A...	Identification of RANTES, MIP-1alpha, and MIP-1beta as the...	1995	Science

Theoretically, the General Citation Search could be used to compare institutional performance in particular fields. As noted above, however, Google Scholar does not have a bibliographic field for affiliation. This means that these searches are not likely to be very accurate as Google Scholar will match the name of the university anywhere in the document (including acknowledgements, main body and references).

In addition, year and field restrictions seem to have rather unpredictable results for institutional searches. Without further experimentation and testing, I would therefore not recommend the use of Publish or Perish for these purposes. The only exception would be very generic searches, such as to establish whether a particular university generates any academic papers at all. Therefore, at present the only way to use Publish or Perish and Google Scholar to measure institutional performance is to run searches for individual academics in a school, department, or faculty and aggregate the results.

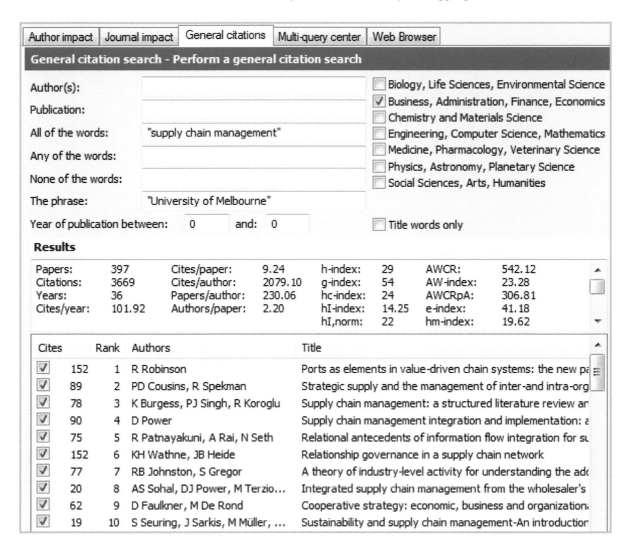

However, in spite of these limitations, Google Scholar does seem to have **some** usefulness to find out whether there are any academics in a particular institution on a specific topic. This could be useful for instance for PhD students looking for a supervisor or for academics looking for an institution to visit on their sabbatical.

The screenshot above shows an example of such a search focusing on "supply chain management" in my own University, the University of Melbourne. In this type of search, it is generally best to sort the results by Google Scholar rank (by clicking on the rank column), rather than the standard sort for the number of citations. The latter privileges publications that have more citations, but these might be less relevant for the search in question.

Out of the first ten hits in the search, seven of the papers were indeed written by one or more authors affiliated with Melbourne, whilst number the book in the 9th place includes a chapter of a University of Melbourne academic. This search might therefore enable the student or academic to more easily identify relevant individuals in a particular university. However, it should be combined with other search strategies, such as perusing university web sites, for the best results.

5.3.6   CONDUCTING A LITERATURE REVIEW

The General Citation Search can also be used to conduct a literature review about any topic. In fact, the search sequence I have described under 5.3.3-5.3.4 already has characteristics of a focused literature review. For a more detailed discussion and examples of the use of Publish or Perish to conduct a literature review, see Chapter 11.

CHAPTER 6:
MULTI-QUERY CENTRE

6.1 INTRODUCTION TO THE MULTI-QUERY CENTER

The **Multi-query center** page contains a list of recently executed queries. It also allows you to add further queries, optionally organized in folders that you want to keep for future reference.

The queries that you perform on this page are identical to the ones on the more specialized query pages.

The **Multi-query center** page contains the following panes:
- Multi-query pane (See Section 6.2)
- Results pane (see Section 2.1.2)

For general search tips, see:
- Chapter 3: Author searches
- Chapter 4: Journal searches
- Chapter 5: General citation searches

6.2 HOW TO USE THE MULTI-QUERY CENTER

6.2.1 MULTI-QUERY PANE

The multi-query pane (see screenshot below) is part of the Multi-query center page. For an overview of the results pane see Section 2.1.2.

The multi-query pane consists of a toolbar across the top, a tree view on the left and a list view on the right, as shown in the following screen shot.

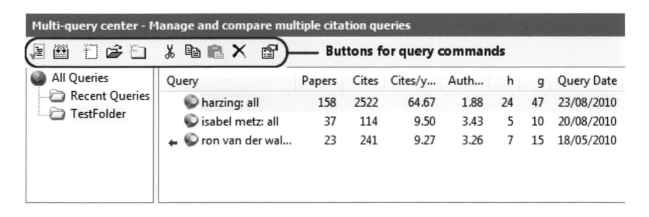

Across the top of the multi-query pane is the toolbar that contains the commands for the Multi Query Center. Not all commands are available at all times; for some commands (for example, **Lookup** and **Lookup Direct**) you must first select a query in the list on the right before the command becomes active. Unavailable commands are grayed out.

LOOKUP (SHORTCUT CTRL+L)

Click this button to perform the query. If possible, the query is satisfied from the local Publish or Perish cache; this saves time and reduces the load on Google Scholar. If no cache entry for the query exists or the entry is older than the maximum cache age, then the query is forwarded to Google Scholar. After the results are received from Google Scholar, the local cache is automatically refreshed.

Warning: If you have more than a few queries selected when you issue this command, then Google Scholar may start refusing the lookup requests because of an excessive number of requests. In that case you must wait a few hours before retrying the queries, preferably with fewer queries selected.

Tip: You can change the maximum cache age in the Preferences - Queries dialog box, which is accessible through the File > Preferences command.

LOOKUP DIRECT (SHORTCUT CTRL+SHIFT+L)

Click this button to send the query directly to Google Scholar, bypassing the local Publish or Perish cache. This may be useful if you suspect that Google Scholar may have newer information available than is available through the local cache. When the results are returned from Google Scholar, the local cache is automatically refreshed.

Warning: If you have more than a few queries selected when you issue this command, then Google Scholar may start refusing the lookup requests because of an excessive number of requests. In that case you must wait a few hours before retrying the queries, preferably with fewer queries selected.

Note: It is not useful to perform multiple direct lookups for the same query shortly after another; this merely increases the load on Google Scholar and increases the chance that your computer may be temporarily denied access by Google Scholar. We recommend that you only use the **Lookup Direct** function as a last resort.

NEW QUERY

Click this button to create a new query. It will be placed in the currently selected folder (or in the parent folder of the currently selected query).

IMPORT QUERY

Click this button to import external query data into Publish or Perish. This command is currently only partially implemented.

NEW FOLDER

Click this button to create a new query folder under the current folder. Please note that you can nest folders, i.e. you can make folders under the main **All Queries** folder, but you can also create as many levels of sub-folders as is useful to you.

CUT (SHORTCUT CTRL+X)

Click this button to copy the currently selected folder or query to the Windows clipboard and delete it from its current position. You can then paste it into a different folder. Be careful if you are using this to move queries. For most users, it might be safer to use the mouse to drag the query or folder to a new folder.

COPY (SHORTCUT CTRL+C)

Click this button to copy the currently selected folder or query to the Windows clipboard. You can then paste it into a different folder.

PASTE (SHORTCUT CTRL+V)

Click this button to paste the folder or query on the Windows clipboard into the current folder.

DELETE (SHORTCUT: USE DELETE BUTTON)

Click this button to delete the currently selected folder or query. If you delete a folder, all queries in it are also deleted.

Be careful if you use this command; once deleted, a folder or query cannot be retrieved. (You can, however, re-create the query and rely on the Publish or Perish cache to quickly retrieve the previous results.)

PROPERTIES (SHORTCUT ALT+ENTER)

Click this button to edit the currently selected folder or query.

The tree on the left displays the available query folders. The folders are containers that help you organize your queries. Query folders can be nested, and they can be rearranged by dragging and dropping with the mouse, just like you would do in Internet Explorer. They can also be copied (**Ctrl+C**), cut (**Ctrl+X**), and pasted (**Ctrl+V**).

The tree always contains the **Recent Queries** folder. This folder automatically receives the queries that you perform on one of the other citation analysis pages. You can also add your own queries to this folder and edit existing queries. However, you cannot delete this folder or change its name.

The screenshot below shows how queries can be nested to create logical containers for your queries. I strongly recommend you to organize your queries if you are planning to run them on a regular basis. It can be easy to get lost in a long list of recent queries.

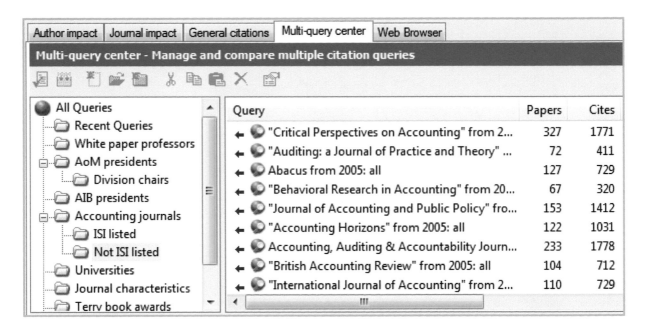

It is also a good idea to clean out your Recent Queries folder periodically, so that even if you do not want to make the effort to organize your queries into folders, you can keep some order in your queries. Simply select the query you want to discard and click on the delete button in the toolbar, or hit the delete button on your keyboard.

TREE VIEW POPUP MENU

If you right-click on any of the folders in the tree view, a popup menu appears with the same commands as found in the toolbar.

See Section 6.2.2 above for a description of the commands.

The list on the right displays queries similar to the queries that you enter on the other pages, but presented in a condensed format. Queries can be moved between folders by dragging and dropping them with the mouse. They can also be copied (**Ctrl+C**), cut (**Ctrl+X**), and pasted (**Ctrl+V**).

The screenshot below shows the full results of the queries for ISI listed Accounting journals shown in the Multi-query centre tree view in the previous screenshot. Please note that the results can be sorted on any column: simply click on the column heading. By default the queries are sorted in the order in which they were executed. The list below has been sorted by h-index.

Query	Papers	Cites	Cites/year	Auth/paper	h
← ◐ "Journal of Accounting Research" from 2005: all	280	6775	1129.17	2.12	43
← ◐ "Accounting Review" from 2005: all	290	4409	734.83	2.11	37
← ◐ "Accounting, Organizations and Society" from 2005: all	251	3835	639.17	1.93	34
← ◐ "Contemporary Accounting Research" from 2005: all	189	3188	531.33	2.38	29
← ◐ "Review of Accounting Studies" from 2005: all	132	3121	520.17	2.40	28
← ◐ "European Accounting Review" from 2005: all	177	1926	321.00	1.92	23

LIST VIEW COLUMNS

The list view displays the following columns. At present it is not possible to change the columns that are displayed, but this might change in a future version of Publish or Perish.

Column	Description
Query	An abbreviated rendering of the query parameters, intended as a reminder about the query. To see all query parameters, press **Alt+Enter** to open the Edit Query dialog box.
Papers	The number of results (~papers) returned by the query.
Cites	The total number of citations returned by the query.
Cites/year	The total number of citations in the query divided by the number of years spanned by the results.
Authors/paper	The average number of authors per paper in the query results.
h	Hirsch's h-index calculated for the query results.
g	Egge's g-index calculated for the query results.
Query Date	The date on which this query was last performed (see Results caching below).
Cache Date	The date on which the query data were last retrieved from Google Scholar (see Results caching below).

If you right-click on any of the queries in the list view, a popup menu appears with the following commands.

A full description of these commands can be found in appendix 6.

6.2.4   EXPORTING THE RESULTS FOR FURTHER PROCESSING

The multi-query center not only makes it easier to **organize** your queries, it also makes it easier to **export** the results for further processing. This is particularly useful if you want to do further bibliometric research with the PoP results (see Chapter 12 for more details on Doing Bibliometric Research on Authors and Journals).

The easiest way to export results is to select the queries you want to export and right-click to access the popup menu. Let's assume you are working with the set of ISI-listed accounting journals as below.

Query	Papers	Cites	Cites/year	Auth/paper	h
← "Journal of Accounting Research" from 2005: all	280	6775	1129.17	2.12	43
← "Accounting Review" from 2005: all	290	4409	734.83	2.11	37
← "Accounting, Organizations and Society" from 2005: all	251	3835	639.17	1.93	34
← "Contemporary Accounting Research" from 2005: all	189	3188	531.33	2.38	29
← "Review of Accounting Studies" from 2005: all	132	3121	520.17	2.40	28
← "European Accounting Review" from 2005: all	177	1926	321.00	1.92	23

If you would like to export the **results**, i.e. the articles included in the six journals for the time period in question, you would select one of the "Save As …." commands, which allow you to save and import the data into for instance Endnote (Save As Endnote), or MS Excel (Save as CSV). See Section 2.3 for more information about exporting.

If you would like to export the **statistics** for the journals in questions, i.e. their number of papers, citations, h-index etc., you would select one of the "Copy Statistics …." commands, which allow you to copy the statistics to the Windows clipboard for pasting into a variety of other programs.

For most users the best option is to use the Copy Statistics for Excel command. In order to ensure you copy the headers with the names of the statistics into your file, select the first journal, use "Copy Statistics for Excel with Header" and paste the results into an Excel worksheet. Then select all remaining journals, use "Copy Statistics for Excel" to copy and paste the remaining journals into the same Excel worksheet. The screenshot below shows part of the resulting Excel worksheet.

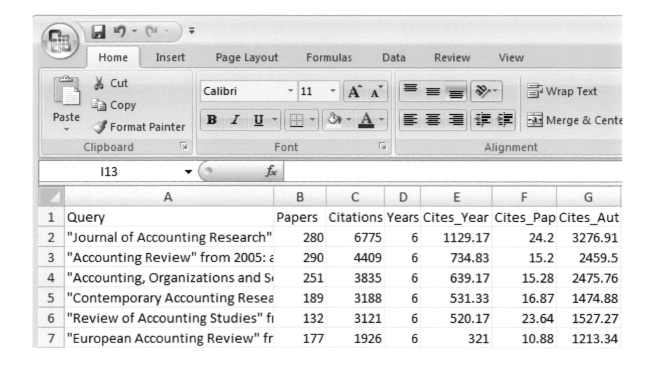

	A	B	C	D	E	F	G
1	Query	Papers	Citations	Years	Cites_Year	Cites_Pap	Cites_Aut
2	"Journal of Accounting Research"	280	6775	6	1129.17	24.2	3276.91
3	"Accounting Review" from 2005: ā	290	4409	6	734.83	15.2	2459.5
4	"Accounting, Organizations and Sᵢ	251	3835	6	639.17	15.28	2475.76
5	"Contemporary Accounting Reseā	189	3188	6	531.33	16.87	1474.88
6	"Review of Accounting Studies" fᵣ	132	3121	6	520.17	23.64	1527.27
7	"European Accounting Review" frᵣ	177	1926	6	321	10.88	1213.34

6.2.5   RESULTS CACHING

Publish or Perish uses a local cache for the data returned by queries. If you re-run a query, then Publish or Perish will retrieve the results data from the local cache instead of contacting Google Scholar again, provided that the cached data is still "fresh". If the cached data is too old, or if no cached data exists, then Publish or Perish sends the query to Google Scholar and stores the new results in the local cache for subsequent use.

The **Query Date** and **Cache Date** columns in the list view show the status of the query and cached data.

- **Query Date** is the date on which you last performed the query, i.e., last issued the **Lookup** [**Direct**] command.
- **Cache Date** is the date on which the data were last retrieved from Google Scholar.

Typically, the **Query Date** is the same or more recent than the **Cache Date**. If the **Query Date** is more recent, this means that the query on that date used the cached results rather than contacting Google Scholar. This is normal behavior.

OUT-OF-DATE CACHED DATA

If the **Cache Date** is too long ago or missing altogether, then the list view will display a small red arrow in front of the query. This means that the **Cache Date** is exceeds the maximum cache age specified in the Preferences - Queries dialog box.

In the case of out-of-date cached data, Publish or Perish will resubmit the query to Google Scholar the next time that you use the **Lookup** command. This happens automatically when you issue that command; you do not have to do anything special for that.

If you want to refresh the cache before the data expires, use the **Lookup Direct** command. This might occasionally turn up some extra results, but there is no point in using **Lookup Direct** more than once every few days; this merely increases the load on Google Scholar and increases the chance that your computer may be temporarily denied access by Google Scholar. Under normal circumstances you should rely on Publish or Perish's automatic caching implementation.

CHAPTER 7:
MAKING YOUR CASE FOR TENURE OR PROMOTION

Many academics using Publish or Perish do so because they have to make a case for tenure, promotion or other types of research evaluation. In this section, I will provide some pointers on how to report your case for citation impact more effectively.

These suggestions are based on my experience with some two dozen applications for tenure and promotion over the past decade. I do not guarantee that my suggestions will lead you to be successful in your application, but you will certainly increase your chances of success by paying attention to them.

Please note that these suggestions refer only to citation impact, whilst touching indirectly on journal quality. They do **not** relate to the **content** of your research, nor to your teaching or service activities. For those, you are on your own, although I am happy to send buyers of this book a copy of my own application for full professor at the University of Melbourne. Just email me at anne@harzing.com with the subject line "Promotion application".

7.1   CREATE YOUR OWN REFERENCE GROUP

First, it is a good idea to compare your case to a **relevant** group of peers. Many evaluators have very little idea of what typical norm scores for the various metrics are. So unless you make an explicit comparison, they will – explicitly or implicitly – use their own reference group, which may not work to your advantage.

As the analysis in Chapter 16 shows, there are vast differences in typical citation scores between disciplines, especially when using Thomson ISI citation data. Therefore, if your university has a tenure or promotion process in which decisions are made by committees composed of people in related or even unrelated disciplines, it is even more important to frame your case for tenure or promotion with an appropriate reference group.

Citation behaviors can also vary dramatically within disciplines or even within sub-disciplines. The area of Human Resource Management – as a sub-discipline of Management – includes scholars working on industrial relations and labor unions as well as scholars working on more psychologically oriented topics such as motivation or job attitudes. The latter academics might be able to publish in a mainstream Psychology journal such as *Psychological Bulletin*, whilst the former academics would feel most fortunate if they published in the top US journal in their field: *Industrial Relations*. At 12.85, the journal impact factor of the former is six times as high as the journal impact factor of the latter (2.05).

Moreover, many Industrial Relations academics will not be able to publish in mainstream US-American Industrial Relations journals as their research is very contextual. Hence they might need to publish their work in even lower impact journals such as British Journal of Industrial Relations (1.38), European Journal of Industrial Relations (1.00), Asia Pacific Journal of Human Resources (0.78), or the Australian journal

Labour History (0.15). Hence, any articles in the area of Industrial Relations can be expected to be cited far less frequently than articles in the area of organizational behavior, which is more closely related to psychology.

Therefore, it is very important to pick your reference group wisely. Your reference group should be narrow enough to reflect any differences in citation behaviors across disciplines. However, it should not be so narrow that it leads your committee to discard your selection as biased or irrelevant. Generally, I have found two strategies to be particularly effective: the international discipline-based strategy and the institution-based strategy.

For the first strategy, you compare your record with a representative selection of other academics at the level you are applying for. To make your case convincing, it is usually best to pick academics at institutions of similar or higher level of prestige. If you can show you are performing at the same level as academics in more prestigious institutions who have been in position for a while, you have a very strong case.

The second strategy is a more local strategy. Here you compare your record with academics in your own institution at the level you are applying for. If you have access to the length of tenure of your academic colleagues, you might be able to compare your performance with that of both long-established academics and that of academics recently promoted to the same level. This strategy might be particularly effective if your institution has more stringent norms for promotion than comparable institutions.

A combination of both strategies might even be more effective. The table below was taken from my own (successful) application for full professor in 2007. I used three reference groups, focused on my strengths (single/first authored articles) and included ISI citations for panel members who don't like Google Scholar. Please note that the Google Scholar data are lower than would be expected now as Google Scholar coverage has increased substantially since 2007.

Bibliometric comparison with other professors, mean and range are given for each indicator.

Reference Group	h-index	1st authored papers in h-index	Single-author papers in h-index	Number of ISI citing articles (2006 only)	Years as professor
2005/2006 promotions in the same department	Mean: 6.3 Range: 4-8	Mean: 4.3 Range: 3-5	Mean: 3.0 Range: 2-4	Mean: 15 Range: 3-34	Recently appointed
IB professors at top Australian universities	Mean: 9.0 Range: 4-16	Mean: 3.3 Range: 1-6	Mean: 1.5 Range: 0-3	Mean: 10 Range: 3-21	15 years (4-28 years)
Established professors in the same department	Mean: 14.0 Range: 6-22	Mean: 5.0 Range: 0-11	Mean: 2.0 Range: 0-4	Mean: 46 Range: 8-102	14 years (10-19 years)
Anne-Wil Harzing	**13**	**13**	**10**	**63**	**N/A**

Please note that you will normally need at least 3-4 academics in your reference group to be able to make a credible comparison and larger numbers are advisable. I would generally advise against listing names of individuals as this can easily lead to antagonistic responses. However, be prepared to substantiate your averages if so requested. You might wish to create folders for your reference groups in the Publish or Perish multi-query center (see Chapter 6), so that you can store and update analyses easily.

In Section 7.7 you will find some "norm" scores for management, marketing and social psychology. Please note that many of these norm scores are aspirational scores as they refer to top academics in the respective fields. Of course if you can show you meet even these norm scores, your case for research impact is very strong.

In general, please realize that it is **your** job to convince and educate your tenure or promotion panel of the impact of your research. Many senior academics, having grown up in an age in which citation metrics were relatively unimportant, have a very limited knowledge of their own or other academics' citation records. Moreover, in my experience many academics have the tendency to subconsciously overestimate what their own records were when they went up for tenure or promotion and hence use an inappropriate reference group.

You might think this is unfair and senior academics should know better, but remember that they are only human and are very busy people as well. Moreover, many processes in academia (e.g. further promotions, job applications, grant applications, applications for research awards, and applications for fellowships) depend on you making the case for the impact of your research. Hence it is not a bad idea to get some skills in "selling" your record!

7.2 PICK YOUR METRICS WISELY

Publish or Perish provides you with a very wide range of metrics. If your university or government prescribed the metrics you need to use, you have little choice but to do so. However, in many cases there is more flexibility. So which metrics do you pick?

The screenshot above shows a summary of my own citation record. Fortunately, my h-index and g-index are relatively high in comparison to other academics in my field (see section on norm scores), so it is relatively easy for me to make my case.

However, if I had the choice and was applying for a professorial position, I would probably point to the fact that my contemporary h-index and my individual h-index are relatively high in comparison to my regular h-index. This would allow me to make the case that:

1. Much of my work is recent. Hence my productivity has not (yet) declined and I am likely to continue making a strong contribution to the field. Academics who have published most of their impactful work long ago will have a low contemporary h-index, even though their regular h-index might be fairly high.

2. My most-cited work is single-authored. This means that it is easy for me substantiate that I have made a significant intellectual contribution. It also shows that my citation record is not inflated by citations from co-authors and their networks. Academics who publish a lot of co-authored work will usually have lower individual h-indices.

Most academics going up for tenure or promotion will benefit from using the contemporary h-index when comparing themselves with current job incumbents as most of their published work will be relatively recent.

Whether it is beneficial to you to use the individual h-index depends on the number of highly-cited single-authored articles. Publish or Perish provides three implementations of the individual h-index, so feel free to pick the one that shows of your case to its best advantage!

7.3   SINGLE OUT INDIVIDUAL PAPERS

It might be useful in your case for research impact to single out individual papers. The screenshot below shows my most highly cited papers. Of those, I would single out the ones that have been published recently, but already have a large number of citations, reflected in a high number of citations per year.

Cites	Per year	Authors	Title	Year
207	17.25	AWK Harzing	Managing the multinationals: An international study of contro...	1999
191	21.22	AW Harzing	Acquisitions versus greenfield investments: International stra...	2002
173	10.81	AWK Harzing	The persistent myth of high expatriate failure rates	1995
170	15.45	AW Harzing	An Empirical Analysis and Extension of the Bartlett and Ghos...	2000
131	18.71	AW Harzing, J Van R...	International human resource management	2004
128	9.14	AW Harzing	Response rates in international mail surveys: results of a 22-...	1997
109	10.90	AW Harzing	Of bears, bumble-bees, and spiders: The role of expatriates i...	2001
106	13.25	AW Harzing, A Sorge	The relative impact of country of origin and universal conting...	2003
87	29.00	AWK Harzing, R van ...	Google Scholar as a new source for citation analysis	2008
76	7.60	AW Harzing	Who's in charge? An empirical study of executive staffing pra...	2001
67	6.09	AW Harzing	Cross-National Industrial Mail Surveys:: Why Do Response R...	2000
66	7.33	AW Harzing	Are our referencing errors undermining our scholarship and c...	2002
60	4.00	AW Harzing, G Hofst...	Planned change in organizations: The influence of national cu...	1996
59	5.90	AW Harzing	An analysis of the functions of international transfer of mana...	2001
58	7.25	AJ Feely, AW Harzing	Language management in multinational companies	2003
56	28.00	NJ Adler, AW Harzing	When knowledge wins: Transcending the sense and nonsens...	2009
53	7.57	JB Hocking, M Brown...	A knowledge transfer perspective of strategic assignment pu...	2004
50	6.25	AW Harzing	The role of culture in entry mode studies: From neglect to my...	2003
46	9.20	AW Harzing	Response styles in cross-national survey research	2006

In addition, I would point to a book and an older paper that have continued to attract citations over the years. [The high level of citations to the 2004 IHRM book is a bit misleading as Google Scholar has combined citations for the first (1995) and second edition to the book, so I would not make a case of that].

This list might also help me making additional claims such as:

1. The high quality of my PhD thesis, given that my most cited work is a book based on my PhD.

2. The research impact of my textbook in International Human Resource Management, which had 135 citations over the two editions.

3. My contribution to several distinct research areas (HQ-subsidiary relationships, expatriate management, entry modes, research methods, and research evaluation) that have all received a significant number of citations.

4. My ability to work alone as well as with co-authors, given that I have highly cited papers in both categories.

Of course the claims you can make depend on your own specific record, so I can't make any general recommendations. I can only encourage you to be creative and look for the gems to be polished in order to make your application shine.

You can also conduct a citations/per year analysis with ISI or Scopus data if your University prefers these data sources. However, the process is a lot quicker and easier with Publish or Perish and Google Scholar data.

7.4   COMPARE YOUR BEST PAPERS TO THE JOURNAL AVERAGE

In Section 7.1, I encouraged you to pick your own reference group. What better reference group than academics who have published in the same journals that you have published in?

The screenshot below compares my paper published in the *Journal of World Business* in 2001 with other papers published in the same journal in the same year and finds it is the most highly cited paper in the journal in that particular year.

A comparison like this can be particularly effective as it automatically corrects for differences in citation behaviors across disciplines and differences in papers of a different age. You could write this up in your application as: My 2001 paper in *Journal of World Business* was the most cited paper out of 28 papers and had three times as many citations as the average paper in the journal that year.

You can be creative in this as well. The screenshot below shows my 2001 publication in the *Journal of International Business Studies*. Unfortunately, it was not the most cited paper in the journal that year, but it was nearly the most cited single-authored paper, which in a top US journal is a significant achievement. Also, given that JIBS published 54 papers that year, I could say that my paper was within the top 15% most cited papers that year.

Journal impact — Journal of World Business

| | Author impact | Journal impact | General citations | Multi-query center | Web Browser |

Journal impact analysis - Perform a citation analysis for one or more journals

Journal title: "Journal of World Business"

Exclude these words:

Year of publication between: 2001 and: 2001

Results

Papers:	28	Cites/paper:	36.54	h-index:	19	AWCR:	102.30
Citations:	1023	Cites/author:	602.09	g-index:	28	AW-index:	10.11
Years:	10	Papers/author:	16.67	hc-index:	13	AWCRpA:	60.21
Cites/year:	102.30	Authors/paper:	2.04	hI-index:	8.60	e-index:	24.37
				hI,norm:	13	hm-index:	11.83

Cites	Authors	Title	Year	Publication
109	AW Harzing	Of bears, bumble-bees, and spiders: The r...	2001	Journal of World Business
95	A Ferner, J Quinta...	Country-of-origin effects, host-country ef...	2001	Journal of World Business
80	M Lazarova, P Cali...	Retaining repatriates: The role of organiza...	2001	Journal of World Business
72	D Angwin	Mergers and acquisitions across European ...	2001	Journal of World Business
69	P Very, DM Schwei...	The acquisition process as a learning proce...	2001	Journal of World Business
54	P Ghauri, T Fang	Negotiating with the Chinese: a socio-cultu...	2001	Journal of World Business
51	H Scullion, C Brews...	The management of expatriates: message...	2001	Journal of World Business
48	S Gherardi, B Poggio	Creating and recreating gender order in or...	2001	Journal of World Business
48	CS Wong, Y Wong,...	The significant role of Chinese employees' ...	2001	Journal of World Business

---

| | Author impact | Journal impact | General citations | Multi-query center | Web Browser |

Journal impact analysis - Perform a citation analysis for one or more journals

Journal title: "Journal of International Business Studies"

Exclude these words:

Year of publication between: 2000 and: 2000

Results

Papers:	54	Cites/paper:	63.07	h-index:	29	AWCR:	309.64
Citations:	3406	Cites/author:	1855.60	g-index:	54	AW-index:	17.60
Years:	11	Papers/author:	32.73	hc-index:	21	AWCRpA:	168.69
Cites/year:	309.64	Authors/paper:	2.09	hI-index:	12.55	e-index:	47.77
				hI,norm:	23	hm-index:	20.70

Cites	Authors	Title	Year	Publication
276	JH Dyer, W Chu	The determinants of trust in supplier-auto...	2000	Journal of International ...
231	AS Thomas, SL Mu...	A Case for Comparative Entrepreneurship:...	2000	Journal of International ...
206	Y Pan, DK Tse	The hierarchical model of market entry mo...	2000	Journal of International ...
190	X Liu, P Siler, C Wa...	Productivity spillovers from foreign direct i...	2000	Journal of International ...
181	J Birkinshaw, N Hood	Characteristics of foreign subsidiaries in in...	2000	Journal of International ...
173	P Ellis	Social Ties and Foreign Market Entry.	2000	Journal of International ...
172	AW Harzing	An Empirical Analysis and Extension of the ...	2000	Journal of International ...

Of course, it will not happen very often that your paper is the most-cited paper in the journal in question. However, even just being able to say that it is within the top-5 or top-10 most cited papers (especially if the journal published quite a lot of papers each year) is a very significant contribution to your case. As above you can also use percentages if this makes your case more impressive.

If you are lucky you have articles that are amongst the most-cited articles in a particular journal over a longer period. If you could say that your article was amongst the top 5% or top 10% most cited articles in a particular journal over its entire history of publication that would make a very strong case, especially if the journal was a particularly well-known journal.

I would not be inclined use this strategy if the journal wasn't particularly well-known. The screenshot below shows that my publication in Ethics in Science and Environmental Politics is the most cited paper in the journal since its inception, even though it was only published in 2008. However, given that most academics in my field will not recognize this journal, this claim would not make my case any stronger.

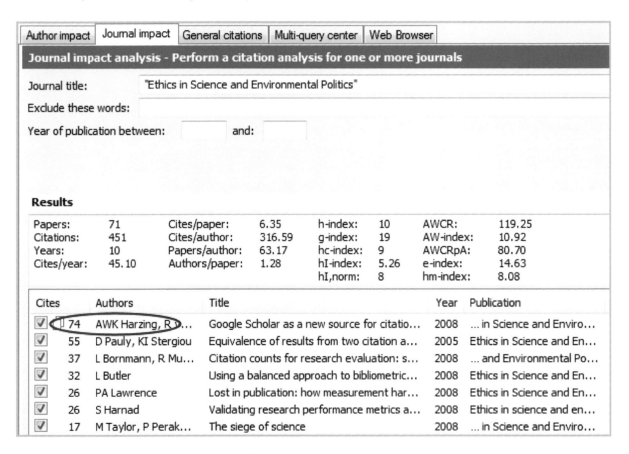

It is not a good idea to use this strategy if your paper was published early in the time period you are reporting on. For instance, if you claim that your paper is amongst the 25% most cited articles in a journal between 2000-2010, and your paper was published in 2000/2001, it is likely that your paper was actually cited less than average for articles in 2000 and 2001. Never boast about papers being in the top 50%, as it just shows your papers are average.

If you do not have any papers that really stand out, but your papers are generally well cited in comparison to the journals they are published in, you could emphasize this. For instance, you could say: on average my articles are amongst the top 20%-30% most cited papers when compared to papers published in the same journal in the same year.

Be careful with this strategy though. Unless you have some papers that have been published in journals that your evaluation committee will recognize as top journals, it will only elicit the comment that you tend to waste your work by publishing in low impact journals.

7.5 PRESENT COMPREHENSIVE CITATIONS FOR EDITED VOLUMES

In some disciplines it is very common to publish edited volumes. In these cases the editor typically invests a significant amount of time in coaching contributors to submit their chapters in time and often provides very significant editorial feedback. Edited volumes can make a major contribution to the field as they typically provide a collection the latest research on a particular topic.

Author impact	Journal impact	General citations	Multi-query center	Web Browser

Journal impact analysis - Perform a citation analysis for one or more journals

Journal title: "International Human Resource Management"

Exclude these words:

Year of publication between: 1995 and: 1995

Results

Papers:	14	Cites/paper:	16.29	h-index:	9	AWCR:	14.25
Citations:	228	Cites/author:	189.83	g-index:	14	AW-index:	3.77
Years:	16	Papers/author:	11.33	hc-index:	5	AWCRpA:	11.86
Cites/year:	14.25	Authors/paper:	1.43	hI-index:	6.23	e-index:	10.77
				hI,norm:	8	hm-index:	7.83

Cites	Authors	Title	Year	Publication
☑ ⧉ 36	H Harris	Women's role in (international) management	1995	International Human Re...
☑ ⧉ 33	K Baumgarten	Training and development of international...	1995	International Human Re...
☑ 26	M Borg, AW Harzing	Composing an international staff	1995	International Human Re...
☑ 26	R Olie	The 'culture'factor in personnel and organi...	1995	International Human Re...
☑ 21	J Paauwe, P Dewe	Human resource management in multinati...	1995	International Human Re...
☑ 20	A Sorge	Cross-national differences in personnel an...	1995	International Human Re...
☐ 14	G Oddou, M Mend...	Expatriate performance appraisal: Proble...	1995	... human resource man...
☑ 13	E Logger, R Vinke,...	Compensation and appraisal in an internat...	1995	International human res...
☑ 13	H Slomp	National variations in worker participation	1995	International Human Re...
☑ 9	W Nijs	International human resource manageme...	1995	International Human Re...
☑ 8	J Paauwe, P Dewe	Organizational structure of multinational c...	1995	International Human Re...
☑ 7	AW Harzing	Strategic planning in multinational corpora...	1995	International Human Re...
☑ 6	A Nadelkerke	European social policy and European indu...	1995	International Human Re...
☑ 6	U Veersma	Multinational Corporations and industrial r...	1995	International Human Re...
☑ 4	M Van der Klink, M...	Human resource development and staff fl...	1995	International Human Re...

Unfortunately, edited volumes are often not appreciated as much as authored books or journal articles in promotion applications. One reason for this might be that the citation impact of these volumes can be quite modest as few authors refer to the edited as a whole. It is more common for authors to refer to individual chapters within an edited volume.

In 1995, I published an edited text-book on International HRM, with new editions in 2004 and 2011. Although a textbook, it generated a lot of citations in academic literature. Many of these citations were to the book as a whole, with a combined number of some 135 citations for the 1995 and 2004 editions.

As the screenshots above and below shows, there were a further 228 citations to the 1995 edition and another 74 citations to the 2004 edition. The 1995 edition was particularly well-cited, with fourteen of the sixteen chapters in the book receiving some citations. Unfortunately, these searches still missed about a dozen citations that didn't have a year attached to them in the Google Scholar results and hence were excluded through the year restriction. Overall, the book therefore had nearly 450 citations, which would allow me to more easily argue the case that it has had a significant impact in the field of International HRM.

Author impact	Journal impact	General citations	Multi-query center	Web Browser

Journal impact analysis - Perform a citation analysis for one or more journals

Journal title: "International Human Resource Management"

Exclude these words:

Year of publication between: 2004 and: 2004

Results

Papers:	12	Cites/paper:	6.17	h-index:	5	AWCR:	10.57
Citations:	74	Cites/author:	59.00	g-index:	8	AW-index:	3.25
Years:	7	Papers/author:	10.50	hc-index:	3	AWCRpA:	8.43
Cites/year:	10.57	Authors/paper:	1.25	hI-index:	3.57	e-index:	6.00
				hI,norm:	5	hm-index:	5.00

Cites		Authors	Title	Year	Publication
✓	20	I Tarique, P Caligiuri	International Staff	2004	... human resource man...
✓	18	T Edwards	The transfer of employment practices acr...	2004	International Human Re...
✓	12	AW Harzing	Composing an international staff	2004	International human res...
✓	6	C Communal, C Br...	HRM in Europe	2004	International Human Re...
✓	5	M Fenwick	Performance management	2004	International human res...
✓	5	T Jackson	HRM in developing countries	2004	International Human Re...

7.6   WHAT TO DO IF YOU HAVE VERY FEW CITATIONS OVERALL?

Of course it is rather difficult to make your case for research impact if you have very few citations, which will often be the case if you are a junior researcher who has started publishing quite recently. In this case, there are several things you can do beyond making the argument that citation scores in your discipline are generally low (only if that's the case of course, see Section 7.1 for details).

7.6.1 ARGUE FOR THE USE OF GOOGLE SCHOLAR

First, if your University prefers ISI as a data source and you have very few citations in ISI, but a respectable number of citations in Google Scholar, you can argue that Google Scholar citations are a more accurate measurement of citation impact for junior scholars. This is true because Google Scholar includes citations in Masters and Doctoral theses, conference proceedings and working papers that, in most cases, will ultimately be reflected in ISI citations. Google Scholar also includes a wider range of journals than ISI, including electronic journals and journals that have shorter publication lags than most ISI-listed journals.

7.6.2 COMPARE YOUR ARTICLES WITH ARTICLES PUBLISHED IN THE SAME YEAR

Second, if you don't have many citations in Google Scholar either, but have one or two articles with more than an incidental number of citations, try to compare these articles with other articles in the same journal that year. This is a defensive version of the same strategy as recommended above for your star articles. Even if your 2009 article has only accumulated 5 Google Scholar citations, if most of the articles in the journal from the same year have no citations so far, you have a pretty good case to make.

The screenshot shows an example where three quarters of the articles published in 2009 had 0 or 1 citation, with 2.16 citations per paper on average. You would be able to make a good case for future impact if you had 5 or more citations. Early citations are usually reflective of high eventual citation counts.

7.6.3 PRESENT ISI BASELINE DATA FOR YOUR FIELD

Third, you can put your lack of citations in context by presenting your evaluation panel with the average number of citations for articles of a certain age published in certain disciplines overall. Unfortunately, this type information is not readily available for Google Scholar as its discipline categories are rather broad. However, it can be found for citations to publications in ISI listed journals only in ISI's database "Essential Science Indicators Baselines".

For instance, if you had published an article in an ISI listed journal in Economics & Business in 2009 that – at the 1st of May 2010 – had even just **one** ISI citation, your article would already be in the top 20% most cited articles. Four citations would even put it in the top 1% most cited articles. Obviously, for articles published in earlier years the number of citations to be in the top 20%/1% will go up.

However, a paper published in an ISI listed journal in Computer Science in 2004 with only **one** citation would still be in the top 50% of most-cited papers for that discipline, i.e. the lack of a significant number of citations would be quite normal. Thus, even though you wouldn't be able convince your tenure or promotion committee your ISI citation record is stellar; if you work in these fields you should be able to convince them that your lack of a significant number of citations is quite normal.

In fact, in Economics & Business, Computer Science, Engineering, Mathematics and the Social Sciences/-General even for papers in ISI listed journals that are 10 years old two to four ISI citations are enough to put an article in the top 50% most cited papers in their fields. As discussed in detail in Chapter 16, this is partly due to the lack of comprehensive coverage of ISI in these disciplines. However, it is also due to differences in citation behavior across fields. To be in the top 50% most cited articles in Molecular Biology & Genetics, you would need your 10-year old paper to have 22 citations at the 1st of May 2010, whilst 64 are needed to be in the top 20%.

7.6.4 ARGUE CITATIONS ARE SLOW TO PICK UP

This is a generic version of the two specific strategies described above. If you do not have many citations in Google Scholar either and do not have any papers with more than an incidental number of citations, your only choice is probably to explain that citations take a long time to pick up. This is particularly true for the Social Sciences and Humanities, where the publication process is generally more drawn-out with many revisions and even accepted publications can take a long time to finally appear in print.

Taking my own case as an example, my current ISI citation record puts me in the top 1% most cited academics for 2000-2010 in my field. However, my citations took rather a long time to take off. My first publication appeared in 1995 and by 2000 I had about a dozen publications printed or in press/accepted. However, at the start of 2000 I only had 9 ISI citations (with 20 new citations in 2000 and 27 new citations in 2001). If I had had to make my tenure case after just 5 years I wouldn't have had much to show for in terms of research impact.

You might be able to apply this strategy by doing some analyses for top people in your field and look at their first five years after they published their first article. This strategy is probably most effective when combined with the next strategy.

Fifth, if you have only a few citations in either ISI or Google Scholar, it might be worth tracking each of them down to see who is citing your work and in which outlets. It is more impressive when many of your citations occur in the top journals in your field or if some famous academics in your field cite your articles. Some of the fame and quality image of the journals and of the academics citing your work might rub off on you in the eyes of your evaluation committee.

This brings me to the sixth and final strategy. If you have very few citations, you may need to focus on the quality of the journals that your work appeared. Whilst in general, this is not appropriate as some papers in top journals never get cited (see Chapter 1 for a discussion on this), on average papers in top journals get cited more than papers in lower-ranked journals. That's why they have higher Journal Impact Factors.

Therefore, if your work has been published in high-impact journals, you can make the case that it is more likely that your work will be highly cited. In addition, you should of course make the argument that these journals have generally higher quality standards for the work they publish and a more rigorous review process. However, that's a quality argument, not a citation impact argument, which is what I am focusing on in this book.

7.7   NORM SCORES FOR DIFFERENT DISCIPLINES

As indicated in Section 7.1, it is usually best to compare yourself to a reference group of peers in your own discipline or university. However, for some of you this might not be possible as there are not enough academics in your peer group or because you do not have the time to research your peer group. In that case, you might find the norm scores in this section useful.

Ever since Publish or Perish has been available, academics have asked me for "norm scores" for the various indices. I have always hesitated to provide these as these scores are so easily taken out of context and can often take on a life of their own. However, currently the only publications providing norm scores for the h-index and related indices deal with academics in the (Natural) Sciences. H-indices in the Natural Sciences are much higher than in the Social Sciences and Humanities. Hence, I felt that in order to support academics in the Social Sciences and Humanities it would be appropriate to provide some systematic evidence that lower citation indices can be expected in these disciplines.

A calculation of citation metrics for an individual academic requires one to be at least familiar with the field in question (in order to eliminate publications by authors with similar names) and preferably with the individual's work. Therefore, my "norm scores" only pertain to the two fields that I am familiar with: Management and International Business.

7.7.1   METHOD

It is difficult to establish an appropriate reference group. However, I think most academics will agree that fellow academics who have been elected as presidents of the peak professional organization in their field would probably constitute an appropriate (if ambitious) benchmark. Therefore, I have calculated the various citation metrics (h-index, g-index, contemporary h-index and individual h-index) for presidents of the Academy of Management (AoM) and the Academy of International Business (AIB) since 1988. Since AIB presidentship only rotates every 2 years, the data are based on 13 individuals, whereas for AoM they are based on 23 individuals.

It is important to note that the record of specific individuals might be both underestimated and overestimated. Most of the publications of academics that were presidents in the early years will be relatively old. Google Scholar does not perform as well for older publications, because these publications and the publications that cite them have not (yet) been posted on the web. Hence their citation metrics might be understated.

On the other hand, given that Google Scholar cannot go back in time, I calculated their citation metrics as of the **current** date, rather than the date at which they **became** president, hence overstating their citation metrics. This overstatement could be very substantial for earlier presidents, and given the rapid increase in citations in the later stages of one's career, could even be quite substantial for later presidents.

7.7.2   RESULTS

Using Publish or Perish I found the following citation metrics as of July 2010. I report the general h-index, the g-index, the contemporary h-index (h_c) and the individual h-index ($h_{I,norm}$). Years active is the number of years since the presidents' first publication.

Obviously, this is a very distinguished group of academics, who on average have been active for 36-39 years. Hence, one should not expect every applicant for a professorial position in Management or International Business (let alone for positions lower down in the academic hierarchy) to meet these norm scores. However, if applicants do meet these norm scores or even come close to them, they should have a strong case for research impact.

Organization	h-index	g-index	h_c	$h_{I,norm}$	Years active
Academy of Management	34	81	20	25	36
Range	(19-69)	(39-145)	(9-38)	(15-44)	(27-42)
Academy of International Business	27	60	15	22	39
Range	(12-60)	(26-157)	(6-35)	(8-54)	(28-56)

As is apparent from the range of scores within these two groups, there are substantial differences in citation scores even **within** these two distinguished groups of academics. Further, since most presidents of AIB and AoM are senior, well-established scholars many of them will have published a lot of their important work a while ago. This means that their **contemporary** h-indices are normally substantially lower than their regular h-index.

There are also two interesting disciplinary differences apparent in these norm scores. First academics in International Business can be expected to have lower citation scores overall than academics in Management. Second, academics in Management typically publish slightly more co-authored papers than academics in International Business, reflected in the more substantial drop in their individual h-index.

On my website, I invite academics to submit norm scores for reference groups in their own sub-discipline with a short description of their search parameters. I would suggest that comparison groups need to include at least 10 academics (and preferably more) to avoid idiosyncrasies. If I am confident that the searches have been done competently, I will post them on my website with attribution to the person who has compiled them. Please submit your results to pop@harzing.com.

Below is a list of norm scores that has been submitted so far. Although I have done a "sanity check" for each of these papers, the ultimate responsibility lies with the authors. Please contact the individual authors if you have any questions about the paper in question.

- Research Performance of Senior Level Marketing Academics in the Australian Universities: An Exploratory Study Based on Citation Analysis, a paper by Mohammed A. Razzaque and Ian F. Wilkinson, presented at the Australia New Zealand Marketing Academy Conference (ANZMAC), University of Otago, New Zealand, Dec 1-3 2007.
- Citation Benchmarks for Articles Published by Australian Marketing Academics, a paper by Geoff Soutar, In M. Thyne, K. R. Deans and J. Gnoth (eds.), Conference Proceedings of the 2007 ANZMAC Conference. Dunedin: Department of Marketing, University of Otago, 3515-3520.
- Measuring the research contribution of management academics using the Hirsch-index by John Mingers, published in *Journal of the Operational Research Society*, applies the h-index to three groups of management scholars: BAM fellows, INFORMS fellows and members of COPIOR.
- Cumulative and career-stage citation impact of social-personality programs and their members by Brian Nosek and co-authors provides benchmarks for evaluating impact across the career span in psychology, and other disciplines with similar citation patterns. In press for PERSONALITY AND SOCIAL PSYCHOLOGY BULLETIN. Supplementary page with career-stage impact calculators: http://projectimplicit.net/nosek/papers/citations/
- In Characterizing author citation ratings of herpetologists using Harzing's Publish or Perish Malcolm L. McCallum analyzed a random sample of herpetologists. He used linear regression to analyze the influence of career length and publication count on their h-score, g-score, e-score, and m-quotient and provides mean scores for each author metric for herpetologists at various career lengths.

CHAPTER 8:
HOW TO EVALUATE OTHER ACADEMICS?

Thus far, I have assumed that you are using Publish or Perish to evaluate your **own** citation record. However, there are plenty of other uses of Publish or Perish that might lead you to evaluate **another** academic's citation record. In this chapter, I will discuss the most common instances and give you some tips and caveats when using Publish or Perish in this fashion.

The examples vary from a 5-minute preparation before meeting someone you don't know, to evaluating editorial board members or prospective PhD supervisors, from writing up tributes (or laudations) and eulogies, to deciding on publication awards and preparing for a job interview.

8.1   GETTING A QUICK IMPRESSION OF SOMEONE YOU ARE MEETING

I am sure many of you will recognize the following scenario. You are due to meet an official guest of some standing, but you do not know the academic in question very well and hence do not have a clear idea of what he or she is well-known for. You only have 5-10 minutes before the meeting. How do you ensure you are well-prepared and don't blunder your way through the meeting?

You could of course start searching on the web for a university staff page. However, these are not always easy to find, especially if the academic has a relatively common name. Moreover, not all universities allow their staff to create their own web pages and even if they do, they often are out of date as most academics are not very diligent in maintaining them. Publish or Perish offers a quick solution. If you know the academic's given and family name you can use these for a very quick author search, which can allow you to deduce quite a lot in just a couple of minutes.

8.1.1   WHAT ARE YOU BEST KNOWN FOR?

Even though the quick-and-dirty search might not give you fully accurate citation statistics, looking at the most cited works will give you a very quick idea of what the academic in question is best-known for. It might also give you some insight into their publication strategy. Do they have a large number of papers that have gathered a reasonable, but not extremely high, number of citations? That might point to a more diversified publication strategy. Do they have one or two papers with a huge number of citations and other less cited work? This might point to a very focused publication strategy?

8.1.2   WHO ARE YOU WORKING **WITH**?

By sorting on the author column, you can quickly find out the academic's co-authors. Maybe you have an academic acquaintance or even collaborator in common? Nothing is better to get a conversation going than talking about people you both know. Looking at an academic's earliest collaborators might also give you a clue about who his/her PhD advisor was. Finding that someone mostly publishes on his/her own is also useful to know. You might not bring up collaborative work in that case, certainly not in a first meeting.

8.1.3   WHAT ARE YOU WORKING ON **RECENTLY**?

Sorting on the year column helps you finding out what the academic in question has been working on most recently. Most academics don't like it if you talk only about a paper they published ten years ago (even if it is a classic) as the research in question might be more than fifteen years old and they might have moved on to completely different topics by now.

8.1.4   HOW LONG HAVE YOU BEEN IN THE BUSINESS?

Reviewing the years active statistic gives you *some* feel for how much academic experience the person you are meeting is likely to have. Of course this might not be of great importance, but again it might change what you will be talking about with this person. Knowing this ahead of time might be helpful. Your conversations with someone in a mid-career stage might be different from those with someone who is close to retirement.

8.1.5   WHAT JOURNALS HAVE YOU PUBLISHED IN?

Sorting on the publication column will also allow you to establish which journals the academic has published in, giving you an idea of his/her disciplinary orientation and publication strategy. Have they published in general or specialized journals, do they publish mostly conceptual or empirical work? Have they published in the top journals in their field? Have they published in lots of different journals or focused their output in a small number of journals.

8.1.6   WORKED EXAMPLE: RABI BHAGAT

In July 2010, two of my colleagues had organized a 2-day workshop on Global Teams. One of the keynote speakers was Rabi Bhagat. Although I had seen his name in press before, I could not recall clearly in what context and I had never met him before. I therefore ran a quick Publish or Perish Author Query. The results for his most cited works are below.

Cites		Authors	Title
☑	322	BL Kedia, RS Bhagat	Cultural constraints on transfer of technology across nations: Implications for res
☑	281	RS Bhagat, BL Kedia, PD …	Cultural variations in the cross-border transfer of organizational knowledge: An i
☑	212	RS Bhagat, SJ McQuaid	Role of subjective culture in organizations: A review and directions for future res
☑	151	TA Beehr, RS Bhagat	Human stress and cognition in organizations: An integrated perspective
☑	150	SE Sullivan, RS Bhagat	Organizational stress, job satisfaction and job performance: Where do we go fro
☑	137	K Leung, RS Bhagat, NR …	Culture and international business: Recent advances and their implications for fu
☑	83	RS Bhagat	Effects of stressful life events on individual performance effectiveness and work
☑	79	RS Bhagat, SJ McQuaid, …	Total life stress: A multimethod validation of the construct and its effects on orga
☑	57	RD Arvey, RS Bhagat, E …	Cross-cultural and cross-national issues in personnel and human resources mana
☑	54	TA Beehr, RS Bhagat	Introduction to human stress and cognition in organizations
☑	45	JM Bailey, RS Bhagat	Meaning and measurement of stressors in the work environment: An evaluation
☑	41	RS Bhagat, KO Prien	Cross-cultural training in organizational contexts
☑	40	RS Bhagat, SM Allie	Organizational stress, personal life stress, and symptoms of life strains: An exam

I could see immediately that he had done influential work on the impact of culture on transfer of technology and knowledge across borders, which is most likely where I had seen his name in print as I have done some work on transfer of management practices across cultures. However, I also noticed that he has a fairly large body of work related to stress and stressors in the workplace. This made me realize that his disciplinary background might be in organizational behavior or even psychology. His work on technology transfer had led me to the erroneous assumption he was a more macro oriented strategy scholar.

That first result also showed me that he has worked with a fairly varied group of co-authors, and acted both as first and second author. The titles of his papers led me to conclude that he seems to prefer conceptual work to empirical work as most of his papers appear to be about building theory, creating frameworks and providing an integrative perspective.

Sorting the results by year (see below) showed me that recently he became interested in the role of Asia in management theories and in global mindsets. I also noticed that he has maintained his interest in stress, but has added a cross-cultural element to it. Further, I noticed that although his most cited (older) work is mostly conceptual, his recent articles seems to include empirical work, with data collected in a lot of different countries. Given that he is the first author on these articles, I conclude he was leading those projects. As I have led several multi-country projects myself, that might be a nice conversation topic.

Authors	Title	Year
RS Bhagat, AS McDevitt, …	On improving the robustness of Asian management theories: Theoretical anchor…	2010
MW Peng, RS Bhagat, SJ …	Asia and global business	2010
RS Bhagat, B Krishnan, T…	Organizational stress, psychological strain, and work outcomes in six national co…	2010
RS Bhagat, RM Steers	Cambridge handbook of culture, organizations, and work	2009
RS Bhagat, CA Davis, ML …	24 Acculturative stress in professional immigrants: towards a cultural theory of …	2009
RS Bhagat, PK Steverson…	International and Cultural Variations in Employee Assistance Programmes: Implic…	2007
RS Bhagat, HC Triandis, B…	On Becoming a Global Manager: A Closer Look at the Opportunities and Constrai…	2007
RS Bhagat, JR Van Scotte…	Cultural Variations in Individual Job Performance: Implications for Industrial and …	2007

Sorting the results by journals showed (amongst others) no less than four articles in the Academy of Management Review (a journal that only publishes conceptual work), three articles each in Human Relations (two of which theoretical) and Journal of Management and two articles each in Journal of Organizational Behavior and Journal of Vocational Behavior. This confirmed my earlier impression that my counterpart was strong in conceptual work. It also confirmed that he was more of a micro Organizational Behavior scholar more so than a macro International Business scholar.

In five minutes, I was ready to meet our keynote speaker. As it turned out, we only talked about Melbourne (the conference location) and Publish or Perish, and more in particular the differences between ISI and Google Scholar citations. But at least I felt prepared for any conversation about his academic work!

8.1.7   CONCLUSION

Even just a 5-minute author search can give you a quick impression of another academic. Obviously, you could do the same type of search in a more rigorous fashion if you were meeting up with someone who could be a potential co-author.

Publish or Perish can be used to provide a quick evaluation tool to assess a specific set of academics for a large variety of functions. I would certainly not advocate it to be used as the **only** evaluation mechanism. However, it can be very useful as a first port of call, because it often allows one to quickly reduce one's options to a smaller group to assess in more detail.

There is a large variety of possible functions one could think of: reviewers for journals or conferences, examiners for Master of PhD theses, key note speakers, discussants or session chairs for conferences, academic mentors, referees, etc. In this section, I will discuss selection as an editorial board member, but the mechanisms involved are very similar for most of these functions. In addition, I will discuss evaluation "from the other side", i.e. prospective PhD or Masters students looking for a supervisor.

8.2.1   EDITORIAL BOARD MEMBERSHIP

Several journal editors told me they are frequently using Publish or Perish to get a quick impression of the publication record of potential editorial board members. There are several things that an editor/evaluator would be interested in.

ACADEMIC CREDIBILITY

The first question would be: Does the prospective editorial board member (or reviewer or examiner or referee…) have a credible publication record? If one is selecting an editorial board member for a prestigious journals there should be some evidence of publications that have had an impact on the field and of a sustained stream of research output. This can be easily evaluated looking at the number of publications and citations that PoP reports.

This does not mean one should always select people with the best publication record. First, academics with stellar publication records are often already serving on many editorial boards. Second, these academics are often so busy that they are not reliable reviewers, sometimes taking months to complete their reviews. Choosing someone who is up and coming and eager to make a name for themselves might be a better choice.

EXPERTISE IN THE AREA IN QUESTION

The prospective editorial board member should also have sufficient expertise in the specific disciplinary orientation of the journal or the sub-discipline that is currently underrepresented. A quick perusal of the titles of the prospective board member's publications should be sufficient to establish this.

For some journals it might be important to have a broad orientation so that one is able to review in a range of different, but related areas. Other journals might prefer specialists, either because the journal is a specialist journal itself (e.g. *International Journal of Nuclear Desalination*), or because the journal has a more general orientation, but only publishes the very best research in each sub-discipline (e.g. *Science*).

EXPERIENCE WITH THE JOURNAL

An editor will also want to know whether the prospective editorial board member has experience with the journal. Most journals will keep systematic files on their ad-hoc reviewers, so if the prospective board member has been a successful ad hoc reviewer, they can be expected to have sufficient experience with the journal. However, editors would normally give preference (or in some cases only consider) academics who have published in the journal themselves. Publish or Perish makes it very easy to run a quick search on this.

GEOGRAPHICAL SCOPE

Many journals in the Social Sciences will publish work conducted in different countries. To the extent that the country context matter for the research in question, it is important to have editorial board members with a broad geographical experience.

Although it is not always possible to deduce this from the articles titles, in many cases a quick perusal of the PoP results should provide the editor with a feel for the experience the prospective board members has with research in different countries. Looking at their co-authors might also give some clues, to the extent one can deduce nationality from names.

CAVEATS

None of these factors can be established with absolute certainly through a simple Publish or Perish search. However, the editor should be able to get a pretty good feel for the prospective board members that are worthy of further investigation.

There are of course many other criteria for selecting editorial board members. First, and probably most importantly, good academics are not always good reviewers. It takes a considerable amount of skill and care to write a well-informed and constructive review. Often academics who possess these skills are successful publishers themselves, but this is not always the case. If these reviewers have consistently provided excellent reviewers' report as ad hoc reviewers, they may be chosen on the editorial board in spite of their lack of academic achievement.

Second, editorial board appointments can function as signaling devices, indicating to the journal's readership that the journal in question welcomes submissions from researchers working in specific subdisciplines or using certain methodological approaches. In that case, an editor might prefer an academic who fulfils this signaling function over someone with a higher level of academic credibility or expertise.

8.2.2   LOOKING FOR A PHD/MASTERS SUPERVISOR

Although some research higher degrees students are pretty happy to just enroll in a program and get a supervisor assigned to them, there are others who are far more proactive and actively search for the most suitable supervisors who are looking for supervisors. I was bemused to see Publish or Perish recommend for this purpose in a variety of blogs visited by PhD students.

Although I would not recommend selecting a supervisor based on the Publish or Perish output alone, there is no doubt that it would allow prospective PhD students to get a feel for the publication record of their prospective supervisors. In fact, a number of academics have told me they use PoP to market their programs to potential PhD students.

My slight concern with this is that not all prospective PhD students might have enough maturity to realize that a successful publication record doesn't guarantee a successful supervisor. There are many personality factors (ability to give constructive feedback, patience, enthusiasm, empathy) that might be more important in the student-supervisor relationship.

Furthermore, although in the Sciences working in a laboratory headed by a successful academic might substantially improve one's career chances, this relationship is not as strong in the Social Sciences or Humanities. In fact, in these disciplines younger or more recent graduates may be better supervisors than famous professors, because the former often have more time and more up-to-date methodological expertise.

8.3   WRITING TRIBUTES, LAUDATIONS OR EULOGIES

Publish or Perish users are also using the program when writing tributes, laudations or eulogies. Although these two tasks will generate diametrically opposite emotions, in both cases it is equally important to get a complete overview of someone's impact on the field. It is all too easy to be heavily influenced by a number of contributions that are well-known to you personally, whilst forgetting the broader impact that the academic in question might have had.

Cites	Authors	Title	Year	Publication
4686	CA Bartlett, S Gho...	Managing across borders: The transnationa...	1998	
4562	J Nahapiet, S Gho...	Social capital, intellectual capital, and the or...	1998	Academy of management revie
1556	W Tsai, S Ghoshal	Social capital and value creation: The role o...	1998	Academy of management Jour
1379	H Mintzberg, S Gh...	The strategy process: concepts, contexts, ...	2003	
1194	S Ghoshal, P Moran	Bad for practice: A critique of the transacti...	1996	Academy of management Revi
980	S Ghoshal, CA Bar...	The multinational corporation as an interorg...	1990	Academy of management revie
825	S Ghoshal	Bad management theories are destroying g...	2005	Academy of Management Lear
823	CA Bartlett, S Gho...	Transnational management: text, cases, an...	2000	
771	S Ghoshal	Global strategy: An organizing framework	1987	Strategic management journal
549	CA Bartlett, S Gho...	Changing the role of top management: bey...	1994	Harvard Business Review
541	S Ghoshal, CA Bar...	The individualized corporation: a fundament...	1997	
496	S Ghoshal, N Nohria	Internal differentiation within multinational ...	1989	Strategic Management Journal
463	CA Bartlett, S Gho...	Tap your subsidiaries for global reach	1986	Harvard Business Review
458	N Nohria, S Ghoshal	The differentiated network: Organizing mult...	1997	
387	CA Bartlett, S Gho...	Beyond the M-form: toward a managerial th...	1993	Strategic Management Journal
358	S Ghoshal, CA Bar...	Creation, adoption, and diffusion of innova...	1988	Journal of International Busine
278	N Nohria, S Ghoshal	Differentiated fit and shared values: Altern...	1994	Strategic Management Journal
278	CA Bartlett, S Gho...	What is a global manager?	2003	Harvard Business Review
268	S Ghoshal, H Korin...	Interunit communication in multinational cor...	1994	Management Science
265	S Ghoshal, N Nohria	Horses for courses: organizational forms fo...	1993	Sloan Management Review
251	CA Bartlett, S Gho...	Managing innovation in the transnational co...	1997	Oxford University Press, New \

As an example of how to use Publish or Perish in writing obituaries (or review works outlining the impact of a scholar's work) I will focus on Sumantra Ghoshal. His *Managing Across Borders* book with Christopher Bartlett, first published in 1989, was the inspiration for my own PhD work on control mechanisms in multinational companies and I was very shocked to learn of his untimely death at only 55 in 2004.

The screenshot above clearly shows that Sumantra Ghoshal's work has had an enormous impact on the field, with more than 20 of his publications generating more than 250 citations and five of them generating more than 1,000 citations. In total, his work generated more than 25,000 citations, even though less than 20 years had passed between his first publication and his untimely death. However, there are several other conclusions we can derive from the Publish or Perish data.

8.3.1   GOOGLE SCHOLAR SHOWS A MUCH BROADER IMPACT

Comparing Ghoshal's Google Scholar citation record with his ISI citation record again shows us how much broader the coverage of Google Scholar is in the Social Sciences (for more details on this see Chapters 13 and 16). Ghoshal's most cited book (*Managing Across Borders*) doesn't even show up in ISI if you search for his name as he is not the first author.

However, even searching for Christopher Bartlett only finds some 800 ISI citations, less than a fifth of the Google Scholar citations. The same is true for their *Transnational Management* book which registers just over 100 ISI citations in ISI, completely negating its important impact on the field. Ghoshal's journal articles fare a bit better in ISI, but even for them Google Scholar citations are generally three times as high.

8.3.2   COMBINING TOP SCHOLARSHIP WITH MANAGERIAL RELEVANCE

The Publish or Perish data clearly illustrate Ghoshal's fairly unique ability to combine rigorous scholarship with work that has managerial relevance. He has published a large number of very influential books that are read beyond the academic community and has published a large part of his work in more managerially oriented journals such as *Harvard Business Review* and *Sloan Management Review*.

However, at the same time, he has published in the very top journals in the field of Management and Strategy, such as the *Academy of Management Review/Journal, Strategic Management Journal, Management Science*, and *Journal of International Business Studies*. There are few academics that have combined rigor and relevance so successfully. Although, I was already aware of this before running the search, the Publish or Perish analysis made me realize that even Ghoshal's earliest work, a working paper on scanning behavior by managers, had a practical slant.

8.3.3   FIGHTING FOR A BETTER WORLD

Many academics and students will have been inspired by Ghoshal's last article, published posthumously in the *Academy of Management of Learning & Education*. Entitled "Bad Management Theories are Destroying Good Management Practice", it is a very dramatic analysis of the potential negative impact of academic theories. However, I was unaware that Ghoshal's interest in this field was long-standing with a critique on transaction cost theory published in 1996.

I was also unaware of another posthumous publication "Scholarship that Endures", that appeared in a little-known research annual *Research Methodology in Strategy and Management*, published by Emerald publishers. As even four years after publication, there is only one citation to this paper (in a paper published the same research annual), I can only assume most people are unaware of it. Hence, I am quoting the first paragraph of the article at length, in the hope that it will offer inspiration for current and future scholars:

> *"As academics, we collectively publish thousands of articles and hundreds of books each year. We spend a large part of our lives producing them, sacrificing, in the process, sleep, time with our families, reading things we want to read, seeing places we wish to see. Most of these books and articles soon vanish without a trace, helping us get tenure perhaps, but talking with them into oblivion very large parts of the best years of our lives. Few – very few – of the outputs of our intellectual endeavors endure. What is it that distinguishes scholarship that endures from scholarship that does not?" (Ghoshal, 2006: 1)*

8.3.4   SERENDIPITOUS FINDINGS

As an aside, finding Ghoshal's "Scholarship that Endures" article in Google Books also led me to stumble upon another article in the same volume of this research annual that is of substantial relevance to me (Bednar & Westphal, 2006). It deals with improving response rates when surveying corporate elites. It is another article that deserves far more attention than its meager 2 citations (one in a Health Care journal, one in a working paper in Accounting) seem to suggest it receives.

I therefore ran a search for articles published in this research annual (screenshot below) and discovered a large number of highly intriguing titles written by well-known scholars. However, most of these articles seem to have generated very little interest so far, with half of the papers having 0, 1 or 2 citations and only a quarter – reproduced in the screenshot – generating more than 10 citations. It is exactly these kinds of serendipitous findings that are facilitated by Publish or Perish and Google Scholar.

Cites	Authors	Title	Year
56	MA Hitt, BK Boyd, D Li	The state of strategic management research and a vision of the future	2004
34	T Felin, NJ Foss	Individuals and organizations: thoughts on a micro-foundations project...	2006
32	JG Combs, TR Crook, ...	The dimensionality of organizational performance and its implications fo...	2004
28	JB Barney, TB Mackey	Testing resource-based theory	2005
18	PS Barr	Current and potential importance of qualitative methods in strategy re...	2004
18	SF Slater, K Atuahene...	Conducting survey research in strategic management	2004
17	HP Bowen, MF Wiersema	Modeling limited dependent variables: Methods and guidelines for rese...	2004
16	RD Ireland, JW Webb...	Theory and methodology in entrepreneurship research	2005
15	LJ Williams, MB Gavin,...	Structural equation modeling methods in strategy research: Application...	2004
13	HR Greve, E Goldeng	Longitudinal analysis in strategic management	2004
12	K Lajili, M Madunic, JT ...	Testing organizational economics theories of vertical integration	2007
11	NP Podsakoff, W She...	The role of formative measurement models in strategic management re...	2006
11	JAC Baum, B McKelve...	Analysis of extremes in management studies	2006
10	BK Boyd, S Gove	Managerial constraint: The intersection between organizational task en...	2006

Many disciplines have publication awards, i.e. awards for particular publications rather than awards for an academic's overall career. Although the importance of the topic and the quality of the scholarship would normally be the most important criterion in deciding on publication awards, the level of impact might be an additional criterion of interest. Below I will discuss publication award for both research books and research articles.

8.4.1   GOOGLE SCHOLAR COMPREHENSIVELY EVALUATES THE IMPACT OF BOOKS

In the Social Sciences and Humanities book awards are a very important signal of academic excellence. In the Humanities, it can even be considered to be one of the **most** important indicators as books are normally seen as the most prestigious research outputs.

Several academics have informed to me that they have used Publish or Perish to propose one of their colleagues or students for a book award. Being able to show impact is especially important for relatively unknown authors. Hence, having a good understanding of the impact of research books is very important for award committees. Publish or Perish can be used to easily get a comprehensive account of citation data for books as the two examples below show.

THE IMPACT OF BOOKS ACROSS DISCIPLINES AND DATA SOURCES

In the detailed comparisons of data sources and metrics across disciplines that is presented in Chapter 16, I noticed that all academics outside the Sciences had published at least one research book. The table below shows the citation impact of these books according to ISI and Google Scholar.

Discipline	ISI citations (cited reference search)	GS citations	% Increase GS citations
Business Academic	66	200	203%
Computer Scientist	None*/538	2599	383%
Education academic	132	797	504%
Linguist	78	518	564%
Political scientist	62	215	247%
Media studies academic	110	538	389%
Total	986	4858	394%

* The academic in question is 2nd author of the book, so the book does not appear when searching for his name in ISI.

Please note that the number of citations for ISI was acquired using the ISI Cited reference functions, as books do not show up at all in ISI's general search function (see Chapter 1 and Chapters 13 and 16 for further details about these differences). The many stray citations for these books (several dozens for the most cited book) were manually added to the counts.

It is abundantly clear that by only looking at ISI citations, I would seriously underestimate the impact of these research books. Even for the Business academic Google Scholar find three times as many citations, whilst for the Linguist Google Scholar finds nearly seven times as many citations. Overall, Google Scholar reports nearly five times as many citations as ISI for these research books.

TERRY BOOK AWARD WINNER DO HAVE IMPACT!

Our second illustration involves a citation analysis for books winning the Terry book award between 1992-2001. I have chosen this award for two reasons. First, the Terry Book award is a prestigious award given yearly by the Academy of Management, the most important professional organization in the field of management.

Second, Pfeffer and Fong (2002) strongly criticized business school research for its lack of impact. One of their arguments was based on an analysis of the impact of books winning the Terry Book award. Pfeffer and Fong (2002) claim that even these, supposedly highly influential, books only had an average of 6.80 citations per year.

Walsh, Tushman, Kimberly, Starbuck & Ashford (2007) subsequently use these data to conclude that this shows that our best books are not particularly well read even by our scholarly peers. I found this conclusion rather surprising and wondered whether the same conclusion would be drawn if I used a more inclusive source of citation impact, i.e. Google Scholar instead of ISI's Web of Science.

INACCURATE CITATION ANALYSIS CREATES MYTHS

In order to assess this, I first repeated the analysis conducted by Pfeffer and Fong (2002). This analysis was conducted in September 2007. Our results show that the Terry Book Award winners on average received 346 citations in the Web of Science for an average of approximately 34 citations a year (calculated by dividing citations by the number of years since publication), not exactly a performance which I would consider to show low impact.

Hence our conclusion strongly contradicts that of Pfeffer and Fong. It is unclear why our analysis resulted in so many more citations. One reason might be the fact that our analysis was conducted five years later than theirs and hence the books had had more time to gather citations. This shows that the impact of books might take some time to effectuate and hence JIF-like indices that use two year time-spans would not be very useful for books or for research fields that take a long time for work to penetrate.

Another reason might be that Pfeffer and Fong did not systematically include misspellings or appearances with different author initials (i.e. the many stray citations in ISI). A final reason might be that in the case of the *Handbook of Organization Studies* they did not include citations to individual chapters.

Whatever the reason, it shows that one should be very careful before drawing rather far-reaching conclusions. Whilst I would not necessarily negate Pfeffer and Fong's general conclusion that business school do not have much impact on practice, their conclusion that even our best books do not have an academic impact or Walsh's even stronger conclusion that *"our best books are not particularly read by business people or by their scholarly peers"* (Walsh et al., 2007: 129) does not seem to be supported by the data.

This note of caution is all the more important since myths are easily created by subsequent citations that seem to endorse the message, making it unassailable (see also Harzing, 2002). The Pfeffer & Fong article had already gathered 57 ISI and 169 GS citations in September 2007, when this analysis was initially conducted. Today (July 2010) it has no less than 165 ISI citations and 576 Google Scholar citations.

GS REPORTS 2.5 TIMES AS MANY CITATIONS AS ISI'S WEB OF SCIENCE

Even more remarkable than the difference between our Web of Science search and that of Pfeffer & Fong, is the difference in impact when using Google Scholar as a base for citations. On average GS reports nearly 2 ½ times as many citations as the ISI WoS, for an average of 833 citations per book and 81 citations per book per year. Both measures show that these books have (had) a very considerable impact on the field.

The differences are particularly large for two books in the area of Strategic Management (those authored by Haspeslagh & Mintzberg), reflecting our observation in Chapter 15 that Strategy journals are not particularly well covered in ISI. In the case of Philip Haspeslagh, the fact that this academic is not working at a North American university might also have led to a modest impact in ISI listed journals, given the focus of ISI on North American journals.

Year	First Author	Title	ISI cites	GS cites	% GS incr.	ISI/ year	GS/ year
1992	Stopford, J.M.	Rival States, Rival Firms: Competition for World Market Shares	166	266	60%	11	18
1993	Haspeslagh, P.C.	Managing acquisitions: creating value through corporate renewal	125	513	310%	9	37
1994	Cox, T.	Cultural Diversity in Organizations: Theory, Research, and Practice	298	587	97%	23	45
1995	Mintzberg, H.	The Rise & Fall of Strategic Planning: Reconceiving Roles for Planning, Plans, Planners	480	1614	236%	40	124
1996	Rousseau, D.M.	Psychological Contracts in Org.: understanding written & unwritten agreements	406	951	134%	37	86
1997	Clegg, S.R.	The Handbook of Organization Studies	1315	2667	103%	132	267
1998	Nohria, N.	Differentiated Network: Organizing Multinational Corporations for Value Creation	101	270	167%	11	30
1999	Brown, S.L.	Competing on the edge: strategy as structured chaos	221	499	126%	28	62
2000	Aldrich, H.	Organizations Evolving	316	917	190%	45	131
2001	Thomas, D.A	Breaking Through: The Making of Minority Executives in Corporate America	35	47	34%	6	8
Average			**346**	**833**	**141%**	**34**	**81**

An update of the Google Scholar citations for these books was done in July 2010 (i.e. nearly three years after the initial data collection), using the PoP general search function (see screenshot below). This showed that on average these books had gathered another 240 Google Scholar citations **per year** and the average total number of citations for the books was 1660 citations, hardly a sign of a lack of impact.

General citation search - Perform a general citation search

Author(s):	Haspeslagh		
Publication:			
All of the words:			
Any of the words:			
None of the words:			
The phrase:	"Managing Acquisitions"		
Year of publication between:	0	and:	0

Results

Papers:	6	Cites/paper:	173.50	h-index:	3	AWCR:	52.05
Citations:	1041	Cites/author:	520.50	g-index:	6	AW-index:	7.21
Years:	20	Papers/author:	3.00	hc-index:	2	AWCRpA:	26.03
Cites/year:	52.05	Authors/paper:	2.00	hI-index:	1.50	e-index:	32.00
				hI,norm:	3	hm-index:	2.50

Cites		Authors	Title	Year
☑	767	PC Haspeslagh, DB Jemison	Managing acquisitions: Creating value through corporate renewal	1991
☑	261	PC Haspeslagh, DB Jemison	Managing acquisitions	1991
☑	5	G Haspeslagh, DB Jemison	Managing acquisitions: creating value through corporate acquisi…	1991
☑	3	C Haspeslagh Philippe, D…	Managing Acquisitions	1991
☑	3	PC Haspeslagh, DB Jemison	Managing Acquisitions–Creating Value Through Corporate Rene…	1991
☑	2	PC Haspeslagh, DB Jemison	Managing acquisitions: creating value through corporate renew…	1991

8.4.2   GOOGLE SCHOLAR SPOTS EARLY CITES FOR BEST JOURNAL ARTICLES

Many journals award some type of best paper award on a yearly basis. One of the factors that are often considered when awarding best journal article prizes is the (citation) impact a particular article has had. This is relatively easy to do when the awards are given 10 years after publications, as is for instance the case with the *Journal of International Business Studies* decade award.

However, most journal article prizes are awarded the 1 or 2 years after the articles are published. Especially in the Social Sciences and Humanities there are few articles that gather significant citation impact in such a short time. For instance this year (2010), my article with Nancy Adler (When Knowledge Wins: the Sense and Nonsense of Academic Ranking) won the 2009 outstanding article of the year for the *Academy of Management Learning and Education* journal in which it was published.

I hope this was mainly because of the article's content which cautioned against an exclusive focus on academic rankings discussed the importance of doing research that has relevance to societal problems. However, it is likely that the decision was at least partially influenced by the article's citation impact.

Unfortunately the ISI Web of Science general search database has so far neglected to incorporate **any** articles published in AMLE for 2009, except for articles in the first (March) issue. Of these there was one article with 18 citations (the awarded paper), two articles with 4 citations and several articles with 1-3 citations for a total of 38 citations for AMLE for 2009. Hence, it is clear that ISI data would have been pretty useless in assessing the impact of articles published in AMLE in 2009.

Looking at Google Scholar data (see screenshot), the picture is entirely different. Although the awarded article is still the most cited article in the journal, there are fourteen (not two) other articles with at least 4 citations and the total number of citations to AMLE articles published in 2009 is 179, not 38. From this, I would conclude that many articles published in this journal do have a fairly substantial immediate impact.

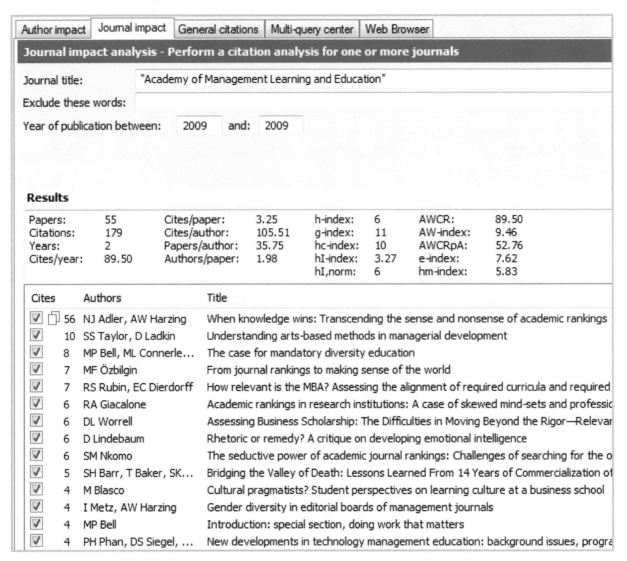

However, even in cases where ISI **does** have complete data for the journal in question, I would recommend using Google Scholar data instead when evaluating papers for publication awards as they are a much better indicator of early impact. This is true because Google Scholar includes citations in conference papers and working papers, most of which will eventually find their way to published articles. For more detailed information on this, see Chapters 7 and 13.

We have all been in this situation: you are invited for an academic job interview and you want to be well-prepared. As part of your search you want to find out what academics in the university you applied for are working on. You might even want to do this **before** applying for the job to decide whether this is the place for you or simply to tailor your application.

Remember that most applicants for the job are well qualified and will do a good job in their research presentation and teaching demonstration. What matters most is that you create a **connection** with the people on your interview or shortlist panel. They should be able to picture you as a person they **could**, and would **want to**, work with.

As far as I know, personal chemistry is impossible to engineer. However, there is a lot you can do to increase the chances of building a connection by being well prepared. There are several ways you could approach this, discussed in more detail below. Please note that I am absolutely not suggesting you should misrepresent your academic record or compromise your own personal values. However, you can easily emphasize different aspects of your academic record depending on who is on your panel.

8.5.1   FIND OUT WHAT YOUR PANEL MEMBERS ARE WORKING ON

Publish or Perish gives you a quick and easy way to find out what the academics on your interview panel are best known for. Simply do an "author impact search" for each of the members of your interview panel. You might also want to read some of these articles in order to be able to make intelligent comments about them.

Just like when you are preparing to meet someone in a more casual setting (Section 8.1), it would also be a good idea to find out what the **recent** research interests of the members on your panel are by sorting their publications by year. You might find out that some of them have similar interests or are even working on papers together. This is something you could comment positively on in your interview as something you aspire to in your job.

This strategy is even more effective if the panel members didn't know they were working on similar topics. Never underestimate how little many academics know about their colleagues! Although comments on this might work out negatively in some institutions, in most cases your panel will be impressed if you have spotted synergies they were not aware of.

8.5.2   FIND OUT **WHERE** YOUR PANEL MEMBERS ARE PUBLISHING

When searching for your panel members' publications through and author impact search, also make sure you sort the results by publication. Many academics have their favorite journals and they will tend to think positively about applicants targeting the same journals. This might be because targeting the same journals automatically reflects a similarity in academic norms and values, or simply because your panel members are more aware of the (high) quality standards of the journals they are personally familiar with.

I am not proposing you should lie about where you are targeting your work. However, doing a quick search to find out which journals your panel members tend to publish in heavily, might give you some clues about which of your research projects to focus on. It might also lead you to emphasize in your job interview that you have been doing ad-hoc reviewing for this particular journal (only if this is true of course).

Reviewing the **type** of outlets that panel members publish in also gives you an idea of what is valued in the institution you are applying to. Are they mainly publishing in top US academic journals, are they publishing in wider variety of journals, do professional journals feature as an outlet, have any of them written books?

None of these publication strategies are inherently superior to other strategies, but it is useful to be aware what seems to be valued most by the institution in question. You could use this as a lead-in to a question of what would be expected of you in terms of publication output if you joined the institution. Most interviews panels **really** appreciate it if you ask questions pro-actively rather than just answer theirs. However, what they appreciate most are **informed** questions.

8.5.3   FIND OUT WHO ARE **CITING** YOUR PANEL MEMBERS WORK

In order to **really** impress, you could try to read some of the articles that have built on the panel members' important works and comment intelligently on how they have done this. Many academics are not very much aware who is citing their work, so that knowledge might make an excellent impression.

You can find these citing articles easily. Simply double-click on the paper in question. This brings you straight to Google Scholar where you can find all citing articles (often even available in full text). Pick one that is related to a topic you know a lot (or at least something) about, so that you can talk comfortably about it. This might be an easy way to give you a connection to a person in the panel.

Or alternatively, pick an article that is written by an academic you know very well. If you are lucky your panel member knows the academic too, but didn't know that he or she cited their work. There is nothing like common acquaintances to build a quick connection!

I can particularly recommend this strategy when some of your panel members are senior administrators such as Deans or Head of Departments/Department Chairs. Oftentimes their heavy administrative load has prevented these academics from publishing much in recent years. They will be very pleased to be reminded that their research is still cited!

8.5.4   FIND OUT MORE ABOUT THE UNIVERSITY

Most junior applicants are too narrowly focused on the job in question and their future department or school. However, showing you know more about the university as a whole indicates you have made a real effort. It also signals that you are potential leadership material as you are able to take a broader perspective.

Find out what is the university well-known for. You can search for the University's most cited publications using a general search. Make sure though that to double-check that the university in question is listed as an affiliation of the author, not in the references or any other part of the publication (see Section 5.3.5 for more details).

Having found out what your panel members are working on, try to establish whether there is anyone else in the university working on similar topics. You can do this in the general search function by including the topic and the university in question. Your interview panel will be mightily impressed if you have identified another academic in their university that shares their research interests, especially if they weren't even aware of him/her.

You could even try to link this to a more general discussion on multi-disciplinarity and your own views on this. Although some universities might equate multidisciplinary research with a lack of depth, many universities acknowledge these days that big world problems can only be solved with multidisciplinary research.

8.6   REFERENCES

- Adler, N.; Harzing, A.W.K. (2009) **When Knowledge Wins: Transcending the sense and nonsense of academic rankings**, *The Academy of Management Learning & Education*, 8(1): 72-95
- Bednar, M.K.; Westphal, J.D. (2006), **Surveying the Corporate Elite: Theoretical and Practical Guidance on Improving Response Rates and Response Quality in Top Management Survey Questionnaires**, in: Ketchen, D. & Bergh, D. (ed.) *Research Methodology in Strategy and Management,* 3: 37-55.
- Ghoshal†, S. (2006), **Scholarship that Endures**, in: Ketchen, D. & Bergh, D. (ed.) *Research Methodology in Strategy and Management,* 3: 1-10.
- Harzing AWK (2002) **Are our referencing errors undermining our scholarship and credibility? The case of expatriate failure rates**. *Journal of Organizational Behavior* 23: 127-148.
- Pfeffer J, Fong CT (2002) **The End of Business Schools? Less Success Than Meets the Eye**. *Academy of Management Learning and Education* 1:78-95.
- Walsh JP, Tushman ML, Kimberly JR, Starbuck B, Ashford S. (2007). **On the Relationship Between Research and Practice: Debate and Reflections**. *Journal of Management Inquiry* 16: 128-154.

CHAPTER 9:
TIPS FOR DEANS AND OTHER ACADEMIC ADMINISTRATORS

Publish or Perish was initially designed to help academics to present their case for research impact to its best advantage. Inevitably, however, it also became popular amongst Deans, academic administrators and chairs of tenure/promotion committees. I am not very comfortable with the mechanistic type of evaluation of that might be promoted by an exclusive focus on citation analysis.

However, I do realize that many tenure or promotion committees use this kind of information. In this section, I therefore provide advice on how to use Publish or Perish for a more systematic evaluation of citation impact. I include four topics: accepting Google Scholar as an alternative data source, the myths about self-citation, the inappropriateness of citation analysis at early career stages, and the differences in citation impact across disciplines.

9.1 TREAT GOOGLE SCHOLAR AS A SERIOUS ALTERNATIVE DATA SOURCE

Many university administrators are fairly conservative in their approach to citation analysis. It is not unusual to see them prefer ISI as "the gold standard" and discard Google Scholar out of hand, simply because they have heard some wild-west stories about its "overly generous" coverage. These stories are typically based one or more of the following misconceptions.

First, the impression that everything on the web citing an academic's work counts as a citation. Second, the assumption that any publication that is not listed in ISI is not worth considering at all. Third, a general impression that Google Scholar citation counts are completely unreliable. Below, I will show that all of these impressions are misconceptions.

9.1.1 NOT EVERYTHING PUBLISHED ON THE INTERNET COUNTS IN GOOGLE SCHOLAR

Some academics are under the misplaced impression that anything posted on the Internet that includes citations will be counted in Google Scholar. This might also be the source behind the misconception that one can put simply put phantom papers online to improve one's citation count. However, Google Scholar only indexes **scholarly** publications. As their website indicates "We work with publishers of scholarly information to index peer-reviewed papers, theses, preprints, abstracts, and technical reports from all disciplines of research."

Some non-scholarly citations, such as student handbooks, library guides or editorial notes slip through. However, incidental problems in this regard are unlikely to distort citation metrics, especially robust ones such as the h-index. An inspection of my own papers shows that two thirds to three quarters of the citations are in academic journals, with the bulk of the remainder occurring in books, conference papers, working papers and student theses.

Very few non-scholarly citations were found. Moreover, I would argue that even a citation in student handbooks, library guides, textbooks or editorial notes shows that the academic has an impact on their field. In a similar vein, Vaughan and Shaw (2008) argue that 92% of the citations identified by Google Scholar in the field of library and information science represented intellectual impact, primarily citations from journal articles.

Hence, although there might be some overestimation of the number of non-scholarly citations in Google Scholar, for many disciplines this is preferable to the very significant and systematic under-estimation of scholarly citations in ISI or Scopus. Moreover, as long as one compares like with like, i.e. compares citation records for the **same** data source, this should not be a problem at all.

9.1.2   NON-ISI LISTED PUBLICATION **CAN** BE HIGH-QUALITY PUBLICATIONS

There is also a frequent assumption amongst research administrators that ISI listing is a stamp of quality and that hence one should ignore non-ISI listed publications and citations. There are two problems with this assumption. First, ISI has a bias towards Science, English-language and North American journals. Second, ISI completely ignores a vast majority of publications in the Social Sciences and Humanities.

ISI JOURNAL LISTING

ISI's listing of journals is much more comprehensive in the Sciences than in the Social Sciences and Humanities. Butler (2006) analyzed the distribution of publication output by field for Australian universities between 1999 and 2001. She found that whereas for the Chemical, Biological, Physical and Medical/Health sciences between 69.3% and 84.6% of the publications were published in ISI listed journals, this was the case for only 4.4%-18.7% of the publications in the Social Sciences such as Management, History Education and Arts.

As is documented in detail in Chapter 15, many high-quality journals in my field (Economics & Business) are not ISI listed. Only 30%-40% of the journals in Accounting, Marketing and General Management & Strategy listed on my Journal Quality List (already a pretty selective list) are ISI listed. There is no doubt that – on average – journals that are ISI listed are perceived to be of higher quality. In the analysis in Chapter 15, journals that **are** ISI-indexed in general had a significantly higher h-index (23.5 versus 11.5; t = 15.002, p < 0.000). However, there are a very substantial number of non-ISI indexed journals that have a higher than average h-index.

VERY LIMITED COVERAGE OF NON-JOURNAL PUBLICATIONS

Second, as has been mentioned many times in this book, even in the Cited Reference search ISI only includes citations in ISI listed journals and ignores any non-ISI publications for which you are not the first author. In the General Search function it completely ignores any publications that are not in ISI-listed journals.

As a result a vast majority of publications and citations in the Social Sciences & Humanities, as well as in Engineering & Computer Science, are ignored. In the Social Sciences and Humanities this is mainly caused by a completely neglect of books, book chapters, publications in languages other than English, and publications in non-ISI listed journals. In Engineering and Computer Science, this is mostly caused by a neglect of conference proceedings.

ISI has recently introduced conference proceedings in their database. However, it does not provide any details of which conferences are covered beyond listing some disciplines that are covered. I was unable to find any of my own publications in conference proceedings.

As a result ISI very seriously underestimates both the number of publications and the number of citations that academics in the Social Sciences & Humanities and in Engineering & Computer Science receive. A detailed analysis can be found in Chapter 16. However, busy Deans and tenure/promotion panel members might just want to read the bullet point conclusion, reproduced below.

- Academics in the Sciences out-perform academics in the Social Sciences and Humanities by a factor of 17.5 if one considers only the traditional performance indicator: **ISI General Search** citations.
- Academics in the Social Sciences and Humanities out-perform academics in the Sciences when using a more comprehensive data-source (**Google Scholar**) and correcting for career stage and the number of co-authors.

9.1.3   GOOGLE SCHOLAR'S FLAWS DON'T IMPACT CITATION ANALYSIS MUCH

Peter Jacsó, a prominent academic in Information and Library Science, has published several rather critical articles about Google Scholar (see e.g. Jacsó, 2006a/b). When confronted with titles such as *"Dubious hit counts and cuckoo's eggs" "Deflated, inflated and phantom citation counts"*, Deans, academic administrators and tenure/promotion committees could be excused for assuming Google Scholar provides unreliable data.

However, the bulk of Jacsó's (2006b) critique is levelled at Google Scholar's inconsistent number of results for keyword searches, which are not at all relevant for the author and journal impact searches that most academics use Publish or Perish for. In addition, most of the metrics used in Publish or Perish are fairly robust and insensitive to occasional errors as they will not generally change the h-index or g-index and will only have a minor impact on the number of citations per paper.

Chapter 13 includes a detailed discussion of the limitations of Google Scholar in comparison with ISI and Scopus. It also discusses most of the specific problems that Jacsó (2006a/b) has identified in his articles. There is no doubt that Google Scholar's automatic parsing occasionally provides us with nonsensical results. However, these errors do not appear to be as frequent or as important as implied by Jacsó's articles. They also do not generally impact the results of author or journal queries much, if at all.

Google Scholar has also significantly improved its parsing since the errors were pointed out to them. However, many academics are still referring to Jacsó's 2006 articles as convincing arguments against **any** use of Google Scholar. I would argue this is inappropriate. As academics, we are only all too well aware that **all** of our research results include a certain error margin. We cannot expect citation data to be any different.

What is most important is that errors are **random** rather than **systematic**. I have no reason to believe that the Google Scholar errors identified in Jacsó's articles are anything else than random. Hence they will not normally advantage or disadvantage individual academics or journals.

In contrast, commercial databases such as ISI and Scopus have **systematic** errors as they do not include many journals in the Social Sciences and Humanities, nor have good coverage of conferences proceedings, books or book chapters. Therefore, although it is always a good idea to use multiple data-sources, rejecting Google Scholar out of hand because of presumed parsing errors is not a rational.

9.2   EXCLUDING SELF-CITATIONS IS NORMALLY NOT WORTHWHILE

Many Deans, academic administrators, and tenure/promotion committees seem to have an almost obsessive fascination with self-citations, i.e. academics citing their own publications in subsequent publications. In my experience, it tends to seen as negative, with academics perceived to be manipulating their citation record. The realisation that Google Scholar does not automatically exclude self-citations is often enough for university administrator to discard Google Scholar completely as a data-source.

However, the inclusion or exclusion of self-citations will not normally make a big difference in someone citation record, especially for robust indicators such as the h-index (Engqvist & Frommen, 2008). For a more detailed analysis of this see Chapter 1. Here I provide a brief analysis of why self-citations are not usually problematic and how one **can** exclude self-citations in Google Scholar if so desired.

9.2.1   WHY SELF-CITATIONS ARE NOT USUALLY PROBLEMATIC

Self-citations are not necessarily bad or a reflection of manipulative behavior. If an academic does programmatic research, with individual studies building upon each other, one would expect him or her to refer back to their earlier work. To not do so would be violating academic integrity as it would make the later research appear more novel than it actually is.

In order to accumulate a significant number of self-citations, an academic also needs to have a significant number of publications in the first place, as one cannot cite oneself unless one publishes. Therefore, having a large **number** of self-citations usually goes hand-in-hand with having a high level of research productivity in general. However, most highly-cited academics have a very modest **proportion** (typically 5% or less) of self-citations.

Only academics with relatively weak citation records and/or junior academics tend to have a high proportion of self-citation. This is especially true in the Social Sciences and Humanities, where, due to publication delays, several years can pass between citing an article and having that citation appear in print. Hence only the authors of the article will be able to provide early citations to their paper as they are aware of it before it appears in print.

However, for both junior academics and academics with weak citation records, the low number of overall citations would already have provided a strong signal. Excluding self-citations wouldn't provide a lot of additional information. Only in very unusual circumstances would a more senior academic be able to game his or her citation record by consistently citing his or her own work.

If you still want to check the number of self-citations in Google Scholar, you can easily do so by double-clicking on the citations in question. I have provided an example below for a colleague, who – understandably given her very recent publication history – had a relatively modest number of citations (see screenshot).

Cites		Authors	Title	Year	Publication
☑	13	A Paladino	Investigating the Drivers of Innovation and New Pr...	2007	Journal of Product Ini
☑ ☐	8	A Paladino	Understanding the drivers of corporate performanc...	2006	Performance Measure
☑	7	W Pride, G Elliott, S R...	Marketing: core concepts and applications	2006	
☑	6	A Paladino	Understanding the green consumer: an empirical a...	2005	Journal of Customer E
☑ ☐	5	DA Chmielewski, A Pal...	Driving a resource orientation: reviewing the role o...	2007	Management Decision
☑	4	A Paladino	Creating an interactive and responsive teaching en...	2008	Journal of Marketing I
☑	3	A Paladino	Analyzing the Effects of Market and Resource Orie...	2008	Journal of Product Ini
☑	3	S Johnston, A Paladino	Knowledge management and involvement in innova...	2007	Management Interna
☑	1	S Smith, A Paladino	Eating clean and green? Investigating consumer m...	2010	Australasian Marketin
☑	1	A Paladino, J Baggiere	Are We 'Green'? An Empirical Investigation of Rene...	2007	Advances of Consumi
☑ ☐	0	S Rundle-Thiele, A Pal...	Lessons learned from renewable electricity marketi...	2008	Business Horizons

We can systematically check her self-citations by double-clicking on each publication. This takes us to Google Scholar and displays all citing articles. From here we can easily identify self-citations, such as the one below. Using your browser search functions ensures you do not miss any self-citations.

Analyzing the Effects of Market and Resource Orientations on Innovative Outcomes Turbulence*

A Paladino - Journal of Product Innovation Management, 2008 - interscience.wiley.com
Innovation and new product success are often a core precursor to superior performance. Although research has examined the resource-based view (RBV) and market orienta- tion (MO) individually, limited research has evaluated and compared their effect on innovation and ...
Cited by 3 - Related articles - All 3 versions

Doing so for all cited publications above, I was able to find out in less than two minutes that 11 of her 51 citations were self-citations, 6 of which to one 2006 paper (the one highlighted in the screenshot above). Since the other 2 citations for this 2006 paper were by one of Paladino's co-authors, the panel would be justified to assume that the wider impact of this particular paper to the academic community was limited.

However, out of the remaining 43 citations, only 5 were self-citations. Whilst at 11% this is higher than for most highly-cited academics, it would normally not be sufficient reason to change one's assessment of the candidate's research impact. Although specific benchmarks are difficult to give, I would normally not be too concerned with anything less than 30% self-citations for junior candidates. Obviously, for candidates with a larger number of citations, one would expect a lower proportion of self-citations.

Most administrators using of the ISI Web of Science list the possibility to generate a citation report that excludes self-citations as one of its big advantages. You first conduct a general search for the number of articles published in ISI listed journals. This is the standard search page displayed by ISI after logging in, so you can't miss it.

On the resulting page (see screenshot), the ISI Web of Science then offers the possibility to create a citation report. One can subsequently exclude self-citations from the citation report by clicking on the *"view without self-citations"* link. To the naive and even not so naive user, this sounds like a really easy way to identify a "clean" citation record, doesn't it?

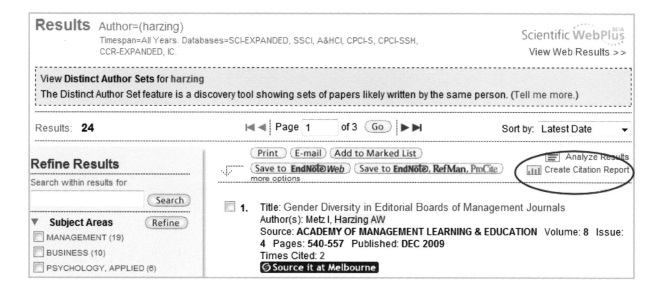

Unfortunately, nothing could be further from the truth. The reasons for this are fairly complicated and require a much longer and more detailed explanation than would be appropriate in this Chapter. Further details are therefore provided in Chapter 14 where I discuss the pros and cons of different data-sources (Section 13.2.2)

Suffice to say here that a naive interpretation of ISI data, using the *"view without self-citations"* link would lead most users to put my self-citation rate at 15%. A more appropriate interpretation would be that around 3% of my citing articles are self-citing articles. However, a fully accurate estimate – which could easily take well over an hour to complete, even if you knew what you were doing – would be that my self-citations lie around 4-5%.

So in fact ISI makes it **more** difficult, not **less** difficult than Google Scholar to accurately exclude self-citations. Hence, there should be absolutely no reason to discard Google Scholar for this reason.

Although one can certainly expect applicants for a prestigious named Chair position to have had an impact on their field, it is not reasonable to expect academics at lower levels to show strong citations records. This is certainly true for tenure cases, but even for promotion applications within the first 5-10 years of one's academic career.

Especially in the Social Sciences and Humanities, citations are not a very meaningful measure of research performance until someone has been publishing for at least a decade (and even then disciplinary differences should be noted, see Section 9.4). In these disciplines, the publication process is generally much more drawn-out than in the Sciences with multiple rounds of revisions that can take years. Even accepted publications can take 1-2 years to finally appear in print.

Therefore, if someone with a relatively brief academic career has gathered a substantial number of citations, this person should be commended for displaying exceptional distinction in this area. However, if someone does not display a strong citation record, this should not bias your evaluation of their research performance.

9.3.1   USING ISI TO TRACK DOWN CITATION RECORDS IN THE PAST

If the tenure/promotion committee is still in doubt, they might want to commission some analyses for acknowledged top academics in the field and look at **their** citation records the first five years after they published their first article. In most cases, you will find it is much lower than you expected.

Unfortunately, it is not possible to use Google Scholar to track down someone's citations at a particular point in time. Google Scholar – and hence Publish or Perish – will always present someone's current publication record. However, ISI's Web of Science data allows us to go back in time.

Taking my own case as an example, my current ISI citation record puts me in the top 1% most cited academics in the field of Economics & Business between 2000 and 2010. However, my citations took quite a while to take off. My first publication appeared in 1995. By 2000 I had a dozen publications printed or in press/accepted. However, at the start of 2000 I only had 9 ISI citations (with 20 new citations in 2000 and 27 new citations in 2001). If I had had to make my tenure case after just 5 years I wouldn't have had much to show for in terms of research impact.

Similarly, my own Dean – an accomplished and currently highly-cited academic in Management Accounting – only had 18 ISI citations a decade after publishing her first post-PhD article. Her citations only really started to take off 15 years after completing her PhD.

9.3.2   BASELINES FOR ISI CITATIONS IN PARTICULAR FIELDS

The slow take up of citations as displayed in the above examples is by no means unusual. ISI's database "Essential Science Indicators Baselines" provides the number of citations one can expect an article in a particular discipline to have at a certain point in time.

If you had published an article in an ISI listed journal in Economics & Business in 2009 that – at the 1st of May 2010 – had even just **one** ISI citation, your article would already be in the top 20% most cited articles. Four citations would even put it in the top 1% most cited articles. Obviously, for articles published in earlier years the number of citations to be in the top 20%/1% will go up.

However, a paper published in an ISI listed journal in Computer Science in 2004 with only **one** citation would still be in the top 50% of most-cited papers for that, i.e. the lack of a significant number of citations would be quite normal. Thus, even though you wouldn't be able convince your tenure or promotion committee your ISI citation record is stellar; if you work in these fields you should be able to convince them that your lack of a significant number of citations is quite normal.

In fact, in Economics & Business, Computer Science, Engineering, Mathematics and the Social Sciences/General even for papers in ISI listed journals that are 10 years old two to four ISI citations are enough to put an article in the top 50% most cited papers in their fields. As discussed in detail in Chapter 16, this is partly due to the lack of comprehensive coverage of ISI in these disciplines. However, it is also due to differences in citation behavior across fields. To be in the top 50% most cited articles in Molecular Biology & Genetics, you would need your 10-year old paper to have 22 citations at the 1st of May 2010, whilst 64 are needed to be in the top 20%.

9.4   CITATION IMPACT CAN DIFFER SUBSTANTIALLY BY DISCIPLINE

As already discussed briefly in Chapter 7 (Section 7.1) and explained in great detail in Chapter 16, citation behaviors can vary dramatically within disciplines or even within sub-disciplines. Differences **between** disciplines are exaggerated when using the ISI Web of Science or Scopus, as they have a far better coverage in the Sciences than in the Social Sciences and Humanities or Engineering and Computer Science.

However, even **within** disciplines differences can be vast. The area of Human Resource Management – as a sub-discipline of Management – includes scholars working on industrial relations and labor unions as well as scholars working on more psychologically oriented topics such as motivation or job attitudes.

The latter academics might be able to publish in a mainstream Psychology journal such as *Psychological Bulletin*. The former academics would praise themselves lucky if they published in the top US journal in their field: *Industrial Relations*. At 12.85, the journal impact factor of the former is six times as high as the journal impact factor of the latter (2.05).

Moreover, many Industrial Relations academics will not be able to publish in mainstream US-American Industrial Relations journals as their research is very contextual. Hence they might need to publish their work in even lower impact journals such as British Journal of Industrial Relations (1.38), European Journal of Industrial Relations (1.00), Asia Pacific Journal of Human Resources (0.78), or the Australian journal Labour History (0.15). Hence, any articles in the area of Industrial Relations can be expected to be cited far less frequently than articles in the area of organizational behavior, which is more closely related to psychology.

GENERIC NORM SCORES ARE NORMALLY A BAD IDEA

It is not advisable to set a general "norm score" of the number of citations that an academic needs to achieve for tenure or promotion to the next level as these typical scores can vary dramatically even **within** a discipline.

If your university insists on these benchmarks, make sure that they are established by referring to what **is** the norm in your field. I have seen many administrators pick a "round number" of out thin air (say 50 citations or 100 citations), without any proper reference to what could be expected in the field.

Further if you **do** decide to apply these norm scores, have the sense to perform a quick reality check. Find out how many academics that are currently at the level the candidate applies for met this norm score when they applied for that level. You would be surprised at the number of academics who do not meet your norms scores even 5-10 years after tenure or promotion.

If you are an academic at the highest level of the hierarchy yourself, be brutally honest and evaluate your **own** record at the time you went up for tenure or promotion. Most senior academics have rather short memories and have a tendency to project their current publication and citation records back to the time when they applied for tenure or promotion.

9.5 CONCLUSION: WHAT SENSIBLE ADMINISTRATORS SHOULD DO

So what advice can I give on citation analysis to administrators who want to maintain rigorous standards, but also want to be fair and equitable? First, especially if you work in the Social Sciences and Humanities or in Engineering and Computer Science, give up your reservations about Google Scholar.

These days, many universities allow or even recommend the use of Google Scholar and Publish or Perish. Institutions such World Bank and Microsoft's research laboratory use it to evaluate their broader impact beyond ISI listed journals. Many US government departments use it to evaluate the impact of particular research projects. You can always ask applicants to provide ISI or Scopus data as well, but do take Google Scholar data seriously.

Yes, some of Google Scholar's results are nonsensical. Yes, occasionally Google Scholar will double-count citations. Yes, some of the citations are not as scholarly as one would want. However, these minor errors are not worth worrying about when comparing them with the systematic and very large underestimation of citations in ISI or even Scopus. For an introduction of the three data sources see Chapter 1. For more detail about their respective advantages and disadvantages, see Chapters 13-15.

Second, give up your fixation with self-citations. Yes, occasionally academics abuse the system and systematically cite their own work. However, there are safeguards against this system as journal editors and reviewers will not like gratuitous citations. Moreover, if academics are so unethical, they probably have bigger problems than their inflated citation record. More importantly, for the majority of academics self-citations do not distort their citation records in any significant way. The hassle and possible inconsistency in excluding self-citations is not worth the small possible gain in accuracy.

Third, be **very** hesitant in applying citation analysis for junior academics, especially again in the Social Sciences and Humanities. It can easily take 5-10 years after an academic's first publication for a significant number of citations to flow in. Hence, if an early career academic shows a large number of citations, make sure you promote them and keep them happy (assuming other aspects of their performance are also at least satisfactory). However, if academics going up for tenure have very few citations, don't hold it against them.

Fourth, realize that citations can vary dramatically between or even within disciplines. Never compare citation (or publication) records across disciplines. If for some inexplicable reason you **have** to do so, use

Google Scholar, not ISI or Scopus. Be **very** hesitant to prescribe norm scores for the number of citations to be accumulated before someone is considered for tenure or promotion to a certain level. If you feel you do need to prescribe norm scores, make sure they reflect current practice in the field and for academics at the same level the candidates apply for.

Fifth, if you have **any** doubts about what you are doing, consult an expert. Academics and administrators at this level are far too busy to try to understand the minutia of citation analysis. Get a proper bibliometric expert involved! You might have access to a librarian with good skills in this respect or you might have academics in your staff who do bibliometric research. If you do not, read the rest of this book as well. If you read it closely, at the end you'll probably know more about citation analysis than 99.9% of the academics.

9.6   REFERENCES

- Butler, L. (2006) **RQF Pilot Study Project – History and Political Science Methodology for Citation Analysis**, November 2006, accessed from: http://www.chass.org.au/papers/bibliometrics/CHASS_Methodology.pdf, 15 Jan 2007.
- Engqvist, L.; Frommen, J.G. (2008). **The h-index and self-citations**. *Trends in Ecology & Evolution*, 23(5): 250–252.
- Jacsó, P. (2006a) **Dubious hit counts and cuckoo's eggs**. *Online Information Review*, 30: 188-193.
- Jacsó, P. (2006b) **Deflated, inflated and phantom citation counts**. *Online Information Review*, 30: 297-309.
- Vaughan, L.; Shaw, D. (2008) **A new look at evidence of scholarly citations in citation indexes and from web sources**, *Scientometrics*, 74(2): 317-330.

CHAPTER 10:
WHERE TO SUBMIT YOUR PAPER?

PoP can be used to assist you when you are uncertain which journal to submit your work to. It can be used to get ideas of the types of journals that publish articles on the topic you are writing on and to compare a set of journals in terms of their citation impact. Finally, once you have decided on the target journal, it can also help you to double-check that you haven't missed any prior work from the journal in question.

10.1 STEP 1: EXAMINING WHICH JOURNALS PUBLISH ON YOUR TOPIC

Let's assume you have written a paper, but are unsure which journal to submit it to. Normally, you would already have a pretty good idea of suitable journals through your literature review, but there might be good reasons why you haven't been able to settle on a journal yet. You might want to ensure you haven't neglected any options. Or you might know what the most suitable journal would be, but you have already published several papers there and you are keen to show the impact of your work beyond your immediate academic peer group. Or maybe the journal that is most appropriate is one with which you have recently had a bad experience in the review process (e.g. long delays or shoddy reviewer reports).

What you can do in this case is use the General Citation Search option in Publish or Perish and do a search by the most important key-words in your paper. For further information on the mechanics of General Citation Searches, see Chapter 5. If you search for a relatively generic topic, many of the hits you get will be books, especially in the Social Sciences and Humanities. Books tend to be highly cited, because they contain more citable material than short journal articles. This is especially true for classic works in the field. As we are not intending to write a book, the best way to find appropriate journals is to sort the results by publication outlet by clicking on the Publication column.

As the default sort for Publish or Perish is always by number of citations, clicking on the Publication column will result in a list that is sorted by publication outlet first and then by the number of citations. Scrolling down the list easily allows one to identify the journals that contain articles on your topic and also shows us which of these are most highly cited.

10.1.1 WORKED EXAMPLE: ETHICAL MARKETING

Let's assume you have written a paper about ethical marketing. You have already noticed that the top-ranked mainstream marketing journals such as Journal of Marketing and Journal of Consumer Research do not seem to publish a lot of papers on this topic and hence are looking for alternative options.

You would enter the words *ethical marketing* in the "The phrase" box. This will provide any articles in which the words *ethical marketing* appear in that particular order. You will get the same results by including the search term *ethical marketing* in quotes ("*ethical marketing*") in the "All the words" field. If you include the search term *ethical marketing* without quotes it provides many more matches as it matches the words in any order. There will be lots of publications that include both these relatively generic words.

As you want to ensure that the journal has published on ethical marketing in recent years, you limit the search to the last ten years. At this stage, you decide not to de-select any of the subject categories as you want to cast the net widely. You can always run the search again with a more restricted number of subject categories if you end up with too many hits. The screenshot below shows the relevant Query pane.

Author impact	Journal impact	General citations	Multi-query center	Web Browser

General citation search - Perform a general citation search

Author(s):	
Publication:	
All of the words:	
Any of the words:	
None of the words:	
The phrase:	ethical marketing
Year of publication between:	2000 and: 0

☑ Biology, Life Sciences, Environmental Science
☑ Business, Administration, Finance, Economics
☑ Chemistry and Materials Science
☑ Engineering, Computer Science, Mathematics
☑ Medicine, Pharmacology, Veterinary Science
☑ Physics, Astronomy, Planetary Science
☑ Social Sciences, Arts, Humanities

☐ Title words only

The search resulted in 874 hits (including duplicates). As expected many of the most-cited works were books, often generic ones on Marketing Research, Consumer Behavior and International Marketing. However, sorting the results by publication allows us to identify the most important journal outlets. Below, you will find screenshots with the most frequently occurring journals in this search, with a brief discussion of the results for each.

JOURNAL OF BUSINESS ETHICS

The Journal of Business Ethics is the most frequently mentioned journal in our search. The screenshot below shows some of the most cited papers.

Title	Year	Publication
A review of empirical studies assessing ethical decision making in business	2000	Journal of Business Ethics
A cross cultural comparison of the contents of codes of ethics: USA, Canada and ...	2000	Journal of Business Ethics
Unpacking the ethical product	2001	Journal of Business Ethics
A partnership model of corporate ethics	2002	Journal of Business Ethics
Cross-cultural methodological issues in ethical research	2000	Journal of Business Ethics
An empirical investigation of the relationships between ethical beliefs, ethical ideo...	2001	Journal of Business Ethics
Ethics in personal selling and sales management: a review of the literature focusi...	2000	Journal of Business Ethics
An ethical exploration of privacy and radio frequency identification	2005	Journal of Business Ethics
Ethics and Marketing on this Internet: Practitioners' Perceptions of Societal, Indu...	2000	Journal of Business Ethics
The questionable use of moral development theory in studies of business ethics: ...	2001	Journal of Business Ethics
Packaging ethics: Perceptual differences among packaging professionals, brand ...	2000	Journal of Business Ethics
International marketing ethics from an Islamic perspective: a value-maximization ...	2001	Journal of Business Ethics
Gender differences in ethical perceptions of salespeople: An empirical examinatio...	2002	Journal of Business Ethics
Ethical judgment and whistleblowing intention: examining the moderating role of l...	2003	Journal of Business Ethics
Is cross-cultural similarity an indicator of similar marketing ethics?	2001	Journal of Business Ethics

However, although there are a number of papers relating to marketing, most of the papers seem to deal mostly with general business ethics. Even so, this could be an option for a marketing academic who wants to reach out to a more general audience interested in ethics.

JOURNAL OF MACROMARKETING

The second most frequently listed journal in our search is Journal of Macromarketing. The screenshot below shows all of the hits in order of the number of citations. The first article in the list is the most frequently cited journal article in the entire search. Unfortunately, this is partly caused by a Google Scholar fluke that attributed the citations to the original 1986 article to the 2006 update. Even so, it is still the most cited article on the topic if we relax the "last ten years" restriction.

Title	Year	Publication
The general theory of marketing ethics: a revision and three questions	2006	Journal of macromarketing
Normative perspectives for ethical and socially responsible marketing	2006	Journal of Macromarketing
Building understanding of the domain of consumer vulnerability	2005	Journal of Macromarketing
Quality-of-life (QOL) marketing: Proposed antecedents and consequences	2004	Journal of Macromarketing
Macro measures of consumer well-being (CWB): a critical analysis and a researc...	2006	Journal of Macromarketing
Globalization and technological achievement: Implications for macromarketing an...	2004	Journal of Macromarketing
Research on marketing ethics: A systematic review of the literature	2007	Journal of Macromarketing
Distributive justice: Pressing questions, emerging directions, and the promise of ...	2008	Journal of Macromarketing
Research on consumer well-being (CWB): Overview of the field and introduction...	2007	Journal of Macromarketing
The small and long view	2006	Journal of Macromarketing
Voluntary codes of ethical conduct: Group membership salience and globally inte...	2007	Journal of Macromarketing
On Economic Growth, Marketing Systems, and the Quality of Life	2009	Journal of Macromarketing
Assessing distributive justice in marketing: a benefit-cost approach	2007	Journal of Macromarketing
Globalization, transformation, and quality of life: Reflections on ICMD-8 and par...	2004	Journal of Macromarketing
Limited choice: An exploratory study into issue items and soldier subjective well-...	2006	Journal of Macromarketing
Handbook of Quality-of-Life Research: An Ethical Marketing Perspective, by M. ...	2003	Journal of Macromarketing
Applying Catholic Social Teachings to Ethical Issues in Marketing	2009	Journal of Macromarketing
Medicalization and Marketing	2010	Journal of Macromarketing

The journal has also published a range of other highly cited papers in this field and as such might be an appropriate outlet. However, much of the published research seems to focus on high-level societal issues, quality of life or consumer well-being. This is also reflected in its editorial statement: *"The Journal of Macromarketing examines important social issues, how they are affected by marketing, and how society influences the conduct of marketing."* Whether or not this suits your paper obviously depends on its topic.

EUROPEAN JOURNAL OF MARKETING

The journal with the third largest number of hits to the search for keywords ethical marketing was the European Journal of Marketing. The screenshot below shows all resulting papers in order of number of citations. Unfortunately, Google Scholar sometimes abbreviates the title of a journal (see the first five hits) for no apparent reason.

This means that the citation order is not perfect as it starts again with the first article for the non-abbreviated journal title, i.e. the *"Grounded theory…"* article has more citations than most of the preceding articles. However, as we are mainly interested in journal outlets at the moment, this is not a serious problem.

Title	Year	Publication
How important are ethics and social responsibility?	2001	European Journal of …
Moral philosophies of marketing managers	2002	European Journal of …
An ethical basis for relationship marketing: a virtue ethics perspective	2007	European journal of …
Corporate social responsibility: investigating theory and research in the marke…	2008	European Journal of …
Children's impact on innovation decision making	2009	European Journal of …
Grounded theory, ethnography and phenomenology	2005	European journal of Marketing
Societal marketing and morality	2002	European Journal of Marketing
Marketing as a profession: on closing stakeholder gaps	2002	European Journal of Marketing
Futures dilemmas for marketers: can stakeholder analysis add value?	2005	European Journal of Marketing
Ethics and value creation in business research: comparing two approaches	2006	European Journal of Marketing
An ethical basis for relationship marketing: a virtue ethics perspective The Aut…	2007	European Journal of Marketing

Perusing the titles, it is clear that the European Journal of Marketing has a rather broad focus, publishing papers in a variety of areas in marketing. This is reflected in its mission statement: *"We welcome novel and ground-breaking contributions from a wide range of research traditions within the broad domain of marketing"*. This statement also mentions: *"The EJM is receptive to controversial topics, and new, as well as developments that challenge existing theories and paradigms."* Hence, at first glance, this might not be a bad outlet for a topic that is not yet part of the mainstream in Marketing.

JOURNAL OF CONSUMER MARKETING

As shown in the screenshot below, the journal of consumer marketing has also published a substantial number of papers containing the key words ethical marketing in the past decade. Not surprisingly, most of these papers focus on the ethical consumer. Hence this journal would be a very appropriate outlet if your paper focused on ethical aspect of consumer behavior.

Title	Year	Publication
Shopping for a better world? An interpretive study of the potential for ethical…	2004	Journal of Consumer …
"To legislate or not to legislate": a comparative exploratory study of privacy…	2003	Journal of consumer …
An inquiry into the ethical perceptions of sub-cultural groups in the US: Hispa…	2002	Journal of Consumer …
Consumers' Rules of Engagement in Online Information Exchanges	2009	Journal of Consumer …
The myth of the ethical consumer-do ethics matter in purchase behaviour?	2001	Journal of consumer marketing
The ethicality of altruistic corporate social responsibility	2002	Journal of Consumer Marketing
Consumer privacy and the Internet in Europe: a view from Germany	2003	Journal of Consumer Marketing
Neuromarketing: a layman's look at neuroscience and its potential application…	2007	Journal of Consumer Marketing

JOURNAL OF PUBLIC POLICY & MARKETING

Another article with a fairly large number of papers on this topic is Journal of Public Policy & Marketing. Perusing the article titles, its topics appear to have a some overlap with the Journal of Macromarketing.

Title	Year	Publication
Does Fair Trade deliver on its core value proposition? Effects on income, e...	2009	Journal of Public Policy & ...
The philosophy and methods of deliberative democracy: Implications for p...	2009	Journal of Public Policy & ...
Marketing to the Poor: An Integrative Justice Model for Engaging Impoveri...	2009	Journal of Public Policy & ...
Consumer online privacy: legal and ethical issues	2000	Journal of Public Policy & Marketing
Antiglobal challenges to marketing in developing countries: Exploring the id...	2005	Journal of Public Policy & Marketing
Ethics and Public Policy Implications of Research on Consumer Well-Being	2008	Journal of Public Policy & Marketing
Principle-Based Stakeholder Marketing: Insights from Private Triple-Bottom...	2010	Journal of Public Policy & Marketing
Ethical Beliefs and Information Asymmetries in Supplier Relationships	2010	Journal of Public Policy & Marketing

This is confirmed when we look at its editorial statement: *Journal of Public Policy & Marketing has adopted the noteworthy mission of publishing thoughtful articles on how marketing practice shapes and is shaped by societally important factors such as ...* Hence it appears as if these two journals would be particularly appropriate if your paper focused on the societal issues surrounding ethical marketing.

JOURNAL OF MARKETING EDUCATION

A rather surprising discovery was the fact that the Journal of Marketing Education had published a fairly large number of papers in this area. Hence if your paper had any links to marketing education or investigated perceptions of marketing students, this might be an appropriate outlet for your article.

Title	Year	Publication
The effects of marketing education and individual cultural values on marketing...	2002	Journal of Marketing Education
Important factors underlying ethical intentions of students: Implications for m...	2004	Journal of Marketing Education
The Impact of Corporate Culture, the Reward System, and Perceived Moral I...	2005	Journal of Marketing Education
Teaching marketing law: A business law perspective on integrating marketing ...	2000	Journal of Marketing Education
Designing discussion activities to achieve desired learning outcomes: Choices ...	2007	Journal of Marketing Education
Group-Based Assessment as a Dynamic Approach to Marketing Education	2009	Journal of Marketing Education

JOURNAL OF THE ACADEMY OF MARKETING SCIENCE

In your literature review you had already discovered that the mainstream marketing journals do not tend to publish much in the area of ethical marketing. It should therefore come as a pleasant surprise to see that Journal of the Academy of Marketing Science, one of the top general marketing journals has published four articles on the broad topic in the past decade.

Concomitant with its general marketing status, its editorial statement indicates that articles in a very broad range of topics are acceptable, including ethics and social responsibility. Hence, if you feel your article is of sufficient quality to merit publication in one of the top journals in marketing, this might be an appropriate choice to reach the widest possible audience in the broad field of marketing.

Title	Year	Publication
Representing the perceived ethical work climate among marketing employ...	2000	Journal of the Academy of ...
Consumer online privacy concerns and responses: a power–responsibility...	2007	Journal of the Academy of Marketing
Marketing with integrity: ethics and the service-dominant logic for marketing	2008	Journal of the Academy of Marketing.
A simulation of moral behavior within marketing exchange relationships	2007	Journal of the Academy of Marketing.

USING THE "TITLE WORDS ONLY" BOX TO FURTHER REFINE RESULTS

Judging from the titles in the results above, some articles didn't really seem to have a major focus on ethical marketing, but instead simply mentioned the words somewhere in the article. Another option therefore is to narrow down your results by clicking the "Title words only" box. The results will only contain articles that have the words ethical marketing (in that order) in their title, although the words do not necessarily appear close together. The screenshot below produces the results in order of the number of citations.

Comparing the journal titles with our previous results shows that most of the same journals appear in the list. However, there are five new journals that appear on the scene: Journal of Business Research, the Academy of Marketing Science Review, Journal of Consumer Affairs, Ethics & Behavior and Journal of International Marketing. These journals did not feature on our list before as they only published one or two papers on ethical marketing. However, if the titles appear relevant to your paper, they might be worth considering.

Title	Year	Publication
Normative perspectives for ethical and socially responsible marketing	2006	Journal of Macromarketing
Representing the perceived ethical work climate among marketing employees	2000	Journal of the Academy of ...
Important factors underlying ethical intentions of students: Implications for ma...	2004	Journal of Marketing Education
Perceived risk, moral philosophy and marketing ethics: mediating influences on ...	2002	Journal of Business research
Ethical guidelines for marketing practice: A reply to Gaski & some observations ...	2001	Journal of Business Ethics
Consumer interests and the ethical implications of marketing: a contingency fra...	2003	Journal of Consumer Affairs
Ethical marketing for competitive advantage on the internet	2001	Academy of Marketing Science
The Impact of Corporate Culture, the Reward System, and Perceived Moral In...	2005	Journal of Marketing Education
An ethical basis for relationship marketing: a virtue ethics perspective	2007	European journal of ...
Ethical trends in marketing and psychological research	2001	Ethics & Behavior
Sustainable Tourism: Ethical Alternative or Marketing Ploy?	2007	Journal of business ethics
The impact of cultural values on marketing ethical norms: A study in India and t...	2006	Journal of International ...

10.2   STEP 2: COMPARING JOURNALS FOR IMPACT

After creating a "short-list" of journals that you might want to publish your paper in, one of the criteria to make your final choice could be the standing or rank of the journal. Of course, the most important criterion should be that your paper suits the focus and editorial aims of the journal. However, if there are a set of journals that meet this criterion, you might as well submit your paper to a higher-ranked journal first.

In general we can distinguish two broad approaches to ranking journals: stated preference (or peer review) and revealed preference (Tahai & Meyer, 1999). Stated preference involves members of particular academic community ranking journals on the basis of their own expert judgments. These are often undertaken by particular universities or departments in order to help make decisions about, for example, library budgets, promotion or tenure, and national research evaluations.

As a result there are hundreds of individual university journal rankings in existence and integrated journal ranking lists have sprung up that combine a range of rankings (see e.g. the British ABS Journal Quality Guide (ABS, 2010) and Harzing's Journal Quality List (Harzing, 2010). Opinions might be based on anything from a large-scale worldwide survey of academics to a small group of individuals with decision-making power, but will always contain some element of subjectivity.

Revealed preference rankings are based on *actual* publication behavior and generally measure the citation rates of journals using Thomson ISI's Web of Knowledge. Most commonly used are the ISI Journal Citation Reports (JCR), which provide the yearly Journal Impact Factors (JIF). For more details on the JIF, see Section 1.4.1. However, any source of citation data can be used. Publish or Perish is ideally suited to measure the impact of journals with Google Scholar data.

Mingers and Harzing (2007) show that there is a high degree of correlation between journal rankings based on stated and revealed preference. However, as Tahai & Meyer (1999) point out, stated preference studies have long memories: perceptions of journals normally change only slowly. As such, revealed preference studies provide a fairer assessment of new journals or journals that have recently improved their standing. Therefore, revealed preference studies present a more accurate picture of journal impact.

10.2.1   WORKED EXAMPLE: ACCOUNTING JOURNALS

For a detailed example of doing a Google Scholar based impact analysis, see Chapter 15 on Journal Impact Analysis, which compares the Thomson ISI JIF and the Google Scholar h-index for some 800 journals. Below I will provide a smaller-scale example of journals in the field of Accounting.

Because of differences in accounting rules across countries, Accounting is a localized discipline. As a result, not many of its journals are listed in the Thomson's Journal Citation Reports. Only 30% of the journals in Finance & Accounting listed on the JQL are included in ISI. In contrast, three quarters or more of the journals on the JQL in Economics or Management Information Systems are ISI listed. Hence, if one wants to compare the citation impact of Accounting journals, using Google Scholar is often the only alternative.

The table below lists a selection of Accounting journals, including the journals generally recognized as the top-5 accounting journals. The table first lists the ISI Journal Impact Factor for 2009 (where available) and the ABDC (Australian Business Dean's Council) rank, a popular journal ranking list in Australia. It then reports on the results of a PoP impact analysis for papers published in the journals between 2005 and July 2010. I report the average number of citations per paper, the Google Scholar h-index and g-index.

In order to get a realistic citations per paper count, I merged duplicate papers, removed book reviews, commentaries, obituaries, conference announcements, call for papers, etc. as these items rarely ever attract citations. Including them would distort comparisons between journals that include these items and journals that do not.

Journal Name	ISI JIF 2009	ABDC ranking	GS cites pp	GS h-index	GS g-index
Jnl of Accounting Research	2.350	A*	24.20	43	74
Review of Accounting Studies	1.500	A*	23.64	28	51
Contemporary Accounting Research	1.087	A*	16.87	28	45
Accounting, Organizations and Society	1.803	A*	15.28	34	49
Accounting Review (The)	1.920	A*	15.20	37	56
European Accounting Review	0.633	A	10.88	23	37
Accounting and Business Research	Not listed	A	9.62	15	25
Jnl of Accounting and Public Policy	Not listed	A	9.23	19	30
Accounting Horizons	Not listed	A	8.45	17	27
Accounting, Auditing & Accountability Jnl	Not listed	A	7.63	22	31
Int Jnl of Accounting Inf Systems	Not listed	A	7.20	16	21
British Accounting Review	Not listed	A	6.85	15	22
International Jnl of Accounting	Not listed	A	6.63	15	21
Critical Perspectives on Accounting	Not listed	A	5.42	20	29
Behavioral Research in Accounting	Not listed	A	4.78	9	14
Issues in Accounting Education	Not listed	A	3.20	11	17

The top-5 accounting journals (all A* ranked in the ABDC ranking) stand apart in terms of their Journal Impact Factor and Google Scholar metrics. However, there is quite a difference in terms of citations per paper for the remaining journals, with *European Accounting Review, Accounting and Business Research* and *Journal of Accounting and Public Policy* having citation per paper rates that are 2-3 times as high as the journals towards the bottom of the list. This is true despite the fact that they were all ranked A on the Australian journal ranking list.

The GS h-index and GS g-index also show similar differences. It is, however, interesting to see that some journals (e.g. *Critical Perspectives on Accounting*) publish a fairly large number of impactful papers, as evidenced by the relatively high h-index and g-index, even though the average number of citations per paper is not very high. Overall though, there is a very strong correlation between the three GS-based impact measures (0.86 between GS cpp and GS h-index; 0.92 between GS cpp and GS g-index; 0.98 b/w the h-index and g-index).

In conclusion, this example shows that even when comparing journals that score similarly in stated preference (peer review) rankings can have very different impact scores. Given that very few Accounting journals have ISI journal impact factors, a Google Scholar based impact analysis is an excellent way to assess the impact of non-IS listed journals. It allows you to make a more-informed choice when you chose a journal to submit your paper to.

There are few things that annoy a journal editor more than to receive a paper for their journal that neglects to refer to relevant papers in the journal in question. I am not talking here about the practice here that some of the less scrupulous journal editors practice: asking you to cite papers from their own journal simply to increase their journal's ISI Journal Impact Factor. This is not a practice I approve of. However, journal editors are rightly annoyed if you have failed to incorporate **relevant** prior papers from their journal. By publishing in a certain journal, you are contributing to a conversation (see also Huff, 1998). Not acknowledging the other conversation partners is plain rude.

If this search finds that the journal you intend to submit your paper to has **never** published anything on the topic of your paper, you might wish to reconsider your choice. Remember: You wanting to submit to the journal, because it is the top-ranked journal in your field is not a good enough reason! If there is no prior published work on your topic in the journal, reviewers of the journal might not be familiar with this field and might not be able to evaluate its merits. It might also mean that the readers of the journal might not be interested in reading your work, even if it does get accepted. Maybe it is a sign you should go back to step 1 to examine which journals publish on your topic?

Of course there can be very good reasons to want to introduce a particular stream of research to a new audience, but realize that this is not usually an easy way to get your paper accepted. Academics (and people in general) often find it difficult to relate to ideas that have no connection at all to their knowledge base. Please note that it is not necessary that your paper is complimentary about prior work published in the journal. One reason you submit to a particular journal might be to critique an important paper published in that journal.

10.3.1   WORKED EXAMPLE: ENTRY MODES OF JAPANESE MULTINATIONAL COMPANIES

So how do you do a final check to establish that you haven't missed any highly relevant papers in the journal you are targeting? You could browse tables of contents on the web or in the library. However, Publish or Perish offers a much quicker way. Simply enter the journal in question in the journal title field of the Journal Impact Analysis. It is usually safe to limit your search to the last ten years, as recent papers – if the authors have done their job properly – will normally have referred to older work in the journal.

Let's assume you have written a paper about entry mode choice (the choice between different ways to enter a foreign market) of Japanese multinational companies and intend to submit to Journal of International Business Studies. The screenshot below lists the Publish or Perish output with the 30-odd most-cited papers in the last 10 years of JIBS.

The one but last paper on the list would certainly be relevant for your paper. However, there are quite a few other papers on entry mode choice or market entry. Furthermore, the highly-cited paper on international acquisitions (which is one particular mode of entry) might also be worth a look. Finally, there are two papers that deal with a theory of international new ventures, which is a topic that is related to entry modes. Please note that these are only the 30-odd most cited papers. To be certain that there are no other relevant papers you would need to work down the entire list of results as even papers that are not highly cited might be relevant to your own work.

Title
Knowledge of the firm and the evolutionary theory of the multinational corporation
Toward a theory of International new ventures
Location and the multinational enterprise: A neglected factor&quest
The economic geography of the Internet age
Knowledge transfer in International acquisitions
The impact of national culture and economic ideology on managerial work values: A study of the United States, Russia, .
Cultural distance revisited: Towards a more rigorous conceptualization and measurement of cultural differences
Innovation, Organizational Capabilities, and the Born-Global Firm.
A Perspective on Regional and Global Strategies of Multinational Enterprises.
Institutional, cultural and transaction cost influences on entry mode choice and performance
The determinants of trust in supplier-automaker relationships in the US, Japan, and Korea
A three-stage theory of international expansion: The link between multinationality and performance in the service secto
MNC Knowledge Transfer, Subsidiary Absorptive Capacity, and HRM.
Corporate Social Responsibility in Europe and the US: Insights from Businesses' Self-Presentations.
Globalization and the environment: determinants of firm self-regulation in China
Institutions, transaction costs, and entry mode choice in Eastern Europe
Corruption and Foreign Direct Investment.
A Case for Comparative Entrepreneurship: Assessing the Relevance of Culture.
The hierarchical model of market entry modes
Reinventing Strategies for Emerging Markets: Beyond the Transnational Model.
Productivity spillovers from foreign direct investment: Evidence from UK industry level panel data
A quarter century of Cultures Consequences: a review of empirical research incorporating Hofstedes cultural values frai
Characteristics of foreign subsidiaries in industry clusters
The impact of inward FDI on the performance of Chinese manufacturing firms
Explaining the national cultural distance paradox
An Empirical Analysis and Extension of the Bartlett and Ghoshal Typology of Multinational Companies.
Social Ties and Foreign Market Entry
A Theory of International New Ventures: A Decade of Research.
Globalisation, economic geography and the strategy of multinational enterprises
Governance infrastructure and US foreign direct investment
Intra-and Inter-organizational Imitative Behavior: Institutional Influences on Japanese Firms Entry Mode Choice
Chinas Transition and its Implications for International Business

KEY WORDS WITHIN A SPECIFIC JOURNAL

Although this process is much quicker than searching through the journal's table of contents, it might still lead you to pursue quite a lot of blind alleys. If your time is scarce and you are fairly confident that you have already done a rigorous literature review, you can speed up the process by searching for keywords **within** the journal. In order to do this, you will need to use the General Citation Search tab of Publish or Perish. For further information on the mechanics of General Citation Searches, see Chapter 5.

Sticking with our paper on entry modes in Japanese multinational companies, I now search for the term *entry mode* in the "The phrase" field of the General Citation Search with "Journal of International Business Studies" in the Publication field. This will provide any articles in which the words *entry mode* appear in that particular order. You will get the same results by including the search term *entry mode* in quotes ("entry mode") in the "All the words" field. If you include the search term *entry mode* without quotes it will provide slightly more matches as it matches the words in any order. The screenshot below reports the results of this query, sorted by the number of citations.

It shows many of the same titles as the earlier search, indicating that entry mode is a topic that features in many articles published in Journal of International Business Studies. However, it also showed that one of the articles I had singled out for further study (*Towards Theory of International New Ventures*) does not include the word entry mode. Hence, it is probably safe to remove this from our list.

Title
Knowledge of the firm and the evolutionary theory of the multinational corporation
Location and the multinational enterprise: A neglected factor&quest
Knowledge transfer in international acquisitions
Cultural distance revisited: Towards a more rigorous conceptualization and measurement of cultural differences
Innovation, Organizational Capabilities, and the Born-Global Firm.
A Perspective on Regional and Global Strategies of Multinational Enterprises.
Institutional, cultural and transaction cost influences on entry mode choice and performance
A three-stage theory of international expansion: The link between multinationality and performance in the service sector
MNC Knowledge Transfer, Subsidiary Absorptive Capacity, and HRM.
Institutions, transaction costs, and entry mode choice in Eastern Europe
Corruption and Foreign Direct Investment.
A Case for Comparative Entrepreneurship: Assessing the Relevance of Culture.
The hierarchical model of market entry modes
A quarter century of Cultures Consequences: a review of empirical research incorporating Hofstedes cultural values framev
Explaining the national cultural distance paradox
Intra-and Inter-organizational Imitative Behavior: Institutional Influences on Japanese Firms Entry Mode Choice
Internationalisation: conceptualising an entrepreneurial process of behaviour in time
Organizational learning about new international markets: Exploring the internal transfer of local market knowledge
Mode of International Entry: An Isomorphism Perspective.

On the other hand, it shows that articles I had not initially marked as including relevant information do refer to entry modes. For instance there are several articles referring to culture or cultural distance. These articles discuss the role of culture in entry mode choice as one of their topics. In the case of *Explaining the national culture distance paradox*, it is even the main topic of the paper, providing an update to the most highly-cited papers on entry mode choice (see below).

USING THE "TITLE WORDS ONLY" BOX TO FURTHER REFINE RESULTS

If the second search still provides you with too many results to cope with, you can narrow down your search even further by repeating the last search, but clicking the "Title words only" box. As the number of matches will be much smaller, I have now removed the "last ten years" condition. The screenshot below provides **all** articles that have been published in Journal of International Business Studies since its inception in 1970 that have *entry mode* in their title, sorted by number of citations. As you can see the topic of entry modes has generated continued interest from international business scholars in the last 20 years.

Title	Year
The effect of national culture on the choice of entry mode	1988
Choice of Foreign Market Entry Mode: Impact of Ownership, Location and Internalization Factors.	1992
Global Strategy and Multinationals' Entry Mode Choice.	1992
Ownership-Based Entry Mode Strategies and International Performance.	1994
Institutional, cultural and transaction cost influences on entry mode choice and performance	2002
Institutions, transaction costs, and entry mode choice in Eastern Europe	2001
Intra-and Inter-organizational Imitative Behavior: Institutional Influences on Japanese Firms Entry Mode Choice	2002
Mode of International Entry: An Isomorphism Perspective.	2000
The impact of order and mode of market entry on profitability and market share	1999
The effect of cultural distance on entry mode choice, international diversification, and MNE performance: A meta-...	2005
Transaction Cost Determinants and Ownership-Based Entry Mode Choice: A Meta-Analytical Review.	2004
CEO Successor Characteristics and the Choice of Foreign Market Entry Mode: An Empirical Study.	2002
Broadening the foreign market entry mode decision: separating ownership and control	2003
FDI by firms from newly industrialised economies in emerging markets: corporate governance, entry mode and loc...	2007
Foreign direct investment mode choice: entry and establishment modes in transition economies	2007
Beyond entry mode choice: Explaining the conversion of joint ventures into wholly owned subsidiaries in the Peopl...	2009

This is a very quick and easy way to ensure that you haven't missed any papers that might be crucial to your topic. However, it does not allow you to find papers that might provide important insights on entry mode choice, but do not list the words in their title. In the previous section, we saw an example of that: the article *Explaining the national culture distance paradox*, which provides an update to the 1988 article that tops the list above. Hence, you might wish to do a less restrictive search as well and at least eyeball the results.

10.4   REFERENCES

1. ABS (2010). **Journal Quality Guide**, downloaded from http://www.the-abs.org.uk/?id=257.
2. Harzing, A.W.K. (2010). **Journal Quality List**, 37th Edition, downloadable from http://www.harzing.com/jql.htm.
3. Huff, A.S. (1998) Writing for Scholarly Publication, London: Sage.
4. Mingers, J. & Harzing, A.W.K. (2007). **Ranking journals in Business and Management: A statistical analysis of the Harzing Dataset**. *European Journal of Information Systems*, 16: 303-316.
5. Tahai, A. & Meyer, M. (1999). **A revealed preference study of management journals' direct influences**, *Strategic Management Journal*, 20: 279-296.

CHAPTER 11:
CONDUCTING A LITERATURE REVIEW

Most academics will use Publish or Perish to evaluate their own impact and make a case for tenure or promotion (see Chapter 7), to evaluate the work of other academics for a variety of purposes, ranging from publication awards to preparing for a job interview (see Chapter 8), in their function as academic administrator (See Chapter 9), to do incidental searches for journals or to decide which journal to submit their paper to (see Chapter 10).

However, Publish or Perish can also be used to do a quick literature review to identify the most cited articles and/or scholars in a particular field. Of course, it can also identify whether any research has been done in a particular area at all (useful for grant applications). Other applications are to evaluate the development of the literature in a particular topic over time. In this chapter, I will discuss some tips and tricks in doing literature reviews.

11.1   HOW TO CONDUCT A LITERATURE REVIEW SEARCH?

To conduct a literature review search you will have to use the General Citation Search. For a general instruction on how to use the General Citation Search see Chapter 5. Depending on how broad you want the results to be, you could use **Any of the words**, **All of the words** or **The phrase** (see Section 5.1.1 General query pane for details). This will match these words anywhere in the resulting publications. If you use **The phrase**, the words will be matched in the order they were entered.

If you want to narrow down the results as much as possible, ticking the **Title words only** box will only provide publications where the words are included in the title. As one would normally expect important publications in a field to include relevant key words in their title, this might be a good strategy.

11.1.1   WORKED EXAMPLE: BORN GLOBAL FIRMS

Let's assume you would like to know what has been written about the relatively new concept of "born global" firms in international business. Born global firms are firms who start operating internationally from their inception, rather than starting out as domestic firms first and only internationalize gradually. To do so enter *"born global" OR "born globals"* in **All of the words**, check the **Title words only** box, and leave all subject area boxes checked. After removing duplicates, this search identifies some 150 papers, ten of which have been cited more than 100 times (see the screenshot below), with two articles having been cited more than 500 times. This shows us that, although this is a relatively new concept, it has attracted quite a lot of attention in the last two decades.

Although there are usually good reasons to limit your search by title words only, it is always sensible to do a quick search without the title words limitation. Especially in new fields, concepts are not yet firmly established and authors might not always mention them in the title. A search for born global without the title limitation produced a much longer list of highly cited works (see screenshot below).

| Author impact | Journal impact | General citations | Multi-query center | Web Browser |

General citation search - Perform a general citation search

Author(s):	
Publication:	
All of the words:	"born global" OR "born globals"
Any of the words:	
None of the words:	
The phrase:	
Year of publication between:	0 and: 0

☑ Biology, Life Sciences, Environmen
☑ Business, Administration, Finance,
☑ Chemistry and Materials Science
☑ Engineering, Computer Science, M
☑ Medicine, Pharmacology, Veterina
☑ Physics, Astronomy, Planetary Sc
☑ Social Sciences, Arts, Humanities

☑ Title words only

Results

Papers:	150	Cites/paper:	28.55	h-index:	28	AWCR:	477.92
Citations:	4283	Cites/author:	2379.32	g-index:	63	AW-index:	21.86
Years:	19	Papers/author:	84.08	hc-index:	23	AWCRpA:	251.67
Cites/year:	225.42	Authors/paper:	2.14	hI-index:	12.25	e-index:	52.02
				hI,norm:	20	hm-index:	18.25

Cites	Authors	Title	Year	Publication
☑ 📋 564	TK Madsen, P Servais	The internationalization of born globals: a...	1997	International Business Review
☑ 📋 549	GA Knight, ST Cavusgil	The born global firm: A challenge to traditi...	1996	Advances in international mar
☑ 335	GA Knight, ST Cavusgil	Innovation, Organizational Capabilities, a...	2004	Journal of International Busin
☑ 📋 266	MW Rennie	Global competitiveness: born global	1993	McKinsey Quarterly
☑ 📋 178	DD Sharma, A Bloms...	The internationalization process of born gl...	2003	International Business Review
☑ 173	Ø Moen, P Servais	Born global or gradual global? Examining t...	2002	Journal of International Mark
☑ 155	Ø Moen	The born globals	2002	International Marketing Revie
☑ 119	J Bell, R McNaughto...	Born-again global'firms:: An extension to t...	2001	Journal of International Mana
☑ 113	S Chetty, C Campb...	A strategic approach to internationalizatio...	2004	Journal of International Mark
☑ 112	S Andersson, I Wictor	Innovative internationalisation in new firm...	2003	Journal of International Entre

Cites	Rank	Authors	Title	Year
☑ 4133	905	L Von Bertalanffy	General system theory: Foundations, development, applica...	1968
☑ 780	602	S Ghoshal	Global strategy: An organizing framework	1987
☑ 674	611	P Phillips McDougall,...	Explaining the formation of international new ventures: The...	1994
☑ 📋 554	2	GA Knight, ST Cavusgil	The born global firm: A challenge to traditional internationali...	1996
☑ 📋 553	1	TK Madsen, P Servais	The internationalization of born globals: an evolutionary pro...	1997
☑ 335	3	GA Knight, ST Cavusgil	Innovation, Organizational Capabilities, and the Born-Global...	2004
☑ 266	824	S Hollensen	Global marketing	
☑ 199	657	BM Oviatt, PP McDo...	Defining international entrepreneurship and modeling the sp...	2005
☑ 193	365	SA Zahra, G George	International entrepreneurship: The current status of the fi...	2002
☑ 📋 187	7	Ø Moen, P Servais	Born global or gradual global? Examining the export behavio...	2002
☑ 175	4	DD Sharma, A Bloms...	The internationalization process of born globals: a network ...	2003
☑ 172	452	A Rialp, J Rialp, GA ...	The phenomenon of early internationalizing firms: what do ...	2005
☑ 170	700	SA Zahra	A Theory of International New Ventures: A Decade of Rese...	2005

As can be established from the "rank" column, providing the original Google Scholar order which is ranked by search relevance, many of these works are not very relevant to the search query. For the first two hits (well-cited books) as well as the Global Marketing book, it is likely that the words born and global were mentioned somewhere in the book, but not in a way that was relevant to our interest in born global firms.

However, there are several other publications that do not have born global in their title, but do appear relevant to our search. They deal with international new ventures, early internationalizing firms and international entrepreneurship, all topics that could easily be related to born global firms. Hence it is can sometimes be worthwhile to broaden your search.

11.1.2   WORKED EXAMPLE: MANAGEMENT IN RUSSIA

Let us assume you are interested in doing research on management in Russia as an extension of your previous research on management in transforming economies. However, you would first like to know whether anything influential has been written about this topic (see below). In this case I limit the subject area, because the search terms are fairly generic. If I didn't limit the subject area, the search would also give us papers on for instance fire, soil and forest management in Russia.

The results (see above) quickly establish that there are only a few papers and authors in this field that received a substantial number of citations. What is also immediately apparent is that most of this work was published quite recently, starting in mid nineties. This is not entirely surprising as it would have been virtually impossible for Western researchers to do research in Russia until the fall of the Berlin wall in 1989.

However, the search does identify a book published by MIT Press in the early seventies, which compares management in France, Britain, the United States and Russia. This might be a useful source for an overview of Russian management in the past.

11.2   IDENTIFY KEY AUTHORS/JOURNALS/PUBLICATIONS IN A FIELD

In addition to doing a quick general search on what has been published in a particular field, Publish or Perish can also be used to do a more in-depth literature search. You can for instance find out who the founding fathers (or mothers) of a particular field are and which countries they come from, what the journals are in which academics most frequently publish about this topic. Also, once you have found a key publication in the field, you can do further research following up on this publication.

11.2.1   FOUNDING FATHERS

I go back to our earlier example about born global firms. Sorting the results by year allows us to identify the "founding author(s)" of the concept. In this case, I can easily identify that the first publication was in 1993 by MW Rennie in McKinsey Quarterly (there is one other publication in 1993, but this turned out to be a Google Scholar processing error).

Cites		Authors	Title	Year
☑ ☐ 266		MW Rennie	Global competitiveness: born global	1993
☑ 11		ST Cavusgil	Born globals: A quiet revolution among Australian export...	1994
☐ 0		J Laing	The'Born Global'Wine Producer-Overcoming the Tyranny ...	1995
☑ ☐ 549		GA Knight, ST Cavusgil	The born global firm: A challenge to traditional internatio...	1996
☑ ☐ 564		TK Madsen, P Servais	The internationalization of born globals: an evolutionary ...	1997
☑ ☐ 90		GA Knight	Emerging paradigm for international marketing: The born...	1997
☑ ☐ 25		ST Cavusgil, GA Knight	Explaining an emerging phenomenon for international ma...	1997
☑ 12		S Kandasaami	Internationalisation of Small-and Medium-sized Born-Glob...	1998
☑ 85		ES Rasmussen, TK Madsen, F Evang...	The founding of the born global company in Denmark an...	1999
☑ 5		C Gurau, A Ranchhod	The 'Born Global'firms in UK biotechnology	1999
☑ 5		P Servais, ES Rasmussen	Born Globals–connectors between various industrial distri...	1999
☑ 80		TK Madsen, E Rasmussen, P Servais	Differences and similarities between born globals and oth...	2000
☑ 78		PD Harveston, BL Kedia, PS Davis	Internationalization of born global and gradual globalizin...	2000
☑ ☐ 35		E Autio, HJ Sapienza	Comparing process and born global perspectives in the in...	2000
☑ 17		J Bell, R McNaughton	Born global firms: a challenge to public policy in support o...	2000
☑ 12		T Almor, N Hashai	Born Global: The Case of Small and Medium-Sized, Knowl...	2000

The paper talks about a McKinsey study amongst Australian firms that identified small and medium-sized companies that successfully competed against large, established players in the global arena without first building a home base. Hence, the phenomenon was first discovered by a consulting firm in Australia.

The second publication is an editorial by a well-known academic in International Marketing, who – in the *Journal of International Marketing* – reports on the results of the McKinsey study that he discovered when spending 6 months as a Fullbright Scholar in Australia. Cavusgil (1994:4) says: "I would like to comment on an interesting phenomenon in the Australian export scene. It is relevant to those of us in other post-industrial economies and, hopefully, should spur some research interests."

Interestingly, the third publication is also about Australian born globals, this time wine producers. However, even after 15 years, the article hasn't generated a single citation. This seems to suggest it has not been picked by researchers, no doubt largely caused by the fact that it was published in a rather obscure and specialized journal (*Australian and New Zealand Wine Industry Journal*). The Australian angle is also apparent in a later unpublished conceptual paper by Kandasaami at the University of Western Australia in 1998.

Cavusgil took his own recommendation to heart and started researching this phenomenon, leading to very highly cited publication – co-authored with Gary Knight – in the research annual *Advances in International Marketing*. Both Knight and Cavusgil went on to publish other papers in this field. They were joined at an early stage by Danish academic Tage Madsen, who with his Danish co-authors Servais and Rasmussen published a number of papers on the topic. In 1999 a comparison of Danish and Australian companies was published, co-authored with Australian academic Evangelista.

In 1999, the phenomenon was also picked up in the UK, where Gurau & Ranchhod researched biotechnology firms. By 2000 the topic had spread to researchers in the USA (Harveston et al.), Ireland (Bell), Finland (Autio), and Israel (Almor & Hashai). Interest remained strong amongst researchers these countries, but after 2000 they were joined by researchers in Sweden, Portugal, and New Zealand. One can observe that with the exception of some researchers in the USA and Israel, the phenomenon attracted most interest from academics in "small" economies at the peripheries of the world.

11.2.2   IMPORTANT JOURNALS

Sorting our earlier results on born global firms (without the title only limitation) by publication allows us to identify the journals that publish articles relating to this topic. All of the mainstream international business journals (*Journal of International Business Studies, Journal of World Business, Management International Review* and *International Business Review*) contained a substantial number of papers on the topic. The results for *International Business Review* are reproduced below and show that since one of the seminal articles was published here, the journal has gone on to publish nearly a dozen articles related to the topic.

Specialized International Marketing journals such as *International Marketing Review* and *Journal of International Marketing* also contain a large number of papers on this topic. Most born global firms are exporters rather than multinationals with subsidiaries abroad. Exporting has traditionally been a topic of interest to the International Marketing community.

Finally, the results also show a large number of papers in the *International Journal of Globalisation and Small Business* and a very large number of papers in the *Journal of International Entrepreneurship*. This illustrates that the born global phenomenon often concerns small and medium sized firms and that the early internationalization decision should be seen in the context of entrepreneurship.

Cites		Authors	Title	Year	Publication
☑	2	S Freeman, K Hutchi...	A model of rapid knowledge development: The ...	2009	International Business ...
☑ 🗇	17	M Gabrielsson, VH Ki...	Born globals: Propositions to help advance the ...	2008	International Business ...
☑	3	A Tuppura, S Saare...	Linking knowledge, entry timing and internation...	2008	International Business ...
☑	0	M Gabrielsson, P Ga...	Internet-based sales channel strategies of bor...	2010	International Business Re'
☑	8	A Tan, P Brewer, P...	Before the first export decision: Internationalis...	2007	International Business Re'
☑	172	A Rialp, J Rialp, GA ...	The phenomenon of early internationalizing fir...	2005	International Business Re'
☑	73	SA Zahra, JS Korri, ...	Cognition and international entrepreneurship: i...	2005	International Business Re'
☑	19	A Majocchi, E Bacchi...	Firm size, business experience and export inte...	2005	International Business Re'
☑	64	M Gabrielsson, VH M...	Born globals: how to reach new business space...	2004	International Business Re'
☑	52	N Hashai, T Almor	Gradually internationalizing 'born global'firms: a...	2004	International Business Re'
☑ 🗇	182	DD Sharma, A Bloms...	The internationalization process of born globals...	2003	International Business Re'
☑	157	H Yli-Renko, E Autio...	Social capital, knowledge, and the international...	2002	International Business Re'
☑ 🗇	564	TK Madsen, P Servais	The internationalization of born globals: an evo...	1997	International Business Re'

11.2.3   FOLLOW UP ON KEY PUBLICATIONS IN THE FIELD

Your literature review will discover the seminal publications in the field. These could be publications that are highly cited or publications that deal with exactly the topic you are interested in. You want to ensure that you also study papers citing this seminal piece of work. They will often show up in your initial search, but if they look at the phenomenon from a different angle and don't refer to the exact some concepts, they will not be captured. How to follow up on publications that cite your seminal publications?

A future version of Publish or Perish will implement an option to display citing publications **within** Publish or Perish when double-clicking on the original publications. However, at this stage double-clicking on the publication in question in Publish or Perish leads you to Google Scholar which lists the citing works. The screenshot below shows the first two citing works.

The first two of the citing articles already occurred in our earlier search. However, the second two did not. The short summary of the article provides a quick way to assess whether it is worthwhile to follow up. Google Scholar has recently implemented a new feature, which allows you to search **within** citing articles. We will implement this feature in a future version of PoP, so you have the choice to do this search within Publish or Perish. The advantage of this is that it enables to sort the results in any possible way.

However, at this stage you can still benefit from this feature by using the Google Scholar interface. Let's assume we want to establish which papers referring to Knight & Cavusgil deal with New Zealand. I would then enter "New Zealand" in the search box and click the "Search within articles citing Knight: the born …". The screenshot below shows the first four results.

Barriers to internationalisation: a study of entrepreneurial new ventures in **New Zealan**
V Shaw, J Darroch - Journal of International Entrepreneurship, 2004 - Springer
Abstract. This paper presents the findings of a study of the perceptions of the barriers to internationalis
by 561 **New Zealand** Entrepreneurial New Ventures (ENVs). Significant differences in the perception
of the barriers are identified according to the level of international activity of **New Zealand** …
Cited by 21 - Related articles - All 7 versions

Learning about Foreign Markets: Are Entrant Firms Exposed to a" Shock Effect"?
T Pedersen, B Petersen - Journal of International Marketing, 2004 - JSTOR
… tional firms from small, open economies (Denmark, Sweden, and **New Zealand**). … Page 3. kets
evolves. The empirical study is based on data obtained from current foreign operations as reported
by managers of international firms in Denmark, Sweden, and **New Zealand**. …
Cited by 33 - Related articles - BL Direct - All 10 versions

The network dynamics of international new ventures
NE Coviello - Journal of International Business Studies, 2006 - ingentaconnect.com
… 1997). The case sites were chosen from a wider set of eight firms resident in an
accelerator facility in **New Zealand**. … 2003). Results The case sites are referred to as
Charlie, Sierra and Tango.7 All three INVs are based in **New Zealand**. …
Cited by 106 - Related articles - BL Direct - All 10 versions

[] Born-again global'firms:: An extension to the [] born global'phenomenon
J Bell, R McNaughton, S Young - Journal of International Management, 2001 - Elsevier
… Their meta-analysis encompasses 16 empirical studies undertaken between 1989 and 1998
in 11 European countries (including the Denmark, Finland, Ireland, Italy, the Netherlands, Norway
and Sweden) and Canada, Hong Kong, **New Zealand** and Pakistan. …
Cited by 117 - Related articles - All 2 versions

11.3 DEVELOPMENT OF THE LITERATURE OVER TIME

Publish or Perish can also be used to analyze the development of the literature on any particular topic over time. Using the General Citation search function you can search for particular key-words and look at how the number of papers published varies over time.

In order to eliminate a potentially large range of irrelevant results it might be a good idea to focus on a small set of journals. Journals can be combined with the OR function in the publication field, although Google Scholar **sometimes** refuses to run searches when more than two quoted journal names are included. It is as yet unclear what triggers this.

At present Publish or Perish does not yet have a way to further analyze for instance the number of publications per year. However, this can be done quite easily by exporting the data to a spreadsheet or statistical program. In addition, by selecting all publications in a year, clicking "unselect" and looking at the reduction in the number of papers, you can easily establish the number of papers per year. I have provided two worked examples in below.

11.3.1 WORKED EXAMPLE: CULTURE IN JOURNAL OF INTL BUSINESS STUDIES

Let us assume you are interested how research into the role of national culture in the field of business and management has developed over the years. In order to limit the number of irrelevant hits, you limit your search to two mainstream international business journals. The screenshot below shows the search and all papers receiving more than 150 citations.

| Author impact | Journal impact | General citations | Multi-query center | Web Browser |

General citation search - Perform a general citation search

Author(s):	
Publication:	"Journal of International Business Studies" OR "International Business Review"
All of the words:	
Any of the words:	
None of the words:	
The phrase:	culture
Year of publication between:	0 and: 0

☑ Biology, Life
☑ Business, A...
☑ Chemistry a
☑ Engineering,
☑ Medicine, Ph
☑ Physics, Ast
☑ Social Scienc

☑ Title words...

Results

Papers:	74	Cites/paper:	87.27	h-index:	29	AWCR:	572.49
Citations:	6458	Cites/author:	3606.59	g-index:	74	AW-index:	23.93
Years:	28	Papers/author:	43.37	hc-index:	21	AWCRpA:	269.75
Cites/year:	230.64	Authors/paper:	2.19	hI-index:	12.19	e-index:	72.08
				hI,norm:	23	hm-index:	18.67

Cites		Authors	Title	Year
☑ ☐ 2069		B Kogut, H Singh	The effect of national culture on the choice of entry mode	1988
☑ ☐ 415		KL Newman, SD Nollen	Culture and Congruence: The Fit between Management Practices an...	1996
☑ ☐ 367		DA Ralston, DH Holt...	The impact of national culture and economic ideology on managerial ...	2008
☑ ☐ 351		NJ Adler	A typology of management studies involving culture	1983
☑ ☐ 283		BW Husted	Wealth, Culture, and Corruption.	1999
☑ ☐ 240		G Hofstede	The business of international business is culture	1994
☑ ☐ 239		JF Hennart, J Larimo	The impact of culture on the strategy of multinational enterprises: do...	1998
☑ ☐ 231		AS Thomas, SL Mueller	A Case for Comparative Entrepreneurship: Assessing the Relevance ...	2000
☑ ☐ 186		R Schuler, N Rogovsky	Understanding Compensation Practice Variations across Firms: The I...	1998
☑ ☐ 183		JL Graham	The influence of culture on business negotiations	1985
☑ ☐ 179		K Leung, RS Bhagat...	Culture and international business: Recent advances and their implica...	2005

The most cited paper – by a large distance – is Kogut & Singh's paper on the effect of national culture on the choice of entry mode. This was a seminal paper in that it introduced culture as a variable to be considered in studies on entry modes. Entry modes concern the way multinationals enter foreign countries and could include acquisitions and joint ventures.

Interestingly, most articles citing this paper do not refer to the study's findings at all, but to the way the study operationalizes culture, i.e. by calculating cultural distance based on scores on Hofstede's cultural dimensions. This shows us that methodological articles can often be highly cited. Other highly cited papers are those providing reviews of the field (e.g. Adler, Hofstede, and Leung et al.).

However, the general study of the impact of culture on managerial work values and practices is also popular (Newman & Nollen; Ralston et al.). Further highly cited papers deal with the impact of culture on specific topics such as corruption (Husted), strategy (Hennart & Larimo), entrepreneurship (Thomas & Mueller), compensation practices (Schuler & Rogovsky) and business negotiations (Graham).

When I sort the articles by year, I find that the interest in the role of culture seems to be increasing. There were only six articles published in the 1980s that had culture in their title. This is not surprising as Hofstede's book Culture's Consequences, first published in 1980 and reprinted in 1984, is often seen as the catalyst for the attention to national culture in the field of business and management. Likewise, in the first half of the nineties, only five articles dealt with culture to such an extent that they included the word in their title.

In the latter half of the nineties, the number of articles published on culture increased to nearly a dozen. The first five years of the 21st century produced 18 articles on culture, with the following five years producing 24. Some of these articles, however, dealt with entrepreneurial or industrial cultures rather than national culture. It is clear, however, that culture is a topic that is of sustained interest to international business scholars.

11.3.2 WORKED EXAMPLE: HIV IN SCIENCE, NATURE AND CELL

Let us assume you are interested on how research on HIV has developed over the years. You focus your search on three core journals that are likely to publish on this topic: Science, Nature and Cell. You would then run the following query.

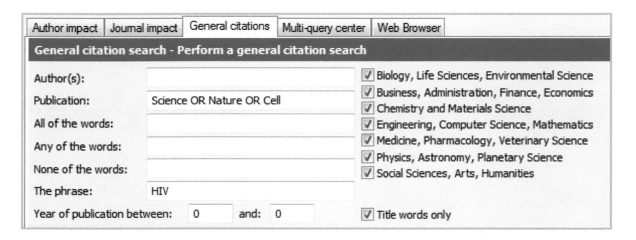

The most highly cited results for this query are shown below. We can see that each of the three journals has published some highly cited articles in this field. We can also observe that most of the highly cited articles were published between 1995 and 1997.

Cites		Authors	Title	Year	Publication
☑	3222	DD Ho, AU Neumann, A...	Rapid turnover of plasma virions and CD4 lymphocytes i...	1995	Nature
☑	2605	HK Deng, R Liu, W Ellme...	of a major co-receptor for primary isolates of HIV-1	1996	Nature
☑	2072	G Alkhatib, C Combadier...	CC CKR5: a RANTES, MIP-1alpha, MIP-1beta receptor ...	1996	Science
☑	1968	JW Mellors, CR Rinaldo ...	Prognosis in HIV-1 infection predicted by the quantity o...	1996	Science
☑	1938	AS Perelson, AU Neuma...	HIV-1 dynamics in vivo: virion clearance rate, infected c...	1996	Science
☑	1918	F Cocchi, AL DeVico, A ...	Identification of RANTES, MIP-1alpha, and MIP-1beta a...	1995	Science
☑	1893	R Liu, WA Paxton, S Ch...	Homozygous defect in HIV-1 coreceptor accounts for re...	1996	Cell
☑	1787	H Choe, M Farzan, Y Su...	The [beta]-chemokine receptors CCR3 and CCR5 facilit...	1996	Cell
☑	1741	M Samson, F Libert, BJ ...	Resistance to HIV-1 infection in caucasian individuals be...	1996	Nature
☑	1643	M Dean, M Carrington, ...	Genetic restriction of HIV-1 infection and progression to...	1996	Science
☑	1552	ES Rosenberg, JM Billing...	Vigorous HIV-1-specific CD4+ T cell responses associate...	1997	Science

However, I am also interested in how the volume of research on HIV has developed over the years. In order to assess this I rerun the search for a single journal: Science. The reason for this is that if I include all journals only the highly cited 1000 results will be shown and this will naturally include fewer recent articles. Running the search for Science alone ensures I also include less-cited articles (there are 50 articles without citations). This reduces the risk of missing most of the more recently published articles.

When I sort the results by year, I first find four articles that were published between 1752 and 1873. These are clearly Google Scholar parsing errors, where Google for instance mistook the page numbers for the year indication. Beyond these four, articles on HIV started to be published in Science in 1986. However, after removing duplicates, I found only four articles published in that year. About a dozen articles were published in 1987, whilst nearly 50 articles were published in 1988. This turned about to be one of the most active publishing year for authors publishing about HIV as between 1989 an 1995 the number of articles had gone down to about 30-40. In 1996, the number of articles reached nearly 50 again, dropping to 30-40 again in 1997 and 1998. From 1999, the number of articles published in Science on HIV went down to about 20 a year, getting closer to a ten a year in recent years.

The name HIV was introduced in May 1986 by the International Committee on the Taxonomy of Viruses. The current treatment for HIV was introduced in 1996, resulting in a declining number of deaths from HIV/AIDS. Studying the scientific interest in HIV (or any illness) thus allows one to understand the development of interest in the disease over time.

11.4   FURTHER EXAMPLES OF LITERATURE REVIEW APPLICATIONS

Several academics have informed me how they use Publish or Perish to conduct literature searches or reviews. Below I very briefly summarize a number of representative studies to further illustrate how PoP can be used in this context. They deal with a general method of literature analysis, research into changing views on alcoholism, research planning in the US environmental protection agency and sourcing literature for meta-analytical studies.

11.4.1 INFLUENTIAL LITERATURE ANALYSIS

Hoepner & McMillan (2009) develop the new concept of Influential Literature Analysis (ILA), using of Publish or Perish to access Google Scholar data. Influential Literature Analysis (ILA) is a four step approach, which the authors claim improves upon existing methods to synthesize research areas. The first step ranks the candidate studies according to their influence and selects the most influential ones to be synthesized. Of course this step is facilitated enormously by Publish or Perish. The second and third steps respectively characterize and categorize the most influential studies. The last step then investigates the (sometimes conflicting) results and interpretations offered by influential studies in depth.

The authors see as the main advantage of ILA that it outsources the assessment of articles to the wider community of researchers by using their average judgment embedded in citations. This contrast with existing approaches in which reviewers would assess the candidate articles themselves. According to the authors, this process therefore offers reviewers a much needed valid and predominantly author independent mean to select studies. Although I am not entirely comfortable to outsource this type of judgment completely, there is no doubt that this process might help many PhD students and young researchers to avoid entering too many dead alleys.

11.4.2 VIEWS ON ALCOHOLISM: GENETIC OR ENVIRONMENTAL

An academic user of PoP wrote to me: "I work in the field of Psychobiology of addictions, where I do most of my lab research. We have just started a project that tries to assess whether a common statement in the field of addiction studies is true or not. Specifically, it has been suggested that the traditional view of alcoholism as a mainly genetic disorder has been replaced by a more environmental view that focuses in how early onset of drinking affects later ethanol abuse and dependence.

If that was true, the number of papers covering the latter "point of view" and the impact of these papers should have been steadily increasing in the last years, while those covering the traditional genetic perspective may be scarcer and perhaps have less impact. As you may imagine, we are using your fabulous program to assess these hypotheses."

11.4.3 RESEARCH PLANNING IN THE US ENVIRONMENTAL PROTECTION AGENCY

Another PoP user working for the US Environmental Protection Agency wrote: "In the last 2 years, a new program (Ecosystem Services Research Program or ESRP) has been implemented as a major objective of the U.S. EPA's Office of Research and Development to transform the way we account for the type, quality, and magnitude of nature's goods and services so that they can be better considered in environmental management decisions.

Within this national effort, a team of aquatic ecological researchers at EPA's Gulf Ecology Division (http://www.epa.gov/ged/) is studying the ways ecosystem services benefit human health and well-being in the Tampa Bay Estuary Watershed as part of a larger research effort to better understand the value of ecosystem services. Within this Tampa project, I am part of a smaller core lead-group that is using PoP as a tool for research planning.

PoP allows us (through a series of targeted topical searches using the "general citation search" function) to better assess and report the "state of the science" based on a complex series of search phrases. Based on the results of our article count analyses using PoP, we are able to better inform the research planning process to either support or challenge research needs previously identified using other more traditional techniques (stakeholder surveys, expert opinion, literature reviews, etc.).

Our current objective involves developing a series of search phrases around a set of societally valued ecosystem services (e.g. fishery production, nitrogen removal, flood attenuation, water supply, carbon storage, etc.) with associated primary habitat/landscape types (e.g. wetland, open water/sea grass, forest, agriculture). For example the search phrase below based on nitrogen removal by wetlands generated a count of 22 articles as published in the journal "Estuaries and Coasts".

> *Example search phrase ("AND" included here only for clarity): wetland AND nitrogen OR nitrate OR nitrite OR loading AND denitrification OR fixation OR "n:p ratio" AND "nitrogen removal" OR sequestration OR "nitrogen burial" AND "water quality" OR "primary production" OR biodiversity"*

11.4.4   FINDING LITERATURE FOR META-ANALYTICAL STUDIES

Canadian-based academic, Vas Taras, describes how he uses PoP for his meta-analytic work. "After I complete the conventional literature search (going through tables of contents of relevant journals, searching scholarly article databases using key words that describe the topic of my interest), I conduct an additional search using PoP. First, I check who cited every publication included in my original meta-analytic database. For every study in the initial dataset, PoP can help find, on average, 0.5 to 1.5 additional studies.

Second, I go through the list of authors of the studies included in my original meta-analytic database and see what names appear there more often. Once the leaders (most published authors in the area) are identified, I run their names through PoP to see if there may be more studies that they have published on the topic of my interest. I could use Google Scholar, but PoP has a much more convenient and streamlined interface. For example, I can easily limit the time range, define the field, etc - things that can be done in Google Scholar, but it would be much more hassle to do it. This strategy yields one to three additional papers per author - people often tend to publish several studies on the same topic. After running these two additional searches, my meta-analytic datasets usually doubles in size."

11.5   REFERENCES

- Hoepner, A. G. F. & McMillan, D. G. (2009), **Research on 'Responsible Investment': An Influential Literature Analysis Comprising a Rating, Characterisation, Categorisation and Investigation** (August 14, 2009). Available at SSRN: http://ssrn.com/abstract=1454793

CHAPTER 12:
DOING BIBLIOMETRIC RESEARCH ON AUTHORS AND JOURNALS

Most academics will use Publish or Perish to evaluate their own impact and make a case for tenure or promotion (see Chapter 7), to evaluate the work of other academics for a variety of purposes, ranging from publication awards to preparing for a job interview (see Chapter 8), to do incidental searches for journals or to decide which journal to submit their paper to (see Chapter 10) or to do a more generic literature search (see Chapter 11).

However, Publish or Perish can also be used to do more far-ranging bibliometric research. The multi-query center (see Chapter 6 for details) is particularly helpful for these types of searches as it allows you to organize your searches in folders, making it much easier to keep track of your results.

Bibliometric research refers to the quantitative analysis of bodies of literature and their references: citations. These bodies of literature can be grouped in different ways, but in this chapter we will focus on the grouping by author or journal and discuss some tips and tricks in doing bibliometric research. When doing bibliometric research it is even more important that your searches are as accurate as possible. For more information on improving accuracy in author and journals searches, please refer to Sections 3.3 and 4.3.

12.1   DOING BIBLIOMETRIC RESEARCH FOR AUTHORS

Ever since 2006 when Publish or Perish was first made available, users have started to compare themselves with other academics. Numerous blogs have published ad-hoc rankings of academics in particular fields. Creating your own reference group is also a strategy that I have specifically recommended in Chapter 7 on "Making your case for tenure or promotion".

However, some academics want to go further than this and are keen to conduct more systematic research on the comparative research impact of academics. This kind of research has been conducted for many decades and had filled the pages of journals such as *Scientometrics* and *Journal of the Society for Information Science and Technology*. The data source for these analyses was almost invariably ISI's Web of Science/Web of Knowledge. The availability of Google Scholar and Publish or Perish now makes a more comprehensive comparison of research impact for authors possible.

Most of the tools and information you need to conduct bibliometric research on authors have been discussed in other chapters. Chapter 1 provides you with a discussion of the range of citation metrics that can be used. Chapter 3 shows you how to conduct author searches effectively and accurately. Chapter 6 explains how to manage your queries in an effective way in the Multi-query center. The most important questions in conducting bibliometric research for authors are what is going to be the population you are studying and which metrics to use to compare academics in your population.

The first important question in doing bibliometric research is which population to study. Of course this is largely dependent on your research question. If your aim is to study the impact of different data sources or different metrics for comparisons across disciplines (see Chapter 16 for an extended example), you will obviously need to select academics from a broad range of disciplines. However, most academic who do bibliometric research on authors aim to create some sort of ranking of individual authors, which necessitates a more focused population. The following options are possible.

PICK A SPECIFIC DISCIPLINE

In order for this ranking to make any sense to your readers, it is usually best to limit your population by discipline. As we have seen in Chapter 7, however, even within disciplines there can be very substantial differences in typical citation scores. Hence your definition of discipline might need to be fairly narrow. The examples given in Section 12.1.3 refer to Economics, Business Administration, (Operations) Management and Social Psychology. In the latter case, the researchers purposefully decided to focus on Social Psychology only, and not include for instance Clinical Psychology, where citation patterns would be very different.

PICK A SPECIFIC COUNTRY

An additional way to narrow down your population is by country. All of the studies discussed in Section 12.1.3 refer to particular countries (Israel, Germany, UK/USA, and USA/Canada). This both limits the scope of the data collection effort and reduces differences caused by different research traditions in different countries. As most of these studies aim to produce norm scores of some sort, this is a good thing. Obviously, if your research question related to comparing the impact of different research traditions on citation patterns, your choice would be different.

PICK ACADEMICS WHO SHARE SPECIFIC ATTRIBUTES

As even narrowing down the population by discipline or country can leave one with a large number of academics a study, most studies narrow down their field even further by studying academics who share specific attributes. These attributes could for instance be:

- Working at the top 5/10/20 universities (however defined) in the country
- Being a fellow of one of the major professional association in the discipline
- Being editor or editorial board member of one of journals in the discipline
- Having been president of a major professional association in the field
- Having won a major research award (e.g. dissertation award, Nobel prize)
- Having done their PhD at a specific set of institutions.

Obviously, your selection would need to make sense in the context of your research questions. There are only so many simple exploratory ranking studies that can be published, even if you are personally very interested in the results.

Obviously, your choice of metrics is also largely dependent on your research question. If you for instance want to study co-authorship patterns across countries or disciplines, the authors per paper would probably be the most appropriate metric. However, as indicated above most bibliometric studies on authors aim to measure research output and/or impact of a group of academics.

In that case, the choice of metrics is to some extent dependent on your personal preferences. Many of the metrics provided by Publish or Perish are highly correlated. This is natural as they are all based to some extent on the number of citations and papers. Therefore some bibliometric researchers decide to simply focus on these raw measures.

NUMBER OF PAPERS OR CITATIONS

Unfortunately, Google Scholar data are not flawless (see Chapters 13-15 for an extensive discussion of different data sources) and using the exact number of papers and citations might suggest a level of accuracy that is not present in the source data. I would certainly caution against using the number of papers or any measure derived from that (e.g. cites/paper) as a measure of research impact unless you are prepared to manually merge all stray references into their master records. This can be quite a tedious process.

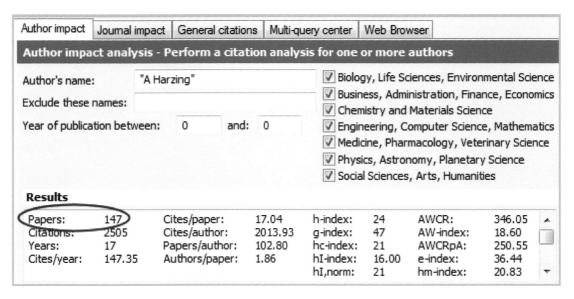

The screenshot above shows my "raw" citation record without any data cleaning and lists no less than 147 papers. The screenshot below shows my "cleaned" citation record after merging all stray references into their master records. The number of papers was reduced by 50% and as a result the number of cites per paper doubled.

Results									
Papers:	74	Cites/paper:	33.85	h-index:	25	AWCR:	353.06		
Citations:	2505	Cites/author:	1994.94	g-index:	49	AW-index:	18.79		
Years:	16	Papers/author:	51.37	hc-index:	23	AWCRpA:	251.64		
Cites/year:	156.56	Authors/paper:	1.74	hI-index:	16.45	e-index:	38.68		
				hI,norm:	20	hm-index:	20.33		

Fortunately, not all scholars will show such a large difference between their "raw" citation record and cleaned citation records. In my case, a large number of stray citations are found, because I have a fairly large number of "non-traditional" publications, such as white papers (e.g. Reflections on the h-index), software (Publish or Perish) and book chapters, that are not always consistently referenced. The problem will generally be smaller for academics who only publish in journals.

The number of citations is not subject to stray citations. However, as indicated above, the number of citations in Google Scholar is not always entirely accurate and there might be some level of double-counting or non-academic citations (see also Chapter 13). This proportion is smaller than some Google Scholar critics seem to believe, but even so I would not recommend placing too much emphasis on the exact number of citations.

Another reason for this is that citations are subject to frequent change. For academics with a substantial publication record, citations will increase with every Google Scholar update. My own citation record has changed dozens of times during the months I wrote this book (hence the slightly different results in the different screenshots). This means that if your data collection period runs over several months, you will be disadvantaging academics whose citation scores are collected at the start of the project.

H-INDEX OR G-INDEX

Because of the inherent inaccuracy and instability of citation and paper counts it might be better to focus on some of the more robust measures, such as the h-index and the g-index. These measures are not as vulnerable to small changes or inaccuracies in the source data. Incidental citations do not normally increase the h-index or g-index very much in relative terms unless the academic in question has a very low h-index or g-index (e.g. the difference between an h-index of 2 or 3).

However, the h-index and g-index can often increase by one or two points by merging stray references, especially if one of the academic's publications is close to becoming part of the h-index. In my case, both the h-index increased by one and the g-index increased by 2 through carefully merging all stray citations, which is an increase of less than 5%.

This is a fairly negligible increase that would not normally influence the ranking of academics to a great extent. Furthermore, stray references – especially those with only one or a couple of citations – are more likely to be dubious citations (e.g. Google Scholar crawling errors) than master records. Hence, when doing bibliometric research, one could consider simply ignoring stray references when using robust measures such as the h-index or g-index.

SELECTIVE MERGING AROUND THE H-INDEX CUT-OFF

There is an alternative strategy that would allow you to minimize the time involved in merging stray references and maximizing the accuracy of the h-index. This involves double-checking for each academic in your sample whether they have any publications that are close to becoming part of the h-index and check whether any stray references can be found for those. An easy way to find duplicates is by sorting the publications by title, publication, author or year. I would normally recommend checking all publications within 5 citations of reaching the required number of citations to be included in the h-index.

Let's work through an example of how this works. The screenshot below shows the publications in my "raw" citation record that might qualify for inclusion in the h-index. The Expatriate Failure article with

Christensen is the last paper to be included in the h-index. The next paper [Response styles in cross-national survey research] has 21 citations, but as is immediately apparent, there is a duplicate paper with an equal number of citations. The duplicate paper does not include the subtitle, but a quick verification of the citing articles shows that they are indeed different from those citing the paper with the subtitle. Hence this would be a prime candidate for merging, which increases the h-index to 24.

☑	25	5.00	AW Harzing, N Noorder...	Knowledge flows in MNCs: an empirical test and extension of Gupta and G
☑	24	3.43	AW Harzing, C Christen...	Expatriate failure: time to abandon the concept?
☑	21	4.20	AW Harzing	Response styles in cross-national survey research: A 26-country study
☑	21	4.20	AW Harzing	Response styles in cross-national survey research
☑	21	2.33	AW Harzing, M Maznevski	The interaction between language and culture: A test of the cultural accd
☑	20	5.00	AW Harzing	Publish or perish
☑	18	2.57	AW Harzing	Journal quality list

The next paper [The interaction between language and culture] does have some stray citations (found by sorting the results by publication), but not enough to enter into the h-index. The Publish or Perish program has a fairly high number of stray citations with academics referring to different versions, and hence when merged becomes part of the h-index. However, as the original last paper included in only has 24 citations, the h-index still remains at 24. Checking the Expatriate failure paper, however, I find some stray citations for that one too. Merging them into the master record results in a h-index of 25. The Journal quality list also has stray citations, but not enough to bring the total up to 25/26.

However, in this process I also noticed that one my most-cited publications – the book Managing the Multinationals – actually appears twice, once with a subtitle and 160 citations and once without a subtitle and 37 citations, thus contributing to the h-index twice. Obviously, these two titles need to be merged, bringing us back to an h-index of 24. Although this whole process sounds fairly involved, with a little practice it can actually be done in a couple of minutes, whilst for some authors a full merge of stray citations can easily take 15-20 minutes. Hence selective merging might be a good compromise.

This process has also taught us two important generic lessons for selective merging:

- Publications with subtitles can often appear twice, once with and once without the subtitle, so it is worthwhile to check them.
- Your most highly cited publications might appear in the h-index twice as the number of stray citations is large enough to enter as a separate publication.

AGE OR AUTHOR CORRECTED METRICS

Another decision to make in terms of indices is whether or not to correct for the age of the publications (using measures such as the contemporary h-index, the Age Weighted Citation Rate or the AW-index), and the length of the academic career of the academics under study (using Hirsch's m quotient). A similar decision needs to be made with regard to co-authorships versus single authorships. Publish or Perish offers three variants for an Individual h-index that can be used to correct for co-authorships.

Whether or not you correct for age and number of co-authors depends on both your population (see above) and your research question. If your population is very diverse in terms of career stage and/or the extent of co-authorship correcting for this might be a good idea if you want to create a fair ranking of academics by research impact relative to opportunity.

However, this is dependent on your research question as well. If you want to find out which academics have had the largest **overall** impact on a field, then correcting by career stage would not be appropriate. However, if you want to identify academics who have written the largest number of **recent** influential articles (rising stars), the contemporary h-index might be more relevant. Similarly, if your research question relates to which **individuals** have had the largest impact on the field, rather than which **papers** or research projects have had the largest impact, metrics correcting for co-authorship *might* be appropriate.

Just like different research questions might require different research **methods**, they might also require different research **metrics.** Hence, as always it is very important to be clear about what your exact research question is, both for the decision on which population to study and for the decision what metrics to use.

12.1.3   EXAMPLES OF BIBLIOMETRIC RESEARCH ON AUTHORS

Many academics have used Publish or Perish to do an impact analysis of authors and create rankings of scholars in their specific field. Below, I discuss a very small selection of these efforts to give you an idea how you can use PoP to do bibliometric analysis for authors. A more detailed example of how to use Publish or Perish for bibliometric research on authors across disciplines can be found in Chapter 16 (Author citation analysis across disciplines).

Most of these examples are in the broad field of Economics & Business. This is probably partly caused by the fact that I am working in this field myself and hence academics are more likely to send me papers in this area. However, it also reflects the fact that Google Scholar and Publish and Perish provide a more comprehensive assessment of research impact in this field (for more details see Chapter 16). However, the basic topics and methods described in these papers are equally applicable in other disciplines.

RANKING ISRAEL'S ECONOMISTS

Ben-David (2010) examined Israel's academic economists and economics departments, ranking them according to the number of citations on their work in Google Scholar. He finds that although in general there is link between the academic rank of a researcher and the number of citations received, there are a large number of individuals at lower ranks who have considerably more citations than those at professorial ranks.

Ben-David argues that promotion rigidities and discrepancies have been a major factor in the unparalleled brain drain of junior academics, especially in Economics. He also indicates that the rise of the Internet, freely available citation data in Google Scholar software such as Publish and Perish software, *"makes it possible to shine many a bright spotlight into areas that were, until now, very difficult – and expensive – to observe."* (Ben-David, 2010: 361). This is exactly the kind of transparency and level of empowerment for individual academics that Publish or Perish was designed for!

GERMAN SCHOLARS IN BUSINESS ADMINISTRATION

Breuer (2009) used Google scholar for a citation-based ranking of more than 100 German scholars in business administration. He found their ranking to be only weakly correlated with existing rankings, which were either based on publications in German language journals only or on publications in top ISI listed journals. Breuer prefers the Google Scholar ranking as it does not create an ex-ante discrimination across different kinds of publication outlets.

He sees the fact that Google Scholar leads to more attention for non-journal publications as a strong positive as books have traditionally been important publication outlets in Germany. He also argues that Google Scholar based ranking may help to reduce the US-American dominance in business administration. Finally, he sees Google Scholar as more in tune with current times where the internet allows the fast dissemination of new knowledge in the form of working papers.

RESEARCH IMPACT OF FELLOWS OF PROFESSIONAL ASSOCIATIONS IN MANAGEMENT

Mingers (2009) applies the Google Scholar h-index and related measures to rank a random sample of 30 members of three groups of management scholars: BAM (British Academy of Management) fellows, members of COPIOR (Committee of Professors in Operations Research) and INFORMS (Institute for Operations Research and the Management Sciences) fellows. Whilst the first two groups mainly consist of British academics, the last group consists mainly of US academics.

Mingers finds that there is a large variance **within** this group of highly distinguished academics, with h-indices ranging from 4 to 38. This leads Mingers to conclude that Fellowships by learned societies are not always awarded on the basis of research output, but presumably also because of contribution in other areas. On average, the first and last group have h-indices of 18, whilst the average for COPIOR members is lower at around 15.

This article is one of the few papers that includes Hirsh's m (called h-rate by Mingers). Using the h-rate instead of the h-index drastically changes the rankings of academics as it improves the scores of those with shorter careers over those with longer career. Mingers concludes that an h-rate of 1 could be seen as reflective of a top scholar. I reach a similar conclusion in the analysis conducted in Chapter 16, where I compare citation metrics across disciplines.

CUMULATIVE AND CAREER-STAGE CITATION IMPACT IN SOCIAL PYSCHOLOGY

Nosek (2010) and his co-authors analyzed citation data for more than 600 academics in the field of social psychology in the US and Canada, using Google scholar and Publish or Perish to gather their data. Data were analyzed both at the individual level and at the departmental level. As the number of citations and the h-index are strongly linked to the academic's seniority, they created new indicators unrelated to the number of years since PhD.

As a result they were able to provide benchmarks for evaluating impact across the career span in psychology, and other disciplines with similar citation patterns. The authors indicate that career-stage indicators can provide a very different perspective on the research impact of individuals and programs than cumulative impact. They can therefore be very useful to predict emerging scientists and programs.

The authors' data management and search procedures are exemplary. Anyone wanting to conduct bibliometric research on authors would be well advised to read their paper. The paper also has an excellent supplementary page with career-stage impact calculators, additional analyses and search tips (http://projectimplicit.net/nosek/papers/citations/)

12.2 DOING BIBLIOMETRIC RESEARCH FOR JOURNALS

There are two main types of bibliometric research one can conduct with PoP: evaluating the impact of journals and comparing a specific set of journals on a range of characteristics. Below I discuss each of these in a bit more detail. For more information on how to improve the accuracy of journal impact queries, please refer to Chapter 4. Unlike our discussion for authors, I will not discuss the selection of the population of journals in any detail as most studies simply focus on journals in a specific discipline.

12.2.1 EVALUATING THE CITATION IMPACT OF JOURNALS

As indicated above, ISI coverage differs substantially by discipline. Butler (2006) analysed the distribution of publication output by field for Australian universities between 1999-2001. For the Chemical, Biological, Physical and Medical/Health sciences between 69.3% and 84.6% of the publications were published in ISI listed journals, this was the case for only 4.4%-18.7% of the publications in the Social Sciences such as Management, History Education and Arts.

ISI estimates that of the 2000 new journals reviewed annually only 10-12% are selected to be included in the Web of Science (Testa, 2004). Publish or Perish can therefore be very helpful if you want to assess the citation impact of a list of journals that are **not** ISI listed or even for journals that **are** ISI listed if your university does not have a subscription to ISI.

WHAT METRICS TO USE?

Publish or Perish offers a wide range of metrics. However, not all of them will be equally useful to evaluate the impact of journals. The screenshot below show the initial Publish or Perish results for the top journal (in terms of ISI Journal Impact Factor) for Industrial Engineering (Technovation).

It shows the same metrics as for an author impact search. However, for a journal impact search, you are probably less interested in metrics that correct for the number of authors or the recentness of citations. The number of co-authors for articles is not very relevant when evaluating journals, although one might be interested in comparing co-authorship patterns across journals (see Section 12.2.2). The speed at which citations pick up is mostly a function of the discipline. If one wanted to remove the impact of different journal ages, one can easily limit the search to a particular time period.

This leaves us with four metrics: cites/year, cites/paper, h-index and g-index. The cites/year metric is probably less useful as it is heavily dependent on the number of papers a journal publishes. Some journals might publish as few as 5 papers a year, whilst others might publish well over 200 papers a year. The cites/paper statistic is closest in nature to Thomson's Journal Impact factor as it measures the average number of citations a typical paper in the journal receives, although using an expanded time period.

Typically the h-index and g-index are very highly correlated for journal searches. In the example of 16 accounting journals in Chapter 9, the correlation was 0.982; for an extended group of 536 journals in Business & Economics (see Chapter 15) it was 0.976. Therefore, for journals we can use these two indices interchangeably. Both the h-index and the g-index include an element of volume (number of papers) as well as impact (number of citations). This could be seen as a disadvantage as a journal cannot have a high h-index or g-index if it only publishes a very limited number of papers, regardless of how well they are cited. If a journal would publish only 5 papers a year, after 10 years its h-index could at a maximum of 50, even if all papers were cited 100 times or more.

However, this is an unlikely extreme and the h-index does not reward journals that publish a lot of papers per se, as they still need to be cited to enter into the h-index. Furthermore, one can easily argue that when evaluating the impact journal, it doesn't just matter how many citations the average paper has, but also how big the body of research is that the journal has created. Theoretically, a journal could have a very high citation per paper rate by being extremely selective and publishing only a few papers a year. However, this journal's overall impact on the field would still be limited.

H-INDEX VERSUS CITES/PAPER

Hence, I would argue that the "cites per paper" and the h-index are the two best metrics to evaluate journals. They are to some extent complimentary as the "cites per paper" metrics only focuses on impact and the h-index focus both on volume and impact. However, the added advantage of the h-index is that it is a more "robust" measure, which is not so dependent on small errors in the data source in question.

The "cites per paper" measure on the other hand is very dependent on the number of stray citations (citations with minor errors that are displayed as separate references), the type of material included in the journal and the number of papers. Stray citations reduce the average number of citations per paper. A lot of book reviews and conference notes (that are normally not cited) also reduce the number of citations per paper. On the other hand, journals that publish a lot of papers per year and/or have been in existence for a long time will easily run up against the maximum number of results returned by Google Scholar (1000) as is evidenced in the Technovation example. This means that only the 1000 most cited papers are returned, thus inflating the "cites per paper" metric.

Returning to our Technovation example, I manually cleaned the results by merging stray citations into master records and removing publications that were book reviews, call for papers or conference notes as they are typically not cited. Cleaning up the results is relatively easy if one sorts by title/author. Reviewing the publications with 0 cites also helps, as they contain many book reviews or conferences notes.

The screenshot below shows that the h-index and g-index for Technovation have changed very little. They increase by only 1 each, an increase of only 1-1.5%. Bontis & Serenko (2009) find identical results in their study of journals in knowledge management. However, the "cites per paper" metric has changed more significantly, from 24.64 to 26.61, an increase of nearly 10%. Although cleaning the results is not terribly time-consuming, it might take 5-15 minutes per journal. Hence, if one wanted to measure the impact of more than a handful of journals it might be better to simply stick to the h-index.

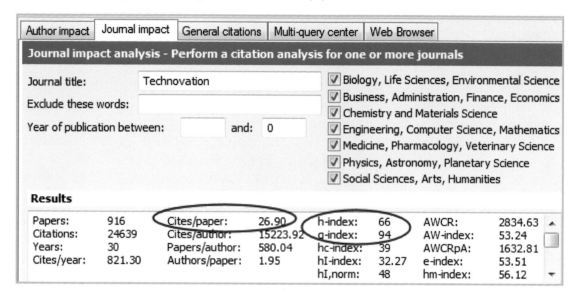

SENSITIVITY OF CITES/PAPER METRIC

If one does want to include the cites per paper metric, it is very important to be conscientious in merging stray citations and removing non-article publications, especially when dealing with a limited number of results. The screenshots below show the results for the *Academy of Management Review* for publications from 2005 onwards, both for the initials results and for the cleaned results.

In the cleaned results the number of papers was reduced drastically by removing book reviews (an important feature of this journal) and merging stray citations. This did not have a significant impact on the h-index, which increased only by 1. Most of the other metrics didn't change much either. However, it nearly doubled the number of citations per paper. Again, this shows that the h-index is a relatively robust index, whilst the "cites per paper" metric requires careful manipulation of the data to provide reliable estimates. Hence, I would suggest that the h-index is probably the most appropriate way to measure journal impact.

Results

Papers:	603	Cites/paper:	21.27	h-index:	64	AWCR:	2886.60
Citations:	12825	Cites/author:	7279.54	g-index:	99	AW-index:	53.73
Years:	6	Papers/author:	383.78	hc-index:	60	AWCRpA:	1634.35
Cites/year:	2137.50	Authors/paper:	1.96	hI-index:	29.47	e-index:	63.47
				hI,norm:	45	hm-index:	47.20

Results							
Papers:	329	Cites/paper:	38.71	h-index:	65	AWCR:	2866.18
Citations:	12735	Cites/author:	7208.30	g-index:	100	AW-index:	53.54
Years:	6	Papers/author:	196.28	hc-index:	60	AWCRpA:	1617.50
Cites/year:	2122.50	Authors/paper:	2.10	hI-index:	29.96	e-index:	63.60
				hI,norm:	45	hm-index:	47.45

EXAMPLES OF JOURNAL IMPACT ANALYSIS

Many academics have used Publish or Perish to do an impact analysis of journals or articles and provide ranking of journals in their specific field. Below, I discuss a very small selection of these efforts to give you an idea how you can use PoP to do bibliometric analysis for journals. A more detailed example of how to use Publish or Perish to assess journal impact can be found in Chapter 15. (A Google Scholar h-index for journals).

Most of these examples are in the broad field of Economics & Business. This is probably partly caused by the fact that I am working in this field myself and hence academics are more likely to send me papers in this area. However, it also reflects the fact that Google Scholar and Publish and Perish provide a more comprehensive assessment of research impact in this field (for more details see Chapter 16). However, the basic topics and methods described in these papers are equally applicable in other disciplines.

Many of the articles discussed below compare different sources of citation data or compare journal rankings based on stated preference with journal rankings based on revealed preference. Stated preference involves members of a particular academic community ranking journals on the basis of their own expert judgments. These are often undertaken by particular universities or departments in order to help make decisions about, for example, library budgets, promotion or tenure, and national research evaluations, such as the Research Assessment Exercise (now Research Excellence Framework) in the UK.

Revealed preference rankings are based on *actual* publication behavior and generally measure the citation rates of journals using Thomson ISI's Web of Knowledge. Most commonly used are the ISI Journal Citation Reports, which provide the yearly Journal Impact Factors (JIF). However, any source of citation data can be used. Publish or Perish is ideally suited to measure the impact of journals with Google Scholar data.

STATED AND REVEALED PREFERENCE FOR JOURNALS IN KNOWLEDGE MANAGEMENT

Bontis & Serenko (2009) compared stated preference and revealed preference for journals in the field of Knowledge management. In order to measure revealed preference the authors calculated Google Scholar h-indices and g-indices using Publish or Perish. Their results find a very strong correlation (0.813, p < 0.000) between the ranking of journals based on stated preference created in a previous study and the ranking based on revealed preference as reported in this study.

The authors used Google Scholar/PoP in their revealed preference study for several reasons. First the field includes practitioners who contribute actively to books and journals, but cannot afford access to the subscription-based ISI Web of Knowledge. Second, the more comprehensive coverage of Google Scholar is beneficial for this relatively new field as none of the twenty main outlets ranked in an earlier study by the authors is ISI listed. Finally, Google Scholar also does a better job in providing coverage of the work published by the many scholars from non-English speaking countries in this field.

GERMAN RESEARCH IN BUSINESS ADMINISTRATION

Breuer (2009) uses PoP to provide an evaluation of German research in Business Administration. I discussed the results of this paper with regard to German academics. With regard to journals, he concludes that Google Scholar is much more useful than ISI's Web of Science for German business administration because of its much broader coverage of potential publication outlets. Again though, this paper shows that rankings of ISI listed journals according to the ISI citation data are highly correlated with rankings according to Google Scholar.

CORE JOURNALS IN EDUCATION AND THEIR IMPACT ON SCHOLARSHIP AND PRACTICE

Goodyear et al. (2009) looked at 126 education journals, with a special focus on 11 core journals. They compared ISI journal impact factors with ISI h-index and GS h-index. The authors found the GS h-index to correlate well with the other ISI impact measures. However, they identify two advantages of the GS h-index that are also signalled in this book.

First, Google Scholar (PoP) is available at no cost and therefore is available to anyone with a computer and Internet connection. Second, Google Scholar and PoP can provide impact data for those journals not indexed by ISI. The article also showed that the impact on scholarship was ranked higher for the 11 core journals than the impact on policy and practice.

WHAT'S NEW IN FINANCE

In *What's New in Finance?* Matti Keloharju (2008) uses PoP to prepare a list of the 300 most cited articles published in the area of Finance during 2000–2006. Rankings are based on the ratio of the number of citations and the number of years since publication. He finds that empirical papers tend to be more highly cited than theory papers and that highly cited papers tend to have a larger number of authors.

He also reports that corporate finance and governance papers are over-represented in the most cited articles and that academics affiliated with top US institutions such as University of Chicago, Harvard Business School, Harvard University, New York University, University of Pennsylvania, Stanford University, Duke University and Massachusetts Institute of Technology publish a disproportionate number of the most-cited papers. Overall, 86% of the highly-cited articles were authored by researchers based in North American institutions.

12.2.2   COMPARING JOURNAL CHARACTERISTICS

In addition to calculating the impact of specific journals or articles, Publish or Perish can also be used to compare a specific set of journals on a number of characteristics or test specific hypotheses on topics such as research collaborations.

CO-AUTHORSHIP PATTERNS

Let's assume for instance that I want to test the hypothesis that North Americans tend to publish more co-authored papers than Europeans. I could conduct a large comparison of North American versus European academics, which would be quite time-consuming.

However, I can also look at this on a journal level, as it has been well-established that North American journals tend to have a larger proportion of North American authors, whilst European journals have a large proportion of European authors. This tends to be true in any discipline, but it is certainly the case the Social Sciences and Humanities whose research topics tend to be more location-bound than the Sciences.

Referring to our earlier example of Accounting journals, of the six ISI-listed journals (see screenshot below), four are North America (JAR, AR, CAR and RAS), whilst the remaining two journals *Accounting, Organizations and Society* and *European Accounting Review* are European. Co-authorship patterns do indeed differ between the North American (2.11-2.40 authors per paper) and the European journals (1.92-1.93 authors per paper).

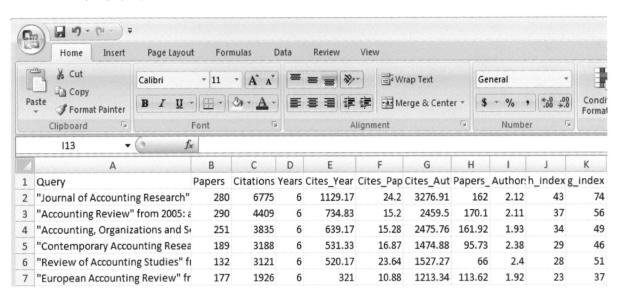

Of course this is only a very small sample of journals, but one could easily expand this to other journals in Accounting or Business in general and the same general pattern will be found. For instance if one compares Organization Science and Organization Studies, two journals in the field of Management with a very similar research domain, I find that the US-based journal has on average 2.27 authors per paper and the European journal 1.91 authors per paper, even when excluding book reviews (that typically only have one author).

CO-AUTHORSHIP PATTERNS ACROSS DISCIPLINES

This same strategy can also be used to compare co-authorship patterns across disciplines. One could for instance take the top-3 journals in every discipline and calculate co-authorship patterns, rather than having to rely on a sample of academics in these disciplines. Doing this, one could not just look at the average number of authors per paper, but also at the number of paper with 1, 2, 3, and more authors as well as the modal number of authors per paper.

A very small-scale comparison looking at co-authorship patterns for articles published between 2005 and 2010 for the above two journals with two top journals in the Sciences and the Humanities already shows very interesting results. Please note that book reviews and other idiosyncratic results (e.g. call for papers, conference announcements, obituaries, apparent Google Scholar parsing errors) were excluded before reporting.

Journal	Mean	Mode
Environmental History	1.08	1
Evolutionary Anthropology	1.39	1
Organization Studies	1.91	1
Organization Science	2.27	2
Science	4.52	5
Nature	4.64	5

Whilst in the Humanities sole authorship is the norm, in the Sciences papers typically have a much larger number of authors. Management – as one of the Social Sciences – falls between these extremes, but is much closer to the Humanities than to the Sciences.

Obviously, these results can also be useful if one wants to make a case for promotion to a panel that is comprised of academics from different disciplines. It helps to explain why it is not realistic to expect the same number of publications from academics in the Social Sciences and Humanities as from academics in the Sciences.

CO-AUTHORSHIP PATTERNS OVER TIME

Another hypothesis that we could test is whether then number of co-authors tends to increase over time, reflecting the more collaborative and competitive nature of academic research and publishing in more recent times.

The table below presents co-authorships for the same set of journals as above for 2000-2004 instead of 2005-2010. Even over the limited time span of five years there has been a small, but noticeable increase in the number of authors for all disciplines, even the modal number of authors hasn't changed.

Journal Title	Mean 2000-2004	Mean 2005-2010	% increase in authors/paper	Mode Both periods
Environmental History	1.04	1.08	3.8%	1
Evolutionary Anthropology	1.31	1.39	6.1%	1
Organization Studies	1.83	1.91	4.4%	1
Organization Science	2.02	2.27	12.4%	2
Science	4.28	4.52	5.6%	5
Nature	4.19	4.64	10.7%	5

CONCENTRATION VERSUS UNCITEDNESS

A second journal characteristic that might be worthy of bibliometric research is the level of concentration of citations versus the level of uncitedness. The concentration of citations is can be measured in a variety of ways. One way is to calculate the percentage of papers required to account for say 50% of the citations in a journal.

Those unfamiliar with citation analysis might be surprised at how low these percentages generally are. An analysis conducted on ISI Essential Science Indicators (Science Watch, 1999) showed that depending on the discipline only 5-10% of the papers accounted for 50% of the citations. The Social Sciences & Humanities generally had a stronger concentration of citations than the Sciences.

The level of uncitedness is the number of papers that – after a time has lapsed – have not been cited at all. The same analysis as above shows that for a 17 year period (1980-1997) this varies from 13%-15% for Immunology, Biology, Neuroscience and Astrophysics to 38%-45% for Economics & Business, Engineering, Education and Computer Science.

Obviously, these differences are partly caused by the fact that citations in the latter fields take much longer to pick up, hence recent papers in these fields will have very few citations. In addition, the rather poor coverage of ISI in the Social Sciences and Engineering means that many citations in non-ISI listed journals, book chapters and conference proceedings are not picked up.

GOOGLE SCHOLAR VERSUS ISI ANALYSIS OF CONCENTRATION AND UNCITEDNESS

In order to address these drawbacks, one can conduct the same analysis on a **journal** level using Publish or Perish. At present, the analyses cannot yet be conducted in Publish or Perish itself, but the easy exporting of data to Excel (see Section 2.3) makes it possible to conduct these analyses relatively quickly. Please note that book reviews and other idiosyncratic results (e.g. call for papers, conference announcements, obituaries, apparent Google Scholar parsing errors) were excluded before exporting the results to Excel.

Science and Nature publish so many papers that when doing an analysis like this, we run into the Google Scholar restriction of 1000 maximum results. This means both that the level of concentration and the level of uncitedness for these journals would be underestimated as only the 1000 most-cited papers would be included. I have therefore substituted Science and Nature with two other journals: Biological Review and Endoscopy.

As the table below shows, the level of concentration is not as strong as in the ISI-based analysis, where 5-10% of the papers provided 50% of the citations. However, I still find that only 6-17% of the papers provide 50% of the citations and that concentration is generally stronger in the Social Sciences and Humanities (average 10.6%) than in the Sciences (average 16.1%).

Journal Title	Concentration: % of papers providing 50% of citations	Uncitedness: % of uncited papers
Environmental History (2000-2004)	16.0%	0%
Evolutionary Anthropology (2000-2004)	6.1%	28%
Organization Studies (2000-2004)	12.0%	0%
Organization Science (2000-2004)	8.5%	0%
Biological Review (2000-2004)	17.1%	0%
Endoscopy (2000-2004)	15.1%	5%

This lower level of concentration might be caused by two reasons. First Google Scholar has a broader coverage and hence includes citations from a wider range of sources. Second, I looked at citations in 2010 to papers published in 2000-2004. Hence our analysis gave papers more time to gather citations, which especially in the Social Sciences and Humanities will reduce the level of concentration.

The broader coverage and longer time-frame also explains why our proportion of uncited papers is much smaller than in the ISI based analysis. For most journals, every paper had at least one citation, so 6-10 years after publication there were no uncited papers. There was only one journal (Evolutionary Anthropology) with a significant number of uncited papers, but with 28% even this proportion is much lower than for the ISI based analysis.

12.3   REFERENCES

- Ben-David, D. (2010) **Ranking Israel's economists**, Scientometrics, 82(2): 351-364
- Bontis, N.; Serenko, A. (2009) **A follow-up ranking of academic journals**, *Journal of Knowledge Management*, 13(1): 16-26.
- Breuer (2009) Google Scholar as a Means for Quantitative Evaluation of German Research Output in Business Administration - Some Preliminary Results, Aachen University - Department of Finance http:/papers.ssrn.com/sol3/papers.cfm?abstract_id=1280033
- Butler, L. (2006) **RQF Pilot Study Project – History and Political Science Methodology for Citation Analysis**, November 2006, accessed from: http://www.chass.org.au/papers/bibliometrics/CHASS_Methodology.pdf, 15 Jan 2007.
- Goodyear, R.K.; Brewer, D.J., Symms Gallagher, K.; Tracey, T.J.G.; Claiborn, C.D.; Lichtenberg, J.W.; Wampold, B.E. (2009) **The Intellectual Foundations of Education: Core Journals and Their Impacts on Scholarship and Practice**, *Educational Researcher*, 38(9): 700–706.
- Keloharju, M. (2008) **What's New in Finance?**, *European Financial Management*, 14(3): 564–608.
- Mingers, J. (2009) **Measuring the research contribution of management academics using the Hirsch-index**, *Journal of the Operational Research Society* 60: 1143-1153.
- Nosek, B. A., Graham, J., Lindner, N. M., Kesebir, S., Hawkins, C. B., Hahn, C., Schmidt, K., Motyl, M., Joy-Gaba, J . A., Frazier, R., & Tenney, E. R. (2010). **Cumulative and career-stage impact of social-personality psychology programs and their members**. *Personality and Social Psychology Bulletin*. Forthcoming.
- *Science Watch*°, January/February 1999, Vol. 10, No. 1, Citing URL: http://www.sciencewatch.com/jan-feb99/sw_jan-feb99_page1.htm
- Testa, J. (2004) **The Thomson Scientific Journal Selection Process**, http://scientific.thomson.com/free/essays/selectionofmaterial/journalselection/, accessed 15 Jan 2007.

CHAPTER 13:
EVALUATING GOOGLE SCHOLAR

In this chapter and the next, I will discuss the two major data sources for citation analysis, Google Scholar and Thomson ISI's Web of Science, in more detail. For a brief summary of these data sources, see Section 1.2. A detailed comparison of the impact of the use of different data sources can be found in Chapter 16: Citation analysis across disciplines: The Impact of different data sources and citation metrics

Instead of the Thomson ISI Web of Science or Elsevier's Scopus, Publish or Perish uses Google Scholar data to calculate its various statistics. This was a conscious choice, guided by a desire to make citation analysis accessible for every academic desirous to use it. Below I will discuss the advantages and disadvantages of Google Scholar in more detail.

13.1   ADVANTAGES OF GOOGLE SCHOLAR

There are four very simple, but important, advantages of using Google Scholar:

1. It is free.
2. It is easy to use.
3. It is quick.
4. It is comprehensive in its coverage.

13.1.1   GOOGLE SCHOLAR IS FREE

An important practical reason for using Google Scholar is that it is freely available to anyone with an Internet connection. The ISI Web of Science and Scopus are only available to those academics whose institutions are able and willing to bear the (quite substantial) subscription costs. As Pauly & Stergiou (2005:34) indicate:

> *"free access to [...] data provided by Google Scholar provides an avenue for more transparency in tenure reviews, funding and other science policy issues, as it allows citation counts, and analyses based thereon, to be performed and duplicated by anyone".*

13.1.2   GOOGLE SCHOLAR IS EASY TO USE

Searches in Google Scholar are intuitive and can be conducted without much knowledge of the underlying database. Publish or Perish has been carefully designed to be able to be used by academics with limited knowledge of bibliometrics or even computers. It presents the Google Scholar interface in an even more accessible format.

13.1.3 GOOGLE SCHOLAR IS QUICK

Google Scholar is also praised for its speed (Bosman et al. 2006). In comparison to searches with ISI's Web of Science and Scopus, searches in Google Scholar/Publish or Perish can be conducted much more quickly. First, there is no need to login to databases and second searches are processed much more quickly.

For instance, for an author with few publications, results are almost instantaneous. Even more complex searches (e.g. John Smith) generally take only 10 seconds. In contrast, Thomson ISI in particular has a rather cumbersome web interface with many separate image files that can take a very long time to load.

13.1.4 GOOGLE SCHOLAR IS COMPREHENSIVE

In addition to free access, ease of use and speed, Google Scholar's major advantage is the comprehensiveness of its coverage. I have already alluded to this in many chapters of this book. A detailed illustration of how Google Scholar's comprehensive coverage benefits the Social Sciences and Humanities in particular can be found in Chapter 16.

As a brief reminder, the reason why Google Scholar is more comprehensive than the two other databases is that it covers not just citations in journals that are listed in the Thomson ISI or Scopus database, but also citations to and in:

1. Books and book chapters.
2. Conference proceedings.
3. Working papers and government reports.
4. Journals not listed in ISI or Scopus, including journals in languages other than English.

13.2 DISADVANTAGES OF GOOGLE SCHOLAR

The disadvantages of Google Scholar are mostly related to the fact that GS is not structured as a traditional bibliographic database in the same way that Thomson ISI and Scopus are. This means that data are not always processed with 100% accuracy. Hence the main drawback in Google Scholar lies in its lower data quality. There are several aspects to this that I will discuss in more detail below. The other drawback is that complex searches that combine a range of bibliographic fields are not possible. However, as we have seen in this book, there are many useful searches that can be conducted with Google Scholar/-Publish or Perish.

13.2.1 INCORRECT IDENTIFICATION OF AUTHORS

Several academics have been critical of Google Scholar's data quality and parsing. In particular, Péter Jacsó discusses a number of Google Scholar failures in great detail in his papers in *Online Information Review* (Jacsó, 2005, 2006a/b). Whereas no doubt some of his critique is completely justified, I was unable to reproduce most of the specific Google Scholar failures detailed in his paper. This suggests that they either resulted from incorrect searches or that Google Scholar has rectified these failures.

Most importantly, the bulk of Jacsó's critique is leveled at inconsistent results for keyword searches, which are not relevant for the author and journal impact searches conducted with PoP. In addition, the summary metrics in PoP (e.g. h-index, g-index) are fairly robust and insensitive to occasional errors. I will discuss the problems he has identified with the identification of authors in some detail below.

PHANTOM AUTHOR I INTRODUCTION HAS DISAPPEARED

Jacsó signals some potentially important problems with the identification of authors, where parts of the text are identified as authors by Google Scholar. He claims (Jacsó, 2006b:299) that GS lists 40,100 documents where the author is 'I Introduction'.

My own search in 2007 only found 956. However, 80% of these papers were not cited at all, whilst the average number of cites per paper for the remainder was 4.69. In many cases the actual author was listed **in addition** to the false 'I Introduction' author. Only about 160 documents had both an incorrect 'I Introduction' as only author and more than zero cites, and only 9 of those had more than 10 citations.

Author impact	Journal impact	General citations	Multi-query center	Web Browser

Author impact analysis - Perform a citation analysis for one or more authors

Author's name: "Introduction"

Exclude these names:

Year of publication between: 0 and: 0

Results

Papers:	43	Cites/paper:	3.72	h-index:	5	AWCR:	8.61
Citations:	160	Cites/author:	97.49	g-index:	9	AW-index:	2.93
Years:	99	Papers/author:	31.00	hc-index:	3	AWCRpA:	5.28
Cites/year:	1.62	Authors/paper:	1.60	hI-index:	3.13	e-index:	6.86
				hI,norm:	4	hm-index:	3.83

Cites		Per year	Authors	Title
☑	49	2.04	T Gaude, C Dumas, I...	Molecular and cellular events of self-incompatibility
☑	6	0.43	Introduction	Politicians on Judges: Fair Criticism or Intimidation
☑	6	0.75	I Introduction	David Sutcliffe African American English suprasegmentals: A stud...
☑	6	0.55	L Labrianidis, I Introd...	Are Greek companies that invest in the Balkans in the '90s Transn...
☑	5	0.16	Introduction	Supreme Court Decisions in Taxation: 1978 Term
☑	4	0.04	Theodore Roosevelt,...	Majority Rule and the Judiciary: An Examination of Current Propo...
☑	4	0.50	CW Dewey, I Introd...	Head-trauma management
☑	4	0.00	RD Van Valin Jr, E Di...	A Bonsai Grammar for German
☑	3	0.13	Introduction	Special Project: Director and Officer Liability
☑	3	0.04	Parrington's Introduc...	The Growth and Decadence of Constitutional Government
☑	3	0.08	Introduction	The Second Decade of Title VII: Refinement of the Remedies
☑	3	0.05	Professor Hazeltine's...	The Medieval Idea of Law
☑	3	0.75	L Cameron, I Introdu...	International humanitarian law and the regulation of private milita...
☑	3	0.09	C. Arthur, introducti...	Law and Marxism: A General Theory

When I conducted a broader search (Introduction instead of I Introduction) in July 2010, I found only 43 documents that had Introduction as one of the authors and more than zero citations (see screenshot above). Only one document had more than 10 citations, and only 18 had more than 2 citations. There were only 14 documents with Introduction as their only author and they had an average of 2.79 citations. Hence, the problem is probably not nearly as big as one would initially believe, and it is certainly not a big issue for citation analysis.

MENU ITEMS AS PHANTOM AUTHORS

In a later paper Jacsó (2009) reports problems with menu items such as "Password", "V Cart" featuring as authors. In July 2010, I was unable to find any authors with these names. When I tried "Username", I did find some rubbish results, but there were only twelve hits (see below) and none of these will have any impact on author or journal impact queries.

Author impact	Journal impact	General citations	Multi-query center	Web Browser

Author impact analysis - Perform a citation analysis for one or more authors

Author's name: username

Exclude these names:

Year of publication between: 0 and: 0

Results

Papers:	13	Cites/paper:	0.15	h-index:	1	AWCR:	0.00
Citations:	2	Cites/author:	2.00	g-index:	1	AW-index:	0.00
Years:	4	Papers/author:	7.78	hc-index:	1	AWCRpA:	0.00
Cites/year:	0.50	Authors/paper:	2.15	hI-index:	1.00	e-index:	1.00
				hI,norm:	1	hm-index:	1.00

Cites		Per year	Authors	Title
☑	2	0.00	Y must enter a Usern...	Password to view and modify the
☑	0	0.00	R Me, F your Username	Most Accessed Articles
☑	0	0.00	U Username	Journal Help
☑	0	0.00	N Classes, O Monday...	St. Joseph's College Mathematics Department Suffolk Campus Co.
☑	0	0.00	E your username pre...	For Queens: http://sqlaptopps1/printers For Staten Island: http:.
☑	0	0.00	D Garg, U Alice	"Access control" refers to enforcement mechanisms that control u.
☑	0	0.00	... , URL Blog, WP Us...	Create your ShareThis Account
☑	0	0.00	D Garg, U Alice	Resource
☑	0	0.00	P Sub cmdOK_Click, ...	本设计根据上面的数据库设计规划出的实体有: 学生实体, 课.
☑	0	0.00	P Sub cmdOK_Click, ...	第一章 选题依据
☑	0	0.00	FTP Username, I Use...	Symantec ManHunt 3.0
☑	0	0.00	D Greeting, D UserN...	Writing a Script in Windows 2000
☑	0	0.00	E your username pre...	To Connect to Printers via Wireless connection in the University.

There does seem to be a serious problem, however, with articles published in The Lancet. When I searched for other likely menu items such as registered, login, options and access, I found a large number of papers in the Lancet where author names had been replaced with menu options. Given that some of them had a very large number of citations, this might rob some legitimate authors of their publications.

Cites		Authors	Title	Year	Publication
☑	870	A Registered, P Login, P Options, SD Access	Prevention of dementia in randomis...	1998	The Lancet
☑	538	A Registered, P Login	Attention-deficit hyperactivity disor...	1998	The Lancet
☑	418	A Registered, P Login	UK and USA breast cancer deaths d...	2000	The Lancet
☑	336	A Registered, P Login, P Options, SD Access	Diagnosis of new variant Creutzfeld...	1997	The Lancet
☑	316	A Registered, P Login, P Options, SD Access	Survival and safety of exemestane ...	2007	The Lancet
☑	287	A Registered, P Login, P Options, SD Access	Oral vitamin D3 and calcium for sec...	2005	The Lancet
☑	239	A Registered, P Login, P Options, SD Access	Effects of cholesterol-lowering with...	2004	The Lancet
☑	210	A Registered, P Login, P Options, SD Access	Tinzaparin in acute ischaemic stroke...	2001	The Lancet
☑	205	A Registered, P Login, P Options, SD Access	Haplotype associated with low inter...	1998	The Lancet
☑	190	A Registered, P Login, P Options, SD Access	Restoration of immunity to chronic ...	1997	The Lancet
☑	174	A Registered, P Login	Concurrent sexual partnerships hel...	2004	The Lancet
☑	174	A Registered, P Login, P Options, SD Access	Potentially high prevalence of prima...	1999	The Lancet
☑	173	A Registered, P Login, P Options, SD Access	Those confounded vitamins: what c...	2004	The Lancet

There are, however, only 359 papers with more than 10 citations and the problem seems to be limited to articles that are parsed from thelancet.com website. Publications parsed from other sources, such as Elsevier do not show the same problem. The Lancet publishes 300-400 articles a year, so although the 359 present a large number of papers, it by no means is a problem for the entire set of Lancet publications.

When limiting the search for the Lancet to publications after 1996 (when the problem seems to be more prominent), I find only 31 of the 1,000 most cited publications carrying inappropriate author names and they make up only 1.2% of the combined citations. So even for a fairly egregious Google Scholar parsing error, the actual impact on author or journal impact searches would be limited, especially when using robust measures such as the h-index.

13.2.2   SOME OF GOOGLE SCHOLAR'S COVERAGE MIGHT BE PROBLEMATIC

There are several potential problems with coverage in Google Scholar, which we will discuss in some detail below. However, it must be said that these problems were mostly present in the early days and Google Scholar has improved its coverage over the years.

NAMES WITH DIACRITICS, APOSTROPHES OR LIGATURES WERE PROBLEMATIC

Both Google Scholar and Thomson ISI Web of Science have problems with academics that have names including either diacritics (e.g. Özbilgin or Olivas-Luján). In Google Scholar a search for the name with diacritics will usually provide some results, but they are not comprehensive (see below). A search for the name without diacritics encompasses both the references with and those without diacritics and is hence recommendable.

Names with apostrophes (e.g. many Irish names) initially also presented problems in Google Scholar. These problems now seem have been resolved, but are still present for ISI (see next chapter). In the early days, a search for "KH O'Rourke" in Google Scholar provided very few results as Google Scholar treated both KH and O as initials and hence searched for KHO Rourke. Adding an additional blank space before O'Rourke solved this problem. More recently, however, searches for "KH O'Rourke" (without the additional blank space) result in more than 3,000 citations.

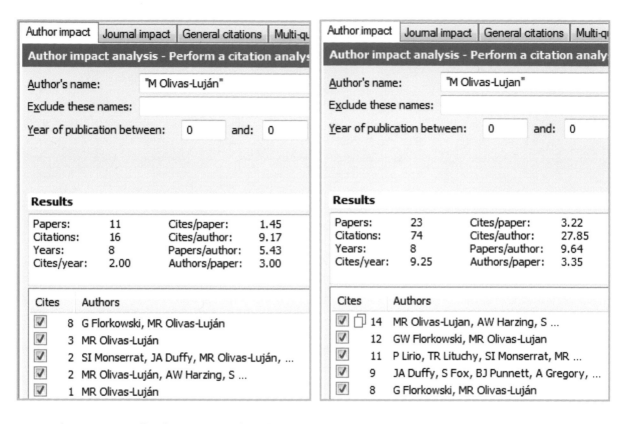

Ligatured names initially also presented problems in Google Scholar. If an academic's name includes a sequence of characters that is ligatured in traditional typesetting ("fi", "ff", "fl", and others in other languages) and he/she prepares papers with LaTeX (as do most academics in mathematics and computer science), Google Scholar did not find their publications.

When searching for "J Bradfield" in 2007, I only found some 190 cites for computer scientist Julian Bradfield, whereas "J Bradeld" resulted in nearly 400 cites for the same person. However, Google Scholar has resolved this problem and a search for J Bradfield" now results in some 900 cites, whereas "J Bradeld" results in only 2 results with a total of one citation.

GOOGLE SCHOLAR INCLUDES SOME NON-SCHOLARLY CITATIONS

Google Scholar does sometimes include non-scholarly citations such as student handbooks, library guides or editorial notes. However, incidental problems in this regard are unlikely to distort citation metrics, especially robust ones such as the h-index.

An inspection of my own papers shows that more than 75% of the citations are in academic journals, with the remainder appearing in books, conference and working papers and student theses. Few non-scholarly citations were found. Moreover, I would argue that even citations in student handbooks, library guides or editorials show that the academic has an impact on the field.

In a similar vein, Vaughan and Shaw (2008) argue that 92% of the citations identified by Google Scholar in the field of library and information science represented intellectual impact, primarily citations from journal articles.

NOT ALL SCHOLARLY JOURNALS ARE INDEXED IN GOOGLE SCHOLAR

Not all scholarly journals seem to be indexed or indexed comprehensively in Google Scholar. Unfortunately, Google Scholar is not very open about its coverage and hence it is unclear what its sources are.

It is generally believed that Elsevier journals are not included (Meho & Yang, 2007), because Elsevier has a competing commercial product in Scopus. However, I was able to find all Elsevier journals I have published in. It is possible that Google Scholar coverage for Elsevier journals has increased in the last three years.

On the other hand, Meho & Yang (2007) did find that Google Scholar missed 40.4% of the citations found by the union of Web of Science and Scopus, suggesting that Google Scholar does miss some important refereed citations. However, it must also be said though that the union of Web of Science and Scopus misses 61.04% of the citations in Google Scholar. Further, Meho & Yang (2007) found that most of the citations uniquely found by Google Scholar are from refereed sources.

GOOGLE SCHOLAR COVERAGE MIGHT BE UNEVEN ACROSS FIELDS OF STUDY

Although Google Scholar generally provides a higher citation count than ISI, this might not be true for all fields of studies.

- The Social Sciences, Arts and Humanities, and Engineering in particular seem to benefit from Google Scholar's better coverage of (citations in) books, conference proceedings and a wider range of journals.

- The Natural and Health Sciences are generally well covered in ISI and hence Google Scholar might not provide higher citation counts. In addition, for some disciplines in the Natural and Health Sciences Google Scholar's journal coverage seems to be patchy. This leads to citation counts in these areas that might well be lower than those in ISI.

In a systematic comparison of a 64 articles in different disciplines, Bosman et al. (2006) found overall coverage of Google Scholar to be comparable with both Web of Science and Scopus and slightly better for articles published in 2000 than in 1995. However, huge variations were apparent between disciplines with Chemistry and Physics in particular showing very low Google Scholar coverage and Science and Medicine also showing lower coverage than in Web of Science.

Based on a sample of 1650 articles Kousha & Thelwall (2007, 2008) found Google Scholar coverage to be less comprehensive than ISI in the three Science disciplines included in their study (Biology, Chemistry and Physics), with Google Scholar showing a particularly low coverage for Chemistry. Google Scholar coverage for the four Social Sciences included in their study (Education, Economics, Sociology and Psychology) as well as Computing was significantly higher than ISI coverage. Similarly, Bar-Ilan (2008) finds the number of Google Scholar citations substantially higher than the WoS and Scopus for mathematicians and computer scientists, but lower for high-energy physicists.

On the other hand, my own recent comparison of coverage across three different databases (see Chapter 16 for details) for a small sample of academics across a large variety of disciplines showed that Google Scholar had higher citation counts than both ISI and Scopus for 9 out of 10 academics. For the 10th academic the citation count in Google Scholar was 10% lower than in ISI, but this might well be caused by the fact that many of his publications were old (see next section).

More detailed comparisons by academics working in the respective areas would be necessary before we can draw general conclusions. However, as a general rule of thumb, I would suggest that using Google Scholar might be most beneficial for three of the Google Scholar categories: Business, Administration, Finance & Economics; Engineering, Computer Science & Mathematics; Social Sciences, Arts & Humanities.

Although broad comparative searches can be done for other disciplines (Biology, Life Sciences & Environmental Science; Chemistry & Materials Science; Medicine, Pharmacology & Veterinary Science; Physics, Astronomy & Planetary Science), I would not encourage heavy reliance on Google Scholar for individual academics working in other areas without doing spot checks with either Scopus or Web of Science.

GOOGLE SCHOLAR DOES NOT PERFORM AS WELL FOR OLDER PUBLICATIONS

Google Scholar does not perform as well for older publications as these publications and the publications that cite them have not (yet) been posted on the web.

Pauly & Stergiou (2005) found that Google Scholar had less than half of the citations of the Web of Science for a specific set of papers published in a variety of disciplines (mostly in the Sciences) between 1925-1989. However, for papers published in the 1990-2004 period both sources gave similar citation counts. The authors expect Google Scholar's performance to improve for old articles as journals' back issues are posted on the web.

Meho & Yang (2007) found the majority of the citations from journals and conference papers in Google Scholar to be from after 1993. Belew (2005) found Google Scholar to be competitive in terms of coverage for references published in the last 20 years, but the Web of Science superior before then. This means that Google Scholar might underestimate the impact of scholars who have mainly published before 1990.

However, these studies are fairly old and with many journals posting back issues on the web, it is expected that this aspect of Google Scholar's coverage will the less important over time.

13.2.3   GOOGLE PROCESSING OCCASIONALLY CREATES NONSENSICAL RESULTS

Google Scholar's processing is done automatically without manual cleaning and hence sometimes provides nonsensical results. For instance there are a range of results for my name where the title starts with K., my last initial (see screenshot).

This generally happened because of one of two reasons. First, some referring authors accidentally put a comma after the first two initials, leading Google Scholar parsing to think the title started with the third initial. Second, referring authors often listed my first two initials as A.-W. (which is actually entirely correct) and then included a large white space before the third initial, again leading Google Scholar parser to think that the author name had finished and the title started with "K."

	3	AW Harzing	K.
☑	2	A Harzing	K. 1997. Response rate in international mail surveys: Results of a 22-country study
☑	2	AW Harzing	K. and Christensen, C.(2004),"Expatriate failure: time to abandon the concept?"
☑	17	AW Harzing	K.(1995)'The persistent myth of high expatriate failure rates'
☑	2	AW Harzing	K.(1999) MANAGING THE MULTINATIONALS, An International Study of Control M...

Most of these errors, however, have little impact on robust citation metrics such as the h-index. As can be seen above, three of the errors only have 2 citations each and they all refer to publications that were already included in my h-index. With 17 citations, the third seems more serious, but this is one of my most cited works and adding the 17 citations does not impact on the h-index, g-index or any of their variations.

Automatic processing can also result in double counting citations when two or three versions of the same paper are found online. Again though, incidental mistakes like this are unlikely to have a major impact on citation metrics, especially those as robust as the h-index. Moreover, Google Scholar is committed to fix mistakes, and will respond (although often slowly) to change requests.

13.2.4   GOOGLE SCHOLAR RESULTS ARE LIMITED TO THE 1000 MOST CITED PAPERS

Google Scholar limits the results of any search to the 1000 most cited papers. This is generally not a problem for author searches as there are few authors who have published more than 1000 papers, even if one includes papers that are double-counted. Moreover, even if they had, the papers that are not listed would generally have no citations or a very limited number of citations.

On the other hand, the upper limit **can** present problems for journal searches as many journals will have published more than 1000 papers over their life-time. Again though, this will not generally impact the h-index or g-index. However, it will impact metrics that are dependent on the number of papers such as citations per paper. Citations per paper would be overestimated for journals that have published more than 1000 papers as their least-cited papers would be omitted.

This is one of the reasons why in Section 12.2.1 I cautioned against the use of citations per paper as a metric to evaluate journal impact. However, one can accommodate the 100 paper limitation to some extent by limiting the journal search to a specific time period. In any case, it would be better to compare journals over a specific time period to avoid an unfair comparison between younger and older journals.

For example, when I searched for *The Academy of Management Journal* without a year limitation, the least-cited papers had 21 citations and papers from 2008 onwards were not included (presumably because they have fewer citations). When I limited the search to the last 10 years, there were some 200 papers without any citations and there was a good spread of papers for each of the ten year.

- Bar-Ilan, J. (2008) **Which h-index? - A comparison of WoS, Scopus and Google Scholar**, *Scientometrics*, 74(2): 257-271.
- Belew, R.K. (2005) **Scientific impact quantity and quality: Analysis of two sources of bibliographic data**, *arXiv:cs.IR/0504036* v1, 11 April 2005.
- Bosman, J, Mourik, I. van, Rasch, M.; Sieverts, E., Verhoeff, H. (2006) **Scopus reviewed and compared. The coverage and functionality of the citation database Scopus, including comparisons with Web of Science and Google Scholar**, Utrecht: Utrecht University Library, http://igitur-archive.library.uu.nl/DARLIN/2006-1220-200432/Scopus doorgelicht & vergeleken - translated.pdf.
- Jacsó, P. (2005) **Google Scholar: the pros and the cons**, *Online Information Review*, 29(2): 208-214.
- Jacsó, P. (2006a) **Dubious hit counts and cuckoo's eggs**, *Online Information Review*, 30(2): 188-193.
- Jacsó, P. (2006b) **Deflated, inflated and phantom citation counts**, *Online Information Review*, 30(3): 297-309.
- Kousha, K.; Thelwall, M. (2007) **Google Scholar Citations and Google Web/URL Citations: A Multi-Discipline Exploratory Analysis**, *Journal of the American Society for Information Science and Technology*, 58(7): 1055-1065.
- Kousha, K; Thelwall, M. (2008) **Sources of Google Scholar citations outside the Science Citation Index: A comparison between four science disciplines**, *Scientometrics*, 74(2): 273-294.
- Meho, L.I.; Yang, K. (2007) **A New Era in Citation and Bibliometric Analyses: Web of Science, Scopus, and Google Scholar**, *Journal of the American Society for Information Science and Technology*, 58(13): 2105–2125.
- Pauly, D.; Stergiou, K.I. (2005) **Equivalence of results from two citation analyses: Thomson ISI's Citation Index and Google Scholar's service**, *Ethics in Science and Environmental Politics*, December, 33-35.
- Vaughan, L.; Shaw, D. (2008) **A new look at evidence of scholarly citations in citation indexes and from web sources**, *Scientometrics*, 74(2): 317-330.

CHAPTER 14:
EVALUATING THOMSON ISI
WEB OF SCIENCE

Thomson's ISI Web of Science, often called ISI for short, has been the traditional data source for citation analysis. It was established by Eugene Garfield in the 1960s and has had a virtual monopoly in this field until the arrival of Google Scholar and Scopus in 2004. For many universities it is still seen as the gold standard of citation analysis.

Below I discuss the advantages and disadvantages of the ISI Web of Science in more detail. This chapter provides a fairly critical analysis of Thomson ISI's Web of Science. I do not in any way mean to imply that this data source doesn't have a useful place in bibliometric analysis. However, given both the high fees that are charged for its use and its dominant position, I feel it is only fair to have high expectations of its accuracy and comprehensiveness.

14.1   ADVANTAGES OF THOMSON'S ISI WEB OF SCIENCE

The main advantage of Thomson ISI Web of Science mirrors Google Scholar's main disadvantage, i.e. it was set up as a bibliographic database. This results in a number of related advantages. Thomson ISI's Webs of Science offers:

1. More complex and focused search options.
2. The option to filter and refine queries.
3. The option to analyze results.
4. Somewhat higher data quality.

14.1.1   MORE COMPLEX AND FOCUSED SEARCH OPTIONS

Since Thomson ISI's Web of Science was set up as a bibliographic database, it offers more extensive options for searching with a wide variety of bibliographic fields (e.g. organization, country, city, document type, funding agency). This allows the user to create very complex and focused searches with the **Advanced Search** function.

With the right search parameters, one can for instance answers complicated questions such as "How many academics affiliated with Australian universities have published in Nature between 1995 and 2005"? or "How many articles have academics affiliated with University X published in field X in the last 5 years?"

However, although these options are very useful for fine-grained bibliometric research, they are not necessary for any of the functions of citation analysis described in this book. In fact, Google Scholar often provides a much more convenient choice in that respect.

14.1.2   ABILITY TO FILTER AND REFINE QUERIES

After running a particular query in ISI's WoS, you can further refine the results by excluding any specific instances of the bibliometric fields. You can exclude for instance editorials and book reviews from the publications or restrict the results to publications in specific years (that do not have to be consecutive). You can also restrict results to specific disciplines only or exclude specific source titles. This ensures that your final search result is likely to be exactly what you are looking for.

Unfortunately, these searches can be quite cumbersome and slow to execute as they involve clicking through multiple screens and options. In addition, ISI's user interface is not particularly intuitive and its help file very concise.

14.1.3   ABILITY TO ANALYZE RESULTS

After conducting a search, ISI's WoS offer the option to further analyze the results. You can for instance run reports for the number and proportion of citations coming from particular countries, authors, source titles (journals). You can also analyze citations per year.

These options can be very useful if you want to show that your citations are increasing by year or that your work is cited in high-quality journals and/or in a large variety of countries. This can useful to include in an application for tenure, promotion or research funding.

Unfortunately, ISI does not actually analyze the number of **citations**. All results in the analyze function are for citing articles, not citations. As one citing article can – and often does – include more than one citation to an academic's work, these analyses can seriously underestimate an academic's citations.

14.1.4   A SOMEWHAT HIGHER DATA QUALITY

As ISI's WoS data processing contains manual checks, the data quality is generally higher than can be offered by Google Scholar's automatic parsing. In particular, ISI generates fewer nonsensical results. However, its number of stray citations is more problematic than Google Scholar (see Section 14.2.3). Many of these stray citations seem to be created by human intervention, i.e. data entry typists making typing errors.

14.2   DISADVANTAGES OF ISI'S WEB OF SCIENCE

ISI's disadvantages also mirror Google Scholar's advantages. It is fairly expensive (my university pays around $120,000/year for its yearly subscription to the Web of Knowledge) and hence only available to academics working at relatively well-resourced universities. Its user interface is fairly cumbersome and tends to be slow, much slower than Google Scholar.

However, ISI's most important disadvantage lies in its lack of comprehensive coverage in some disciplines, resulting in an underestimation of citation impact. I will discuss this in more detail in Section 14.2.1. In addition, ISI has a number of idiosyncrasies that are discussed in later sections: its difficulty in reliably establishing self-citations (Section 14.2.2), its poor handling of stray citations (Section 14.2.3), and its frequent misclassification of original research articles as review articles and proceedings articles (Section 14.2.4).

14.2.1 THOMSON ISI UNDERESTIMATES CITATION IMPACT

The major disadvantage of the Web of Science is that it often provides an underestimation of an academic's citation impact. For example, the current (August 2010) number of citations to my own work is around 400 with ISI's "general search" function, around 900 with ISI's "cited reference" function and 2500 with Google Scholar.

Differences will not be as dramatic for all scholars, but many academics show a substantially higher number of citations in Google Scholar than in the Web of Science. For instance Nisonger (2004) found that (excluding self-citations) Web of Science captured only 28.8% of his total citations, 42.2% of his print citations, 20.3% of his citations from outside the United States, and a mere 2.3% of his non-English citations.

At the same time both sources (Web of Science and Google Scholar) have been shown to rank specific groups of scholars in a relatively similar way. Saad (2006) found that for his subset of 55 scientists in consumer research, the correlation between the two h-indices was 0.82. Please note that this does not invalidate the earlier argument as it simply means most academics' h-indices are underestimated by a similar magnitude by Web of Science.

There are a number of specific reasons that all contribute to a greater or lesser extent to the underestimation of citation impact by Thomson ISI Web of Science. I will discuss each of them in some detail below.

WEB OF SCIENCE GENERAL SEARCH IS LIMITED TO ISI-LISTED JOURNALS

In the General Search, the Web of Science only includes citations to journal articles published in ISI listed journals. Citations to books, book chapters, dissertations, theses, working and conference papers, reports, and journal articles published in non-ISI journals are **not** included.

Whilst in the Sciences this may give a fairly comprehensive picture of an academic's total output, in the Social Sciences and Humanities (SSH) only a limited number of journals are ISI listed. Also, in both the Social Sciences and the Humanities books and book chapters are very important publication outlets. Google Scholar includes citations to all academic publications regardless of whether they appeared in ISI-listed journals.

ISI CONFERENCE PROCEEDINGS PROVIDE LIMITED COVERAGE

Since 2008 ISI has integrated their database of conference proceedings into the Web of Science. This partially accommodates the problem of not counting conference proceeding papers. However, ISI does not provide an overview of conferences that are covered beyond a generic list of topics, so it is unclear which conferences are covered. I was not able to find any of my own proceedings papers. Also, only conferences from 1990 onwards are covered.

In general, conference coverage seems to be much more comprehensive in the Sciences than in the Social Sciences and Humanities. A search for English-language conferences in the Sciences between in 2009 only resulted in > 100,000 hits (i.e. hitting the maximum results), mostly in Engineering and Computer Science.

In the Social Sciences and Humanities the same search results in some 25,000 conference papers. Nearly half of these are in Management or Business, with the bulk of the remainder made up of Education, Operations Research, Economics and Computer Science. However, many of the results are not actually conference proceedings, but journal special issues with papers that were initially presented at conferences or articles misclassified as proceedings papers (see Section 14.2.4 for details).

A search for common author names allows us to better gauge comparative coverage. Zhang results in 1,433 hits in the Social Sciences and Humanities and 16,037 hits in the Sciences for English language publications in 2009. Smith results in 53 hits in the Social Sciences and Humanities and 2,462 hits in the Sciences for English language publications in 2009. Hence, it appears that the Social Sciences and Humanities might be even more underrepresented in ISI listed conference proceedings than they are in ISI listed journals.

WEB OF SCIENCE CITED REFERENCE LIMITED TO CITATIONS FROM ISI-LISTED JOURNALS

In the Cited Reference function Web of Science **does** include citations to non-ISI publications. However, it only includes citations from journals that are ISI-listed (Meho & Yang, 2007). As indicated before in SSH only a limited number of journals are ISI-listed.

Butler (2006) analysed the distribution of publication output by field for Australian universities between 1999-2001. She finds that whereas for the Chemical, Biological, Physical and Medical/Health sciences 69.3%-84.6% of the publications are in ISI listed journals, for Social Sciences such as Management, History Education and Arts only 4.4%-18.7% of the publications are published in ISI listed journals. ISI estimates that of the 2000 new journals reviewed annually only 10-12% are selected to be included in the Web of Science (Testa, 2004).

Archambault and Gagné (2004) found that US and UK-based journals are both significantly overrepresented in the Web of Science in comparison to Ulrich's journal database. This overrepresentation was stronger for the Social Sciences and Humanities than for the Natural Sciences. Further, in many areas of engineering, conference proceedings are very important publication outlets. For example, in a search conducted in 2007, one of the most cited computer scientists (Hector Garcia-Molina) gathered more than 20,000 citations in Google Scholar, with most of his papers being published and cited in conference proceedings. In Web of Science he had a mere 240 citations to his name!

In contrast to the Web of Science, Google Scholar includes citations from all academic publications regardless of where they appeared. As a results Google Scholar provides a more comprehensive picture of recent impact, especially for the Social Sciences and Humanities where more than five years can elapse between research appearing as a working or conference paper and research being published in a journal.

This also means that Google Scholar usually gives a more accurate picture of impact for junior academics. However, it must be acknowledged that although Google Scholar captures more citations in books and book chapters than the Web of Science (which captures none), it is by no means comprehensive in this respect. Google Book Search may provide a better alternative for book searches.

WEB OF SCIENCE CITED REFERENCE COUNTS CITATIONS TO NON-ISI JOURNALS ONLY TOWARDS FIRST AUTHOR

Whilst the Cited Reference function of Web of Science **does** include citations to non-ISI journals, it only includes these publications for the first author. Hence any publications in non-ISI journals where the academic in question is the second or further author are not included.

Google Scholar includes these publications for all listed authors. For instance, my 2003 publication with Alan Feely in Cross Cultural Management shows no citations in the Web of Science for my name, whilst it shows 58 citations in Google Scholar. A more disturbing case is discussed in Chapter 16, where our computer scientist is "robbed" of some 700-odd ISI citations to a book for which he is the second author.

CITATION RECORDS FOR ACADEMICS WITH "FOREIGN" NAMES ARE UNDERESTIMATED

Thomson ISI seems to have some difficulty with names that deviate from traditional English names. Below I describe five variants of this problem: names with diacretics, names with apostrophes, hyphenated names, names with prefixes and names with Asian characters.

NAMES WITH DIACRITICS

Thomson ISI's Web of Science has problems with names including <u>diacritics</u> (e.g. Özbilgin or Olivas-Luján). A search with diacritics provides an error message (*Search Error: Invalid query. Please check syntax*) and no results (see below). A search without diacritics is the only way to get results.

Web of Science ® – with Conference Proceedings

NOTICE
Search Error: Invalid query. Please check syntax.

Search for:

Özbilgin   in   Author

Example: O'Brian C* OR OBrian C*
Need help finding papers by an author? Use Author Finder.

NAMES WITH APOSTROPHES

Thomson ISI's Web of Science has problems with names with apostrophes. A search for "O'Rourke K*" in the Web of Science Cited Reference function results in only eleven citations to the work of the economic historian Kevin H O'Rourke, whereas a search for "ORourke K*" gives more than 500 citations.

Strangely enough, the search for "O'Rourke K*" in the General search seems to provide a comprehensive record, although of course his influential books and book chapters are not included. As we saw earlier

Google Scholar has fixed its problems with names with apostrophes and would hence be a better option for this type of searches.

HYPHENATED NAMES

Thomson ISI's Web of Science has problems with hyphenated names. Even though most academics refer to these names correctly, ISI data entry staff apparently prefers to enter these names without hyphens. As a results citation scores for academics with hyphenated names can be seriously underestimated.

A naïve user would search for Charles Baden-Fuller as "Baden-Fuller C*" and would find only about 200 citations. However, searching for Badenfuller would unearth another 800-odd citations. Google Scholar doesn't have any problems with hyphenated names and finds nearly 4,000 citations for Baden-Fuller and only two citations for Badenfuller, presumably caused by referencing errors by the citing authors.

NAMES WITH PRE-FIXES

There are many languages in which family names are preceded by pre-fixes. For instance in Dutch common examples are "van" (as in van Raan), "van der" (as in van der Wal). In both French and Spanish "de la" is common. In Dutch, the correct way of listing these pre-fixes in a list of references is behind the family names, i.e. when ordering alphabetically the prefix is ignored, such as "Wal, R. van der" and "Raan, F. van".

However, Thomson ISI's Web of Science has difficulty with these prefixes. More than 90% of the citations to the work of bibliometrist Anthony van Raan are incorrectly listed as Vanraan, even though in most cases the referring author listed the name correctly as van Raan.

Results								
Papers:	2	Cites/paper:	25.00	h-index:	2	AWCR:	2.44	
Citations:	50	Cites/author:	50.00	g-index:	2	AW-index:	1.56	
Years:	21	Papers/author:	2.00	hc-index:	1	AWCRpA:	2.44	
Cites/year:	2.38	Authors/paper:	1.00	hI-index:	2.00	e-index:	6.78	
				hI,norm:	2	hm-index:	2.00	

Cites		Authors	Title	Year	Publication
☑	47	AFJ VanRaan	Fractal dimension of co-citations	1990	Nature
☑	3	AF vanRaan	J (1996),'Advanced bibliometric methods as quantita…	1996	Scientometrics

Again Google Scholar doesn't have any problems with names with prefixes. A search for "A van Raan" results in nearly 4,000 citations, whilst a search for "A Vanraan" only finds 50 citations (see screenshot above), 47 of which to an article in Nature that indeed incorrectly lists the last name as Vanraan.

NAMES WITH ASIAN CHARACTERS

In Google Scholar it is possible to do a search in any language, including character based languages such as Chinese, Japanese and Korean. A search for Wang Ying (王英) for instance results in a large number of hits in Google Scholar(see screenshot below).

| Author impact | Journal impact | General citations | Multi-query center | Web Browser |

Author impact analysis - Perform a citation analysis for one or more authors

Author's name: 王英

Exclude these names:

Year of publication between: 0 and: 0

Results

Papers:	1000	Cites/paper:	7.79	h-index:	25	AWCR:	974.70
Citations:	7786	Cites/author:	7727.33	g-index:	38	AW-index:	31.22
Years:	91	Papers/author:	992.83	hc-index:	17	AWCRpA:	966.19
Cites/year:	85.56	Authors/paper:	1.02	hI-index:	24.04	e-index:	23.24
				hI,norm:	25	hm-index:	24.50

Cites	Authors	Title	Year
☑ 142	谢奕汉，王英兰	白云鄂博矿床流体包裹体中稀土矿物的发现	1995
☑ 123	王英鑑，徐寄遥	提高地对空大气红外遥感能力的新方法	1990
☑ 67	万淑芝，王英娟	手部静脉穿刺不宜握拳	1996
☑ 64	王英民，刘豪，李立诚，齐雪峰，王 …	准噶尔大型坳陷湖盆坡折带的类型和分布特征	2002
☑ 61	王英鹏	对在大学英语教学中培养学生社会文化能力…	1999
☑ 56	…赵立双，吴瑞芹，韩芳，刘李承，王英…	承德市区居民睡眠呼吸暂停低通气综合征患…	2003
☑ 50	王英民，金武弟，刘书会，邱桂强，李群…	断陷湖盆多级坡折带的成因类型,展布及其…	2003
☑ 48	张善文，王英民，李群	应用坡折带理论寻找隐蔽油气藏	2003
☑ 46	王英剑，常敏慧，何希才…	新型开关电源实用技术	1999
☑ 45	王英林，王卫东，王宗江，佟平，许萌，…	基于本体的可重构知识管理平台	2003
☑ 40	王英，蒙张敏，黄丹莉	压疮评估和预防的循证医学证据	2006

In ISI's Web of Science this same search will result in the same error messages provided for names with diacritics as information is only stored in English (see screenshot below).

Web of Science® – with Conference Proceedings

NOTICE

Search Error: Invalid query. Please check syntax.

Search for:

王英   in   Author

Example: O'Brian C* OR OBrian C*

Need help finding papers by an author? Use Author Finder.

The Web of Science includes only a very limited number of journals in languages other than English (LOTE). Hence citations in non-English journals are generally not included in any Web of Science citation analysis. Whilst Google Scholar's LOTE coverage is far from comprehensive, it does include a larger number of publication in other languages and indexes documents in French, German, Spanish, Italian and Portuguese (Noruzi, 2005).

Meho and Yang (2007) found that 6.94% of Google Scholar citations were from LOTE, while this was true for only 1.14% for the Web of Science and 0.70% for Scopus. Archambault and Gagné (2004) found that Thomson's ISI's journal selection favours English, a situation attributable to ISI's inability to analyse the content of journals in LOTE.

As an example, Gérard Charreaux, a French accounting scholar, accumulated a grand total of 15 ISI citations in his lifetime. As the screenshot below shows he has a very respectable number of citations in French language journals and books that **are** indexed Google Scholar.

| Author impact | Journal impact | General citations | Multi-query center | Web Browser |

Author impact analysis - Perform a citation analysis for one or more authors

Author's name:	"G Charreaux"
Exclude these names:	
Year of publication between:	0	and:	0

Results

Papers:	158	Cites/paper:	11.81	h-index:	23	AWCR:	147.04
Citations:	1866	Cites/author:	1634.00	g-index:	40	AW-index:	12.13
Years:	27	Papers/author:	129.74	hc-index:	15	AWCRpA:	128.92
Cites/year:	69.11	Authors/paper:	1.44	hI-index:	18.89	e-index:	29.66
				hI,norm:	22	hm-index:	22.00

Cites		Authors	Title	Year
☑	312	G Charreaux	Le gouvernement des entreprises: Théories et faits	1997
☑	147	G Charreaux, P Des...	Gouvernance des entreprises: valeur partenariale contre valeur actio...	1998
☑	103	G Charreaux	Vers une théorie du gouvernement des entreprises	1997
☑	80	G Charreaux	«La théorie positive de l'agence: lecture et relectures...»	1999
☑	64	G Charreaux	«Variation sur le thème: A la recherche de nouvelles fondations pour l...	2002
☑	63	G Charreaux	Structures de propriété, relation d'agence et performance financière ...	1991
☑	58	G Charreaux, JP Pit...	Le conseil d'administration	1990
☑	54	G Charreaux, P Des...	Corporate governance: stakeholder value versus shareholder value	2001
☑	53	G Charreaux	«Le conseil d'administration dans les théories de la gouvernance»	2000

In the General Search function Web of Science does not include citations to the same work that have small mistakes in their referencing (which especially for books and book chapters occurs very frequently). In the Cited Reference function Web of Science does include these citations, but they are not aggregated with the other citations.

For a rather amusing example refer to the screenshot below. It shows the many different variants of Geert Hofstede's highly cited book Culture's Consequences. There are still dozens of other variations included in the ISI database that are not shown below. For further details on this see Section 14.2.3.

CULTURES CONSEQUENCS		
CULTURES CONSEQUENES		CHULTURES CONSEQUENC
CULTURES CONSEQUENSE	CULTURES CIONSEQUENC	CHULTURES ORG SOFTWA
CULTURES CONSEQUNCES	CULTURES CONCEQUENCE	CLOTURES CONSEQUENCE
CULTURES CONSEQUNCES	CULTURES CONEQUENCES	CLTURES CONSEQUENCES
CULTURES CONSEUENCES	CULTURES CONSEAQUENC	CLTURES CONSEQUENCES
CULTURES CONSEUQUENC	CULTURES CONSEQUCNES	CLTURES ORG
CULTURES CONSEZUENCE	CULTURES CONSEQUECE	CLTURES ORG SOFTWARE
CULTURES CONSQUENCES	CULTURES CONSEQUECES	CLULTURAL CONSEQUENC

In many cases these errors were caused by data entry errors and not by mistakes in the original reference. Of course given the large number of entries that ISI has to cope with, incidental errors are inevitable. However, in a commercial product I would have hoped for a more active quality control system.

Google Scholar appears to have a better aggregation mechanism than Web of Science. Even though duplicate publications that are referenced in a (slightly) different way still occur regularly, Google Scholar has a grouping function that resolves the worst ambiguities.

Belew (2005) confirms that Google Scholar has lower citation noise than Web of Science. In the Web of Science only 60% of the articles were listed as unique entries (i.e. no citation variations), while for Google Scholar this was 85%. None of the articles in his sample had more than five separate listings within Google Scholar, while 13% had five or more entries in the Web of Science.

14.2.2   ACCURATE SELF-CITATION COUNTS ARE DIFFICULT TO ACHIEVE IN ISI

As I discussed in Section 9.2 many university administrators seem to be obsessed with the presumed need to exclude self-citations from someone's citation record. They often assume ISI's Web of Science offers an easy and fool proof way to do so. In the process Google Scholar is often discarded as a datasource, because they think it doesn't allow an easy option to exclude self-citation.

I have already argued in Chapter 1 that excluding self-citations is almost always a waste of time. I have also shown in Section 9.2.2. that excluding self-citations with Google Scholar is in fact fairly easy, especially for academics with a modest citation record. Here I will discuss the enormous difficulty in getting accurate self-citation scores from ISI that are comparable across candidates.

ISI'S CITATION REPORT: AN EASY OPTION?

Most users of the ISI Web of Science list the possibility to exclude self-citations as one of its big advantages. The ISI Web of Science offers the possibility to create a citation report (see screenshot) where one can subsequently exclude self-citations. Understandably, to most people, this sounds like a really easy way to extract a "clean" citation record.

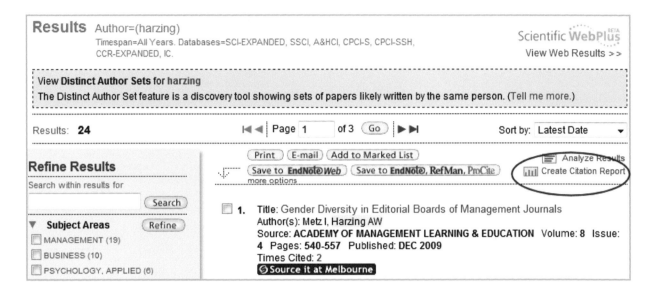

However, in reality this is a very cumbersome and error prone process, that – unless carried by someone with substantial expertise in using the ISI database – is likely to lead to highly diverging interpretations by different applicants and evaluators.

The first problem is that the citation report can only be created in ISI's general search, which only reports citations to ISI listed journal articles, not to books, book chapters, conference proceedings, or non-ISI listed journals (see Section 14.1.1 for details).

A *General Search* for my own publication record lists only 389 citations, even though in the *Cited Reference Search* my work has gathered a total of 914 citations, an increase of no less than 135%. As Chapter 16 shows, differences can be much more dramatic in Social Sciences and Humanities.

ISI USES CITING ARTICLES, NOT CITATIONS FOR MOST OF ITS ANALYSES

The second problem is that even if one would accept this limitation in coverage, the proportion of self-citations would be likely to be drastically overestimated with this function. The reason is that ISI performs any of its analyses only on citing **articles**, not on citations. As a single article **can** and often **will** contain more than one citation to an academic's work, this again underestimates the academic's impact.

In my own case the 914 cited reference citations come from only 667 articles. My 389 citations in the general search come from 341 articles. If one subsequently clicks the link *"view without self-citations"* (left-hand picture) link only 331 articles remain (right-hand picture below). This means that 10 of the 341 articles citing **articles** were written by myself, a self-citation rate of 3%. However, many searchers will conclude that 58 of my 389 citations are self-citations (i.e. 15%) as they see the number of "citations" going down from 389 to 331.

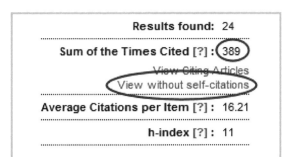

WHY WE ARE STILL NOT THERE?

The third problem is that even the 3% self-citation rate could be incorrect. Why is this so? Because this is the proportion of self-citing **articles**, not the proportion of self-citations. Of course my articles could contain more than one reference to my own work.

Hence in order to find out my **actual** self-citation rate, one would need to check the citations of every single self-citing article. To do so, one would need to go back again to the previous page, click on *"view citing articles"* (instead of *"view without self-citations"*), and then refine the citing articles by author (see screenshot on the left).

One would then be presented with a list of articles of the academic in question that are citing his or her own work, the first three of which are reproduced above. In order to establish the actual number of self-citations contained in these articles, one would need to go through the reference list of each article and identify the number of references to the academic's work.

This is a very time-consuming process, even if your library – like the University of Melbourne – has an integrated electronic database. For most articles I would only need to click on the full text button to access the article electronically. Although this would still take several minutes per paper, it would be relatively quick. However, for journals where full-text is not available (e.g. the first) I would need to go to the University library to access the article in question, which could easily take an hour if your library is not within the same building.

The fourth problem is that when counting the number of self-citation in these ten articles, I would need to remember to **only** count self-citations to ISI-listed journal articles, as citations to non ISI publications were not included in the initial count anyway. I would also need to remember to search for all articles where I am not the first author. Even if someone would get this far, it is likely that one would mistakingly count **all** self-citations, hence again overestimating the proportion of self-citations, or forget some of the articles that they have not first-authored.

Fortunately, I do keep electronic copies of all my publications, so in my case I could fairly quickly verify that I had cited fifteen ISI listed articles that were (co)-authored by myself. This means that my accurate number of **self-citations** in this data-set would be nearly 4%, slightly higher than one would conclude from looking at the proportion of **self-citing articles**, but nowhere near as high as a naive interpretation would assume.

NO, WE ARE STILL NOT THERE: GOING BACK TO THE CITED REFERENCE SEARCH

As I indicated above, the first problem is that the ISI General Search underestimates an academic's citation record substantially, especially in the Social Sciences and Humanities (see Chapter 16 for more details). Therefore, if one wanted to get a **really** accurate estimate of someone's self-citations, one would need to use the Cited Reference search.

To continue the example of my own citation record, I have 914 ISI citations in ISI's *Cited Reference Search*. We thus need to establish how many of these citations were self-citations. In order to do so, we need to go through a five-step procedure.

First we need to search for my name in the Cited Reference Search. Second, we need to establish which of resulting publications are mine and which are written by other academics with the same name. In my case this is not a problem, but for academics with a more common name, this can take a long time. We select all relevant articles and then click "Finish Search" (see screenshot).

This presents us with all citing **articles** (please note, this is not the same as citations). In order to identify the self-citing articles from this set, as a third step we need to again refine the search by author in the same way as above. In my case, this identifies 21 self-citing articles (or just over 3% of the total number of 667 citing articles).

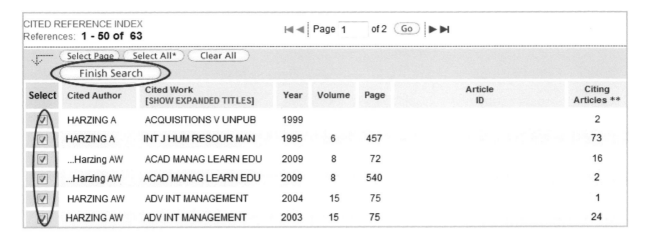

Select Page   Select All*   Clear All

Finish Search

Select	Cited Author	Cited Work [SHOW EXPANDED TITLES]	Year	Volume	Page	Article ID	Citing Articles **
☑	HARZING A	ACQUISITIONS V UNPUB	1999				2
☑	HARZING A	INT J HUM RESOUR MAN	1995	6	457		73
☑	...Harzing AW	ACAD MANAG LEARN EDU	2009	8	72		16
☑	...Harzing AW	ACAD MANAG LEARN EDU	2009	8	540		2
☑	HARZING AW	ADV INT MANAGEMENT	2004	15	75		1
☑	HARZING AW	ADV INT MANAGEMENT	2003	15	75		24

In order to find out the number of self-citations, as a fourth step we need to go through the reference lists of each of these 21 articles. Obviously, this is a fairly tedious procedure. This time, we need to re-member to count **all** citations, not just citations to ISI listed articles, as our base rate is now all citations. We also still need to remember to include all articles where we are not the first authors. Doing for all 21 articles, resulted in a total of 47 self-citations, i.e. just over 5% of the total number of citations.

CONCLUSION

Even if someone would be **willing** to go through this extremely time-consuming and cumbersome process, it is quite likely that most applicants will not really understand how to do this. More importantly, it is very unlikely that university administrators or research officers will understand these procedures and hence candidates will most likely be instructed to simply use the *"view without self-citations"* link. This leads almost certainly to a an underestimation of their real number of **citations** (as it only counts citing articles), and most likely to a substantial overestimation of their self-citations.

So why bother with removing self-citations in the first place? It is a time-consuming and error prone process. In the vast majority of cases, the error margin introduced by removing self-citations will be larger than the error margin present by including self-citations. It is likely that different applicants will interpret the instructions differently, hence leading to inequitably comparisons. For most applicants and administrators, the difference between ISI's *General Search* and *Cited By Search* is difficult enough as it is. Why include even more complexity?

In the example above, my self-citation rate ranged from 3-5%, or 15% in the very naive and inaccurate interpretation. Would it have made any difference in evaluating my ISI citation record whether I had 867 or 914 citations, or even 331 or 389 citations? Most probably not. So why bother?

14.2.3   STRAY CITATIONS ARE VERY COMMON IN ISI

Stray citations are citations that refer to a publication that is also listed correctly in ISI, but have small errors in their referencing. This can be caused either because of the sloppiness of the referring academic or because of data entry errors by ISI staff.

The problem of stray citations in ISI can be quite significant. One of the most-cited academics in the field of Management – Geert Hofstede – has published a book called Culture's Consequences. This book was first published in 1980, reprinted in 1984, and published in a 2nd revised edition in 2001. These three versions of the same book respectively have 4677, 664 and 1422 citations.

However, there are also some 150 additional stray citations in ISI's Cited Reference search, all referring to the same book. Some of these entries refer to specific page numbers in the book and hence have been entered as separate entries. Others refer inaccurately to different publication years or misrepresent the book's title as Cultural Consequences. In contrast Google Scholar has less than 30 variations of this title.

Many stray entries in ISI are simple misspellings of the title, with some of the weirdest being "CULTURES CIONSEQUENC", "CULTUES UCULTURES CO", and "CULTURES OCNSEQUENCE". In many of these cases, the references were correct in the referring works, but spelling errors were made by ISI data entry staff. Most of these inaccurate references only occur once or twice, but a substantial number has a double-digit number of citations, with three accumulating more than 50 citations. Ironically, **none** of the more than 7000 citations to this work was correctly entered as the title is Culture's Consequences, not Cultures Consequences. However, as we have seen above, ISI does not seem to be able to deal with apostrophes.

Fortunately, for most authors the problem of stray citations is more modest, but nevertheless annoying. The screenshots below refer to two articles by Margaret Abernethy, with the last three columns referring to the volume of the journal, the first page of the article and the number of citations respectively. Please note that these screenshots were specially constructed for this book. In reality, the different incarnations of the same paper would not normally appear neatly listed together.

The first screenshot refers to a paper in Accounting, Organizations & Society, which is an ISI listed journal. There is a master record which with 27 citations has the bulk of the total number of citations. The second line shows the same article, but without the issue of the journal and with journal name not following the ISI standard notation for this journal, a data entry error. The third line also refers to the same article, but includes a wrong volume and only lists one of the author's initials. The fourth and fifth line respectively are identical to the master record, safe for the fact that the referring author included the wrong year.

ABERNETHY MA	ACCOUNT ORG SOC	1995	20	1	27
ABERNETHY MA	ACCOUNTING ORG SOC	1995	20		2
ABERNETHY M	ACCOUNT ORG SOC	1995	29	1	1
ABERNETHY MA	ACCOUNT ORG SOC	1996	20	1	1
ABERNETHY MA	ACCOUNT ORG SOC	1994	20	1	2

The second screenshot refers to an article in Accounting & Finance, a journal that is not ISI listed. Hence, there is no official master record for this article in the ISI data-base and citations are spread rather evenly over different versions of the paper, which differ mainly in terms of the journal volume and issue that are listed. The first line shows a very interesting variant of the paper. In addition to missing the author's second initial, the referrer seems to have accidentally included the volume and issue number of one of Abernethy's other papers.

ABERNETHY M	ACCOUNT FINANC		1994	20	241	1
ABERNETHY MA	ACCOUNT FINANC		1994		49	6
ABERNETHY MA	ACCOUNT FINANC		1994	34	9	2
ABERNETHY MA	ACCOUNT FINANC		1994	34	49	9
ABERNETHY MA	ACCOUNT FINANC		1994	33	49	5

If all of these stray citations were correctly merged into one record, the number of citations for the first paper would be 33 instead of 27. The second paper would have a total of 23 citations, even though currently the record with the largest number of citations is 9. So what does it matter? That depends on whether the journal in question is ISI listed or not. If a journal is ISI listed, the stray citations are not reported in ISI's (General) Search function or ISI's citation report. This means that:

- the academic's citation record is understated, even for publications in ISI listed journals. [The General Search will always understate one's overall citation record as citations to non-ISI listed journals, books, book chapters and conference proceedings are not included]
- the academic's listing in the Essential Science Indicators (which includes citations to ISI listed journals only) is understated.
- the University the academics is affiliated with misses out on citations, thus understating its position in the Essential Science Indicators, especially in terms of citations/per paper.

If the journal in question is not ISI listed, the consequences are not as serious as these citations are not counted in any of ISI's other databases or analytical tools anyway. However, having your citations to a particular article spread over many different records – which are not always easy to match – makes it rather difficult to assess the citation impact of individual articles. Therefore, it underestimates the unique contribution that a particular author has made to the field by publishing impactful articles, rather than publishing a lot of articles with only a small of citations.

DATA CHANGE REQUEST

Fortunately, there is a way to get your ISI Cited Reference citation report cleaned up. You can submit a Data Change Request to Thomson Reuters with the references to be corrected at http://science. thomsonreuters.com/techsupport/datachange/. Please make sure you indicate the master record that the stray references need to be merged into. If the article in question is published in an ISI listed journal, the master record will be clickable link highlighted in blue. If the article was not published in an ISI listed journal, you can designate the master record yourself. It is usually best to choose the record with the largest number of citations, as that would normally be the most "correct" reference to the paper.

Requests normally take 3-5 weeks to be processed. In my experience, Thomson Reuters nearly always makes the changes that are requested, provided of course that the records do indeed refer to the same paper. You might think this is quite a lot of work for little reward. However, submitting data change requests is fairly quick, especially if you use the back button on your browser to avoid having to enter all the general information (name, university, email address etc.) again.

I cleaned up my own record by spending about an hour to submit various data changes and now spend five minutes once a month to submit any further changes if necessary. The result is that rather than having citations to my work spread over three full pages with some publications found on three different pages (because referrers used one, two or three initials when referring to the work), my publications now nearly fit on one page. Some publications had more than a dozen different incarnations.

For instance the Journal Quality List that can be downloaded from my website (http://www.harzing.com/jql.htm) was referred to in 16 different ways, with 1-4 citations each. Collecting all these citations into one master record now show 38 citations for this "publication". Likewise, the numerous stray citations to the Publish or Perish program were collated to 17 citations. As a result, it is much easier for me to convince research evaluators of the significant contribution that these resources make to the academic community. Whether or not cleaning up your ISI Cited Reference citation record is beneficial in your case is something only you can tell. However, I do encourage you to at least check it out.

14.2.4   ISI SUFFERS FROM DOCUMENT TYPE CLASSIFICATION PROBLEMS

In the ISI Web of Knowledge each item is categorized into a particular "document type" category. Overall, there are nearly 40 different document types, but the most frequently used are: "article", "review", and "proceedings paper". This section deals with ISI's frequent misclassification of journal articles containing original research into the review or proceedings paper category.

The ISI Web of Knowledge does not provide a definition of any document type in their helpfile, but in various documents (e.g. Journal Citation Report Quick Reference Card), Thomson contrasts "review articles" with "original research articles". There is no commonly agreed definition of review articles and different disciplines might value them differently. However, in general parlance review articles are defined as articles that do not contain original data and simply collect, review and synthesize earlier research.

Thomson does not define proceedings papers either, but one can only assume them to be papers published in conference proceedings. Conference proceedings are a very common and respected outlet in some disciplines, such as computer science. However, in Business & Economics they are normally seen as mere stepping stones to future publication in a peer reviewed journal. The more prestigious conferences (such as the Academy of Management and the Academy of International Business) either do not publish proceedings or publish only short abstracted papers.

In general, in most of the Social Sciences neither review articles or proceedings papers would be considered worthy of the quality stamp reserved for original research published in a peer reviewed journal.

TWO EXAMPLES OF THIS CATEGORISATION PROBLEM

I will give two specific examples in the field of Management to illustrate the extent of this specific categorization problem. First, Michael Lounsbury, co-editor of *Organization Studies*, has published seventeen articles in ISI listed journals. However, no less than ten of these seventeen articles are categorized as reviews (6) or proceedings papers (4), leaving him with a much less impressive seven pieces of original research (see left-hand picture below).

Two of Lounsbury's six "review papers" were published in *The Academy of Management Journal*, a journal that is well-known for only accepting papers that make a very strong original theoretical **and** empirical contribution. The other four papers were published in *Strategic Management Journal*, *Organization*, *Organization Studies* and *Social Forces*, all journals that would definitely **not** publish any articles that simply synthesized previous research. So why were these articles categorized as review papers?

Two of Lounsbury's four "proceedings papers" were published in the *American Behavioural Scientist*, whilst the other two appeared in *Accounting, Organization & Society* and *Journal of Management Studies*. Clearly none of these journals would be categorized as collections of conference proceedings. So why were these articles categorized as proceedings papers?

 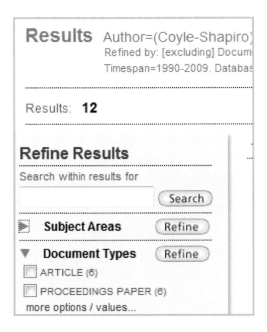

My second example concerns Jacqueline Coyle-Shapiro, Senior editor of *Journal of Organizational Behavior*. She has published 12 articles in ISI listed journals. However, half of them are categorized as proceedings papers (see right-hand picture above). These papers were published in the following journals: *Journal of Vocational Behavior* (twice), *Journal of Applied Psychology*, *Journal of Organizational Behavior*, and *Journal of Management Studies* (twice). As anyone in the field knows, none of these journals are collections of conference papers. So why were these articles categorized as proceedings papers?

WHY DOES ISI CATEGORIZE REGULAR JOURNAL ARTICLES AS PROCEEDINGS PAPERS?

The answer to this question presented itself in an FAQ (Why has the number of articles in the Web of Science gone down and the number of proceedings papers gone up) provided by Thomson Reuters. According to Thomson Reuters a 'Proceedings Paper' is:

> *a document in a journal or book that notes the work was presented - in whole or in part - at a conference. This is a statement of the association of a work with a conference. Prior to October 2008, these items displayed as "Article" in the Web of Science product.*

Indeed, when verifying the "proceedings papers" by Lounsbury and Coyle-Shapiro, I found that the acknowledgements in their articles carried innocent notes such as *"A portion of this paper was presented at the annual meeting of the Academy of Management, San Diego, 1998"* or *"An earlier version of this paper was presented at the Annual Meeting of the Academy of Management, Chicago, 1999"* or *"This paper builds on and extends remarks and arguments made as part of a 2006 Keynote Address at the Interdisciplinary Perspectives on Accounting Conference held in Cardiff, UK"*. Most of these papers were published before 2008. Hence ISI seems to have changed these classifications retroactively.

So simply presenting an early version of your ideas in a 10-15 minute (or shorter) slot at a conference or workshop (some of the acknowledgments even referred to small workshops), perhaps attended by less than a dozen people, appears to mean that your paper is downgraded by ISI to be a "conference proceedings paper" even though the conference in question doesn't even publish proceedings?

Does that mean that from 2008 onwards all of the papers published in these top journals are categorized as conference papers? No, this appears to happen only to those papers whose authors were honest enough to acknowledge that early versions of the paper had been presented at a conference, or to papers whose authors were kind enough to thank participants of a particular workshop for their input. A nice reward for being professional and collegial!

This categorization process also appears to shows a rather limited understanding of the review process in top journals in the Social Sciences and Humanities. Yes, early versions of a paper might have been presented at conferences. However, the paper that is subsequently submitted to a journal will normally be vastly different from the paper that was earlier presented at a conference. Conferences and workshops are often used as a means to test and polish ideas. Even if authors submit fairly polished papers to conferences, these papers will still generally need to go through two to four rounds of revisions before they are accepted for the journal.

A longer and more extensive process of revision is likely for the many papers that are not accepted by the first journal approached. As acceptance rates of top journals in this field are well below 10%, the reality is that papers are often submitted to several journals before they get their first revise & resubmit. Maturation of the author(s)' ideas, reorientation toward different journals, as well as the review process itself means that virtually every paper published has been substantially revised. Hence, the end-product published by a journal often bears very little resemblance to the paper that was originally presented at a conference, years before publication.

WHY DOES ISI CATEGORIZE ORIGINAL RESEARCH ARTICLES AS REVIEW PAPERS?

With the conference proceedings problem "resolved", this leaves us with the puzzling review category. Why are papers that clearly present original research, published in the top journals in our field, categorized as derivative work that synthesizes work of other academics? According to Thomson: simply because they have more than 100 references! No, I am not joking. Thomson says:

> In the JCR system any article containing more than 100 references is coded as a review. Articles in "review" sections of research or clinical journals are also coded as reviews, as are articles whose titles contain the word "review" or "overview."

When verifying this criterion for articles published by Michael Lounsbury, I found Thomson to have applied their criteria absolutely as described. Lounsbury's 2001 *Administrative Science Quarterly* article has 95 references and is categorized in the "article" document type, thus acknowledging it is original research.

His 2004 article in *Social Forces* with 101 references is categorized in the "review" document type, even though the paper has sections titled "Theory and Hypotheses" and "Data and Methods". In addition, the abstract and even the title clearly refer to empirical work. If this scholar wanted Thomson to recognize his work as original, maybe he should have been a bit less conscientious in identifying the contributions of other authors in his literature review?

Thomson does not list any particular rationale for why papers with more than 100 references should be considered to be review articles that do not contain original research. It is true that a "real" review article providing, for instance, a literature review of 30 years of publications in a particular field will tend to have many references.

However, the reverse certainly does not hold true, there are many papers with more than 100 references that are not review articles. One cannot presume that there is a direct relationship between the number of references contained in a paper and its level of originality. Thomson also does not provide any rationale for the seemingly arbitrary cut-off point. Perhaps Thomson simply saw 100 as a nicely convenient round figure?

If – for some inexplicable reason – one wanted to classify articles as review papers based on the number of references, one should at the very least relate them to the length of the paper. It is one thing to punish a 3-page paper with >100 references, it is quite something else to do the same for a 40-page article.

WHAT CAUSED THE INCREASE OF PROCEEDINGS PAPERS AND REVIEWS?

This then brings us to our final question. Why has the number of papers categorized as proceedings papers and review articles increased over time? For proceedings papers, the answer to this question is very simple. In 2008 ISI integrated their separate conference proceedings database into the Web of Science in 2008. At that point in time many journal articles were retrospectively categorized as conference papers.

The reason for the increase of review papers is also fairly straightforward: the number of papers with more than 100 references has increased. If we look at one of the very top journals in Management, the Academy of Management Review, we find that whilst in 1990 only 1 out of the 31 published articles was categorized as a review, in 2008 no less than half of the 42 published articles were categorized as reviews (because they had more than 100 references).

With an average of 109 references per article (84 for papers categorized as articles and 134 for papers categorized as reviews) in 2008, it appears to be only a matter of time before ISI will consider none of the research published in AMR to be "original research work". That would be rather a shame as some of the most original and groundbreaking work in the field of Management is published in AMR.

Of course there could be many reasons for the increasing number of references in articles, such as the increasing availability of relevant literature online, the increase of multi-disciplinary research, the ever increasing rigour of the reviewing process, which is likely to make reviewers suggest that additional bodies of literature that should be covered, the increasing tendency for both reviewers and journal editors to ask for additional references to their own work or that of the journal they are reviewer/editor for.

Whatever the reason, it is clear that classifying articles as review articles simply because they reached an arbitrary number of references is inappropriate. More disturbingly, it shows a very limited understanding of the research process in the Social Sciences and Humanities.

14.3   REFERENCES

- Archambault, E.; Gagné, E.V. (2004) **The Use of Bibliometrics in Social Sciences and Humanities**, Montreal: *Social Sciences and Humanities Research Council of Canada* (SSHRCC), August 2004.

- Belew, R.K. (2005) **Scientific impact quantity and quality: Analysis of two sources of bibliographic data**, *arXiv:cs.IR/0504036* v1, 11 April 2005.
- Butler, L. (2006) **RQF Pilot Study Project – History and Political Science Methodology for Citation Analysis**, November 2006, accessed from: http://www.chass.org.au/papers/bibliometrics/CHASS_Methodology.pdf, 15 Jan 2007.
- Meho, L.I.; Yang, K. (2007) **A New Era in Citation and Bibliometric Analyses: Web of Science, Scopus, and Google Scholar**, *Journal of the American Society for Information Science and Technology*, 58(13): 2105–2125.
- Nisonger, T.E. (2004) **Citation autobiography: An investigation of ISI database coverage in determining author citedness**, *College & Research Libraries*, 65(2): 152-163.
- Noruzi, A. (2005) **Google Scholar: The New Generation of Citation Indexes**, *LIBRI*, 55(4): 170-180.
- Saad, G. (2006) **Exploring the h-index at the author and journal levels using bibliometric data of productive consumer scholars and business-related journals respectively**, *Scientometrics*, 69(1): 117-120.
- Testa, J. (2004) **The Thomson Scientific Journal Selection Process**, http://scientific.thomson.com/free/essays/selectionofmaterial/journalselection/, accessed 15 Jan 2007.

CHAPTER 15:
A GOOGLE SCHOLAR H-INDEX FOR JOURNALS

A revised and condensed version of this chapter was published as: Harzing, A.W.K.; Wal, R. van der (2009) **A Google Scholar H-Index for Journals: An Alternative Metric to Measure Journal Impact in Economics & Business?**, *Journal of the American Society for Information Science and Technology,* vol. 60, no. 1, pp 41-46.

<table>
<tr><td>**15.1**</td><td>**INTRODUCTION**</td></tr>
</table>

Traditionally, journal quality has been assessed through the ISI Journal Impact Factor (JIF). This chapter proposes an alternative metric – Hirsch's h-index – and data source – Google Scholar – to assess journal impact. Using a comparison between the Google Scholar h-index and the ISI JIF for a sample of 838 journals in Economics & Business, I argue that the former provides a more accurate and comprehensive measure of journal impact.

The h-index has several advantages over the Thomson ISI JIF. First of all, it does not have an artificially fixed time horizon. The metrics used in the present chapter were computed in October 2007 over a five-year period (2001-2005) in order to enable a comparison with the average JIF for 2003-2007 (for further details see the section on procedures). However, any time horizon could be used, rather than focusing on citations in one particular year to the two preceding years as is the case with the Thomson ISI JIF[1].

Second, the h-index attenuates the impact of one highly-cited article, because – unlike citations-per-paper measures such as the JIF – the h-index is not based on mean scores. In a citations-per-paper metric even one highly-cited article can cause a very strong increase in the average number of citations per paper for the journal in question, leading to possibly highly idiosyncratic and variable results. When we choose to evaluate journal impact through citation impact measures, we are interested in the **overall** citation impact of the journal, not in the citation impact of one or two highly cited individual papers in that journal.

Third, the h-index is influenced by the number of papers that a journal publishes. A journal that publishes a larger number of papers has a higher *likelihood* – though by no means certainty – of generating a higher h-index since every article presents another chance for citations. This may be seen as a disadvantage when evaluating the standing of individual *articles* in a journal (or an individual academic based on this metric) as this measure should *not* be dependent on the number of articles published in that journal. However, one cannot deny that a journal that publishes a larger number of high-impact papers has a bigger impact on the field. Given that impact on the field is what we attempt to measure, this feature of the h-index and g-index is an advantage rather than a disadvantage.

---

[1] We do acknowledge that a 2-year citation window is not inherent to the JIF. Thomson now even publishes a 5-year JIF. However, the traditional JIF used by thousands of universities around the world as a measure of journal impact or quality, uses a 2-year window.

Since our aim was to cover a broader range of journals than in most previous studies I took the Harzing's Journal Quality List (Harzing, 2007) as our basis. This list includes a collation of twenty different rankings of 838 journals in the broad area of Business and Economics.

The metrics used in this chapter were calculated using Publish or Perish. Searches were conducted in the first week of October 2007. Where relevant I searched for spelling variations of a journal (e.g. British vs. American spelling, the use of and vs. the use of &, spelling of composite words with or without a hyphen). Some journals also have abbreviated titles that are commonly used (e.g. all SIAM journals and many Psychology journals) and hence these were included as alternatives. If a title included very common words, e.g. *Journal of Management*, I conducted searches with the ISSN instead. Unfortunately, Google Scholar's results for ISSN searches seem to be rather erratic and hence this alternative was only used if the ISSN search provided a comprehensive result for the journal in question.

The results of all search queries were inspected for incomplete or inconsistent results. This process left us with only two dozen journals (out of 838) that had substantially incomplete coverage and for which metrics could not be calculated. Eight of these were research annuals in book format (the Elsevier *Advances in …* series and the *Research in….* series). For other journals our visual inspection might have overlooked occasional missing articles, but this is unlikely to impact much on robust measures such as the h-index and g-index unless they happen to be highly cited. I have no reason to believe that this was the case. On the contrary, highly cited articles appear to be less likely to be missing from the Google Scholar database than lowly cited or uncited articles.

Our Google Scholar searches included citations to articles published between 2001-2005. This timeframe was chosen to be broadly comparable with a five-year average for the Journal Impact Factors of the last five available years (2003-2006). These impact factors refer to citations in articles published between 2001 and 2005. Ideally, I would have preferred to include the JIF for 2007, but that metric did not come out until half a year after the analysis conducted for this chapter. Moreover, given that Google Scholar displays some delay in its data processing for some journals, using the 2006 JIF is likely to give a dataset that is fairly comparable to Google Scholar in October 2007.

Supplementary analyses reported below with regard to the extent of concentration of citations within a particular journal were conducted in October 2007 with the general search function of ISI that allows the user to rank articles by citation.

15.3   RESULTS AND DISCUSSION OF THE BENCHMARKING ANALYSIS

15.3.1   OVERALL COMPARISON OF JIF AND H-INDEX

There are 536 journals in the Journal Quality List that have both an ISI JIF for 2003-2006 and a Google Scholar h-index or g-index. The Spearman correlation — used because both the JIF and h/g-index have non-normal distributions - is strong and very significant:

- 0.718 ($p < 0.000$) between the ISI JIF and the h-index,

- 0.717 (p < 0.000) between the ISI JIF and the g-index, and

- 0.976 (p < 0.000) between the h-index and g-index.

Given that these two sets of indices have different data sources (ISI Thomson JCR versus Google Scholar) and provide different metrics (a mean citations per paper count over 2 years for the ISI JIF and a combined quantity/quality measure over 5 years for the h-index and g-index) this strong correlation is quite remarkable. Given the extremely high correlation between the h-index and g-index, in the remainder of this chapter I will focus on the h-index and provide a comparison between the ISI JIF and the h-index.

Figure 1 (see the end of this chapter) shows a scatterplot of the average ISI JIF for 2003-2006 and Google Scholar h-index for articles published between 2001 and 2005. A line shows the regression equation. Outliers above the line are journals that have a high JIF in comparison to their h-index. Most of the major outliers above the regression line are Psychology journals, which generally – similar to journals in the Sciences – have very high immediacy index, i.e. a lot of citations to these journals occur quickly after publication.

For example, the 2006 immediacy index for the *Annual Review of Psychology* (4.091) is more than ten times as high as that of the *American Economic Review* (0.335). This means that when comparing these two journals over a 2-year period the *Annual Review of Psychology* will always show a higher impact factor than the *American Economic Review*, whereas the difference will be much smaller if I consider a 5-year period. This example clearly illustrates the folly of comparing ISI JIFs between disciplines.

The other major outlier is *ACM Computing Surveys*, which had wildly varying JIFs over the years, from .64 in 2001 and 2.77 in 2002 to impact factor between 7.4 and 10.0 2003-2005. However, the very high impact factors in these years appear to be mainly caused by two very highly cited articles published in 2002 and 2003 (for an even more striking case of this phenomenon see the discussion of SIAM Review below), whilst most of the relatively small number of papers published in this journal (63 over five years) are not particularly well-cited.

The two main outliers below the regression line are *The Journal of Finance* and *The American Economic Review* that have a very high h-index in comparison to their JIF. This difference is probably caused by the fact that articles in these journals are cited heavily in working papers (e.g. papers from the *National Bureau of Economic Research* or the *Tinbergen Institute*) and government policy documents, neither of which are included in Thomson ISI JIF.

15.3.2   OVERALL COMPARISON W/H PSYCHOLOGY JOURNALS AND MAJOR OUTLIERS

Figure 2 (see the end of this chapter) shows a scatterplot of the average ISI JIF and Google Scholar h-index with the exclusion of Psychology journals and the three outliers discussed above: *ACM Computing Surveys*, *Journal of Finance* and the *American Economic Review*.

In this figure the most striking outlier is *SIAM Review*, with several Sociology/Geography journals also showing a high JIF in comparison to their h-index. Other less striking outliers are also visible in Figure 2, but these will be discussed in the review of the sub-disciplines below. *SIAM Review* had an average JIF of 2.75 between 2001 and 2003 and a JIF of 2.67 in 2006. However, in 2004 and 2005 its JIF was 6.12 and 7.21 respectively causing a very high average JIF between 2003 and 2006.

Reviewing the JIF for 2004 and 2005 in detail showed that the very high impact factor was nearly entirely caused by the very large number of citations to **one** particular journal article published in 2003 (The structure and function of complex networks by MEJ Newman). In October 2007 this particular article had been cited 998 times, twelve times more than the next highest cited article published in 2003. In fact, in October 2007 the Newman paper alone makes up for 80% of the citations to *SIAM review* in 2003; the other twenty papers published in 2003 together have only 249 citations. This example clearly shows the danger of relying on mean-value metrics, which can be heavily influenced by individual outliers.

The Sociology/Geography outliers are caused by a less extreme occurrence of the same problem, i.e. very concentrated citation scores. For the *Annual Review of Sociology* for instance, the top 3 (out of 104) papers make up nearly one third of the total number of citations. Hence whilst its JIF may be reasonably high, its h-index is modest, as citations taper off quickly after the first highly-cited papers.

15.3.3 ANALYSIS OF INDIVIDUAL SUB-DISCIPLINES

The Journal Quality List includes journals in fifteen different sub-disciplines. However, for some of these sub-disciplines only a small number of journals are included, either because the sub-discipline is a very specialized area (e.g. Innovation, Entrepreneurship, Tourism) or because the Journal Quality List only includes a small subset of journals in the sub-discipline in question (e.g. Psychology/Sociology) that are relevant to Economics & Business. Overall, there are seven sub-disciplines that have a substantial number (more than 60) journals included in the JQL. These seven sub-disciplines cover 75% of the journals in the Journal Quality List.

- Economics
- Finance & Accounting
- General Management & Strategy
- Management Information Systems & Knowledge Management
- Management Science/Operations Research/Production & Operations Management
- Marketing
- Organization Studies/Behavior; Human Resource Management & Industrial Relations.

Table 2 provides some summary statistics for these seven sub-disciplines and show there is significant variability in terms of the proportion of ISI-indexed journals in the different fields, ranging from a low of 30-43% for Finance & Accounting, Marketing and General Management & Strategy to a high of 74-80% for Economics, Management Information Systems and Management Science & Operations Research/Management.

The sub-disciplines also differ in terms of the strength of correlation between the h-index and the JIF, varying from 0.633 for Organization Behaviour/Studies; Human Resource Management & Industrial Relations to 0.891 for General Management & Strategy, but in all cases this correlation was significant at p < 0.000. Below I provide a detailed benchmarking analysis for each of these sub-disciplines.

Table 2: Summary statistics

Sub-field	No. of journals in the JQL	No. of ISI-indexed journals	Spearman correlation b/w h-index & JIF
Economics	158	122 (74%)	0.732***
Finance & Accounting	94	28 (30%)	0.721***
General Management & Strategy	63	27 (43%)	0.891***
Mgmt Information Systems & Knowledge Mgmt	81	61 (75%)	0.774***
Mgmt Science; Operations Research & Mgmt	87	70 (80%)	0.733***
Marketing	65	25 (38%)	0.841***
Org. Behaviour/Studies; HRM & Industrial Relations	71	45 (63%)	0.633***
Others	209	158 (76%)	0.764***
Total	838	536 (64%)	0.718***

*** $p < 0.000$

ECONOMICS

Figure 3 (see the end of this chapter) shows the relationship between the Google Scholar h-index and the JIF for Economics journals. Most journals cluster around the regression line. Two important outliers that show higher journal impact factors than h-indices are the *Journal of Economic Literature* and the *Quarterly Journal of Economics;* both have a JIF above 4.5, but modest h-indices.

- *Journal of Economic Literature* publishes a relatively small number of articles per year (15-20), so that even though most of these are highly cited, it will be difficult for the journal to achieve a very high h-index. This is almost an exact counter case to the *American Economic Review*, which publishes around 160-170 articles per year that on average are not as highly cited as articles in the *Journal of Economic Literature*. Overall, however, the *American Economic Review* has a much larger total number of articles that are highly cited and I therefore argue that the h-index correctly identifies its more substantial contribution to the field of Economics.

- In the case of the *Quarterly Journal of Economics*, it seems that Google Scholar is at fault as it misses a number of highly cited papers in this journal. Its automatic parsing mechanism seems to have misclassified them under the wrong journal. For instance "Understanding social preferences with simple tests" by Charness and Rabbin (2002) is assigned to the (non-existing?) journal *Technology*. Several other papers are listed under their earlier (and highly cited?) publications as a

NBER working paper. In this case it is clear we should ignore the Google Scholar results and give preference to the ranking presented by the ISI JIF[2].

The other outliers are less prominent, though we can distinguish a number of health economics journals that are likely to display the high immediacy of Science journals and hence fare better on the 2-year JIF.

- The *Journal of Economic Geography* and the *Journal of Economic Growth* also publish a relatively small number of papers (15-25/year) and hence their JIFs are quite heavily influenced by a rather small number of highly cited papers. As a result their h-index is relatively low in comparison to their JIF.
- The JIFs for *Journal of Economic Geography* for 2004 and 2005 also seem to have been inflated by a highly cited editorial. As explained above citations to editorial materials and book reviews are included in the numerator of the JIF, but they are not included in the denominator, thus artificially inflating the JIF.
- *Demography* publishes a larger number of papers (app. 200 in 5 years), but also has a highly concentrated citation pattern, with its most cited paper between 2001 and 2005 taking up nearly 10% of total citations.

On the other side of the spectrum are *Review of Economics & Statistics*, *Research Policy* and *European Economic Review* that have a relatively high Google Scholar h-index in comparison to their more modest ISI JIF. The main reason for this appears to be that all three journals show a large number of citations in working papers and policy documents, or journals not covered by ISI. Hence the h-index captures their significant impact beyond academic journals.

FINANCE & ACCOUNTING

As Table 2 shows there are 94 journals in the Finance & Accounting category (93 excluding the *Journal of Finance*), but only 28 have both an ISI JIF and a Google Scholar h-index; only 30% of the Finance & Accounting journals listed in the JQL are ISI indexed. The correlation between the ISI JIF and the GS h-index for these journals is slightly higher than average at 0.721 (p < 0.000). Figure 4 (see the end of this chapter) shows that although many journals cluster close to the regression line, there are a number of significant outliers. Two important outliers on the left-hand side (i.e. higher JIF than h-index) are *Journal of Accounting & Economics* and *Review of Accounting Studies*.

- *Journal of Accounting & Economics* has rather variable JIFs. In 2001-2002 and 2004-2005 its average JIF was around 1.7 which would place it very close to the regression line. However, in both 2003 and 2006 its impact factor more than doubled. Reviewing the individual articles revealed a small number of highly cited papers in 2001 and 2005, which – given the limited number of papers published yearly in this journal – have a significant impact on its JIF.
- *Review of Accounting Studies* was only ISI indexed recently and only has a JIF for two years (2005/ 2006). Its JIF for 2006 is substantially higher than that for 2005. A review of individual articles published in 2005 showed one highly cited paper (The role of analysts' forecasts in ac-

---

[2] When we repeated the search for this journal in April 2008, its h-index had increased to 102 and all of the originally articles missing were correctly ascribed to the journal. It appears that Google Scholar is continuously upgrading its service.

counting-based valuation: A critical evaluation by Q Cheng) that with 78 cites in October 2007 made up nearly two thirds of the total citations to articles in 2005; the remaining fifteen articles on average had only 3 cites each. Again a concentrated citation pattern, combined with a small number of published papers (51 in 5 years) results in a high JIF without a similar impact on the h-index.

Important outliers on the right-hand side (i.e. higher h-index than JIF) are: Journal of Money Credit & Banking, Journal of Banking & Finance, Journal of International Money & Finance and International Journal of Finance & Economics. Papers in these journals often deal with issues relating to stock markets, credit rating and exchange rates and tend to be cited quite often in working papers (e.g. from the National Bureau of Economic Research) and policy documents (e.g. from the Federal Reserve Bank), or in journals not covered by ISI. As a result their Google Scholar h-index is much higher than their JIF that only measures impact in academic journals listed in ISI.

GENERAL MANAGEMENT & STRATEGY

As Table 2 shows out of the 63 journals in the General Management & Strategy category, there are only 27 (43%) that have both and ISI and a Google Scholar Ranking. However, for those journals that are ISI indexed the correlation between the JIF and their GS h-index is 0.891 (p < 0.000), the highest of all sub-disciplines.

It is therefore not surprising that there are relatively few important outliers in Figure 5 (see the end of this chapter). The main outliers on the left-hand side (high JIF in comparison to h-index) are two of the absolute top journals in the field of Management: *Administrative Science Quarterly* and *Academy of Management Review*, which have the highest impact factors of any journal in General Management & Strategy, but have a relatively lower h-index.

ADMINISTRATIVE SCIENCE QUARTERLY

With regard to *Administrative Science Quarterly*, this appears to be caused mostly by the limited yearly number of papers published. Even though most of the articles published in this journal are fairly well-cited, *Administrative Science Quarterly* only published a total of 92 papers (excluding editorials and book reviews) in the 5-year period and hence its ability to achieve a very high h-index is limited.

One should also consider that even in a top journal such as *Administrative Science Quarterly*, the citations received by individual articles are highly skewed: the ten most highly cited papers received 30% of the total citations, whilst the twenty most cited papers received 50% of the total number of citations.

Journal of Management, *Journal of Management Studies* and *Journal of International Business Studies* show h-indices comparable to *Administrative Science Quarterly*, even though they are generally seen to be slightly lower in standing. However, these journals publish about two (for *Journal of Management* and *Journal of International Business Studies*) to three times (for *Journal of Management Studies*) as many papers per year as *Administrative Science Quarterly* and hence have a higher likelihood of reaching a high h-index.

ACADEMY OF MANAGEMENT REVIEW

With regard to the *Academy of Management Review*, citations are even more heavily skewed than for *Administrative Science Quarterly*. The top 4 most cited papers (dealing with key concepts such as social capital, absorptive capacity and the resource-based view (2x)) provide 21% of the total number of citations. Surpassing even *Administrative Science Quarterly*, the 10 most cited papers provide 34% of the total citations and again the twenty (out of 153) most cited papers received 50%.

Hence even though at 46 *Academy of Management Review* has one of the highest h-indices for General Management journals, its concentrated citation pattern means that its h-index is low in comparison to its JIF. And even though with around 150 papers (excluding editorials and book reviews) over five years it publishes more articles per year than ASQ, its empirical counterpart (*Academy of Management Journal*) publishes twice as many papers as *Academy of Management Review* and hence has a higher likelihood of reaching a high h-index.

Furthermore, more than half of the *Academy of Management Review* papers are classified as either editorials or book reviews. Citations to these non-source materials are included in the numerator of the JIF, but the non-source materials are not included in the denominator. Normally, this would not result in a significant distortion of the JIF as these non-source materials tend not to be highly cited in the field of Management, but the paper-length introductions to the many special issues and forums are also classified as editorials and these pieces tend to be highly cited.

HIGH H-INDEX IN COMPARISON TO JIF

The larger number of papers published (200-550 papers over 5 years) is also likely to lie behind the relatively high h-index for *Strategic Management Journal, Harvard Business Review, Sloan Management Review, Journal of Business* and *Journal of Management Studies*.

Further, the two practitioner journals (*Harvard Business Review* and *Sloan Management Review*) are also likely to be more highly cited in scholarly policy documents that are not incorporate in ISI. The same is likely to be true for *Journal of Business* that has many papers that would be cited in working papers (e.g. from the National Bureau of Economic Research) and policy documents (e.g. from the Federal Reserve Bank). Further, the UK-based *Journal of Management Studies* is likely to be more heavily cited in non-ISI listed European journals.

Harzing and Van der Wal (2008) also showed that *Strategic Management Journal* scores much better in Google Scholar than the general management journals, because many Strategy and IB journals that would heavily cite articles in SMJ are not ISI listed. As a result *Strategic Management Journal* has a higher h-index than *Academy of Management Journal* even though its JIF is lower.

MANAGEMENT INFORMATION SYSTEMS; KNOWLEDGE MANAGEMENT

As can be seen in Figure 6 (see the end of this chapter), the various ACM Transactions (on Data Base Systems, on Software Engineering and Methodology, on Information Systems) generally have low h-indices compared to their JIF. The same is true for Information Systems, Information Systems Research, Human Computer Interaction, MIS Quarterly and the Journal of Database Management.

- For the *ACM Transactions* this is most likely caused by the fact that they publish relatively few papers (between 60 and 90 over 5 years). This means on the one hand that an individual highly cited paper can substantially increase the JIF for certain years and on the other hand that it is more difficult to achieve a high h-index.
- The same is true for *Human Computer Interaction* which has highly variable JIFs ranging from 1.95 to 4.78. Again, a small number of published papers (60, excluding editorials), combined with individual highly-cited outliers and a substantial proportion of non-source materials (editorials) which account for 10% of the citation count, drive up the JIF, whilst not having the same impact on the h-index.
- *Information Systems, Information Systems Research* and *MIS Quarterly* also have widely varying JIFs (0.90-3.33, 1.17-3.51 and 1.80-4.98 respectively) and although they publish a larger number of papers than HCI, the number of published papers is still relatively small (100-150) and individual highly-cited outliers as well as highly cited editorials can still have a substantial impact on the JIF in some years. In *MIS Quarterly* for example, the top 4 most cited papers published between 2001-2005 (out of 138 papers) make up 25% of the total number of citations in October 2007.
- The *Journal of Database Management* has only been ISI-indexed in 2006 and hence its high JIF score might be idiosyncratic. It also publishes few papers (about 15 a year) and hence its ability to achieve a high h-index is limited.

The various *IEEE Transactions* and *Communications of the ACM* have a high h-index in comparison to their relatively modest JIF. This is partly due to the fact that articles in these journals are often cited in conference proceedings, which are the most important publication outlets in this field, but are not included in the ISI citation count. However, this is true to a large extent for the ACM Transactions as well.

The main difference between the two groups of journals is the number of articles they publish. For the various *IEEE Transactions* this lies in the 350-600 range for a five-year period and for *IEEE Transactions on Automatic Control* even exceeds 1400, while for *Communications of the ACM* it approaches 1000. As a result, JIFs do not fluctuate as widely as for the other group of journals as they are not influenced by individual highly cited papers. On the other hand, the larger publication base makes it easier to achieve high h-indices, reflecting these journals' substantial impact on the field.

MANAGEMENT SCIENCE; OPERATIONS RESEARCH, OPERATIONS MANAGEMENT

As Table 2 shows out of the 87 (86 without SIAM Review) MS/OR/POM journals in the Journal Quality List 70 (80%) are ISI indexed. The correlation between the ISI JIF and the GS h-index for these journals lies slightly above the average at 0.733 (p < 0.000). and is highly significant.

As Figure 7 (see the end of this chapter) shows, both of the journals of the *Royal Statistical Society* as well as *Annals of Statistics* have relatively high JIFs in comparison to their Google Scholar h-index. This is caused by the fact that even though they publish a reasonably large number of papers, citations are highly concentrated.

For JRSS-A and Annals of Statistics 25% of the citations go to the top 5 most cited papers (out of some 150), for JRSS-B it is even only the two most cited papers (out of some 235) that make up 25% of total citations, with top-10 most cited papers making up 50% of the total number of citations. As we have seen before, a concentrated citation score will always artificially inflate the JIF and lead to a lower h-index in comparison to the JIF.

At the other end of the spectrum *Management Science, European Journal of Operational Research* and *Operations Research* have Google Scholar h-indices that are relatively high in comparison to their JIF.

- *Management Science* publishes a large number of papers (nearly 600 over five years) and has a very evenly spread citation pattern with the top 10 most highly cited papers in ISI in October 2007 having a very similar number of citations (between 41 and 55) and making up less than 10% of the total number of citations.
- *European Journal of Operational Research* publishes even more papers (nearly 2000 over five years) and show a similarly even spread in citations, with the top 10 most highly cited papers making up less than 5% of the total number of citations.
- *Operations Research* publishes fewer papers than the other two (but still nearly 400 over five years), but again has a very evenly spread citation pattern, with the top 10 most highly cited papers all having between 23 and 29 citations for a total of 13% of the total number of citations.

As a result the JIFs for these journals are generally very stable and not influenced by individual highly-cited papers. The large number of papers and even spread of citations ensures a high h-index, reflecting these journals' substantial impact on the field.

MARKETING

As Table 2 shows there are only 25 journals in the Marketing category that have both and ISI and a Google Scholar Ranking, 40% of the 65 Marketing journals in the Journal Quality List. However, for those journals that are ISI indexed the correlation between the JIF and their Google Scholar h-index is 0.841 (p < 0.000), the second highest of all sub-disciplines. It is therefore not surprising that there are relatively few important outliers in Figure 8 (see the end of this chapter).

The two top journals in Marketing, *Marketing Science* and *Journal of Marketing*, have JIFs that are relatively high in comparison to their Google Scholar h-index.

- *Marketing Science* has experienced an important increase in its JIF over recent years, from an average of 1.90 between 2001 and 2003, which would locate it close to the regression line, to an average of 3.72 between 2004 and 2006. This increase seems to have been caused by a dozen of well-cited papers, few of which, however, were cited often enough to become part of the h-index. However, with *Journal of Marketing, Journal of Marketing Research* and *Journal of Consumer Research, Marketing Science* is still one of the four journals with the highest h-index in Marketing.
- *Journal of Marketing*'s JIF has also increased substantially over recent years. After an average of 2.35 in 2001-2002, it was 2.85 on average in 2003-2004, which would pretty much locate it right on the regression line. It then jumped up to an average of 4.5 in 2005-2006. A more detailed analysis showed that this high recent JIF was mainly due to two highly-cited articles published in 2004 (which are in fact the two most highly-cited papers in the entire 2001-2005 period) that dealt with two key new issues in marketing: return on marketing and the service dominant logic. In October 2007 these two articles had a combined total of 200 citations, whilst the remaining articles in 2004 on average had about 10 citations. The recently released JIFs for 2007 show that *Journal of Marketing*'s JIF dropped from 4.83 to 3.75.

Industrial Marketing Management and *Journal of Business Research* are the two most important outliers at the other end of the spectrum with a relatively high Google Scholar h-index in comparison to their modest JIF. Both journals publish a relatively large number of papers (350 to 600 over five years) increasing their chances of reaching a high h-index. They are also cited quite often in journals that are not ISI indexed, such as *European Journal of Marketing*, *Journal of Business to Business Marketing* and *Journal of Business & Industrial Marketing*, which increases their Google Scholar h-index over their JIF and better reflects their overall impact on the field of marketing.

ORGANIZATION BEHAVIOUR/STUDIES; HRM & INDUSTRIAL RELATIONS

At 0.633 (p < 0.000) this sub-discipline has the lowest correlation between the JIF and the GS h-index, but it is still high and very significant. Excluding the *Human Resource Management* and *Journal of Organizational Behavior Management* outliers (see below) raises this correlation to 0.685 (p < 0.000).

As Figure 9 (see the end of this chapter) shows several journals have a high JIF in relation to their Google Scholar h-index. The most striking cases are *Human Resource Management* and *Journal of Organizational Behavior Management*.

HUMAN RESOURCE MANAGEMENT

Harzing & Van der Wal (2008) already noted the discrepancy between *Human Resource Management*'s JIF and h-index. Further investigation and an extensive email exchange with Thomson ISI representatives revealed that Thomson's search query for this journal's JIF included a substantial number of homographs referring to *Human Resource Management Review*, *Human Resource Management Journal* as well as books with Human Resource Management in their title.

As a result the JIF for *Human Resource Management* was erroneously inflated. In fact at 0.64 the recently released 2007 JIF for *Human Resource Management* is very substantially lower than the 2002-2006 JIF average of 2.00.

JOURNAL OF ORGANIZATIONAL BEHAVIOR MANAGEMENT

The JIF for *Journal of Organizational Behavior Management* has fluctuated wildly, standing at for instance 1.79 in 2003 and 0.11 in 2004. In 2004 there were only **two** citations to articles published in 2003 and 2002. In 2003 there were no less than 52 citations to articles published in 2002 and 2001. **All** of the 34 citations to JOBM in 2002 came from JOBM articles (i.e. a 100% self-citation on a journal level), whilst 11 of the 18 citations to articles published in 2001 came from within the journal. Further investigation showed that a very large proportion of the citations to papers in 2002 consisted of within-issue citations in a special issue. The third and fourth most cited of all papers in JOBM between 2001 and 2005 were published in this issue.

- For the first paper seven out of its eleven citations were in the same special issue (the other four being in later issues of the **same** journal).

- For the second paper four of its ten citations were in the same special issue (five of the remaining six were in later issues of the **same** journal).

- Two other papers in this special issue had four (three) of their four (three) citations within the same issue. Three more papers in this special issue each had two of their two citations in this special issue.

- The 8th paper in this issue had four of its four citations in one and the same later issue of JOBM. The ninth paper in this special issue had no citations[3].

Coincidentally, the special issue's topic was "The Search for the Identity of Organizational Behavior Management". Calling this special issue might well have been the best thing the editor ever did for the identity of the journal.

The journal's relatively low Google Scholar h-index is due to Google Scholar's less than complete records for this journal. Google Scholar appears to have processed the papers published in the special issue, but does not seem to have parsed the citations in these papers. In this case, however, I would argue that this is probably for the best and even though Google Scholar is to some extent at fault, it provides a more realistic assessment of this journal's low impact beyond a seemingly rather small academic circle.

OTHER JOURNALS

On the other end of the spectrum we find journals that have a high h-index in comparison to their JIF. *Journal of Human Resources* publishes many policy oriented pieces dealing with the public sector that are heavily cited in working papers and policy papers as well as books not included in ISI. As a result the h-index better reflects its impact beyond academia.

The *Journal of Business Ethics*, *Human Relations* and *International Journal of Human Resources Management*, all published out of Europe, combine a relatively large number of published papers with citations that are evenly spread across papers, as well as a high number of citations in European journals not indexed in ISI, all three of which increase their Google Scholar h-index in comparison to their JIF. Hence the h-index provides a more accurate reflection of their relatively broad impact on the field.

OVERALL CONCLUSIONS ABOUT SUB-DISCIPLINE ANALYSIS

Overall, we have seen that there is a very substantial agreement between the ISI JIF and the Google Scholar h-index for most sub disciplines. This means that for those sub-disciplines that have very limited ISI coverage (Finance & Accounting, Marketing and General Management & Strategy) the Google Scholar h-index could provide an excellent alternative for the 56-70% of journals not covered in ISI, especially given that for these disciplines the correlation between JIF and h-index for journals that did have ISI coverage ranged between .72 and .89. However, even for the other sub-disciplines the additional coverage provided by Google Scholar could be useful. Where the ISI JIF and the Google Scholar h-index diverged this was generally caused by one of two factors.

---

[3] It appears that the 22 within-issue citations were counted in 2003 rather than in 2002 and hence erroneously contributed to the 2003 JIF. An independent search with the cited reference function in the Web of Science only shows 2 citations to 2002 articles in 2003 (both in the same article, published in JOBM) rather than the 34 citations listed in the JCR.

FACTOR 1: JIF'S SENSITIVITY TO ONE-HIT WONDERS

The sensitivity of the JIF to individual highly cited papers, which - especially for journals that publish relatively few papers – artificially inflates the JIF in comparison to the h-index. Using mean scores produces distorted results if distributions are non-normal. In this respect, the h-index is a more robust measure. It is true that the h-index is influenced by the number of papers published and hence that journals that publish a lot of papers have a better chance to reach a high h-index. However, journals producing a larger number of highly cited papers have more impact on the field even if the average article in this journal is less highly cited than the average article in a journal that publishes fewer articles.

Journals such as Strategic Management Journal, the Academy of Management Journal, Organization Science and Management Science have higher h-indices than the Journal of Marketing and the Academy of Management Review (on average 55 versus on average 46), whereas they have much lower JIFs (on average 2.32 versus on average 3.95). However, as we have seen above, the high JIFs of the latter two journals are mostly caused by a very limited number (2-4) highly cited papers. Hence, I would argue that the h-index provides a more accurate picture of the generally very similar standing of these six journals.

FACTOR 2: GOOGLE SCHOLAR'S BROADER COVERAGE

The key reason why some journals showed a relatively high h-index in comparison to their JIF lies in the broader coverage of Google Scholar. There are four main aspects to this broader coverage:

- Some journals have a strong policy impact and their articles are highly cited in policy documents or NBER working papers, neither of which are included in ISI.
- Articles in other journals, often published outside North America, are heavily cited in non North-American journals that are often not ISI indexed.
- Articles in some journals, especially in the area of computer science/information systems, are highly cited in conference papers, which tend to be the most important publication outlets in this field.
- Finally, some sub-disciplines such as Strategy and International Business generally have a low coverage in ISI. As a result the h-index better reflect the broad coverage of these journals.

Overall, I therefore argue that the Google Scholar h-index provides a more comprehensive measure of journal impact, in terms of both the number of journals and the number of citations covered.

15.3.4   NUMERICAL ANALYSIS OF THE DIVERGENCE BETWEEN JIF AND H-INDEX

Above, I have documented a number of cases where the JIF and h-index diverged in considerable detail. Table 3 provides a summary of the 50 most prominent cases of divergence. It was constructed by standardizing both the JIF (after giving a 0 score for all journals without a JIF) and the h-index and subtracting the JIF from the h-index. Since Psychology journals differed considerably from all other journals and would make up most of the top 25 on the left-hand side, I excluded them from the analysis.

Most of these journals have been discussed in some detail above. Apart from apparent errors in the ISI JIF and one deficiency in Google Scholar coverage, the major reason for a high JIF in comparison to the h-index appears to relate to journals that publish a small number of papers and/or have highly concentrated citation papers, where the top 10 most cited articles provide the bulk of citations. As a result the mean-type the JIF presents a less accurate reflection of a journal's overall impact than the h-index.

Table 3: the 50 most prominent cases of divergence between JIF and h-index

JIF exceeds h-index (top 25)		h-index exceeds JIF (top 25)	
ACM Computing Surveys	-6.65	American Economic Review	5.30
SIAM review	-4.90	Journal of Finance	3.93
Quarterly Journal of Economics	-3.81	European Economic Review	2.77
ACM Transactions on Information Systems	-3.52	Communications of the ACM	2.70
Human Computer Interaction	-3.46	Review of Economics & Statistics	2.38
Journal of Economic Literature	-2.74	Research Policy	2.24
Academy of Management Review	-2.28	European Journal of Operational Research	2.10
Progress in Human Geography	-2.26	Econometrica	2.03
Human Resource Management	-2.09	Journal of Banking & Finance	1.89
Journal of Economic Geography	-2.08	Management Science	1.79
Annual Review of Sociology	-2.03	Journal of Public Economics	1.78
Marketing Science	-1.89	Journal of Political Economy	1.76
MIS Quarterly	-1.89	World Development	1.65
Journal of Economic Growth	-1.72	Journal of Financial Economics	1.63
ACM Trans. on Softw. Eng. and Methodology	-1.68	IEEE Trans. on Knowl. & Data Engineering	1.61
Journal of Database Management	-1.68	Economic Journal	1.59
Journal of Marketing	-1.58	European Journal of Political Economy	1.54
Annals of the Assoc. of American Geographers	-1.45	International Organization	1.50
Review of Accounting Studies	-1.45	International Jnl of Project Management	1.46
Environment & Planning D	-1.44	American Journal of Public Health	1.40
Journal of Org. Behavior Management	-1.40	Journal of Econometrics	1.39
Journal of Rural Studies	-1.36	Journal of Money, Credit & Banking	1.38
American Sociological Review	-1.28	ACM Trans. on Comp. Human Interaction	1.38
Administrative Science Quarterly	-1.26	Journal of Knowledge Management	1.38
Structural Equation Modeling	-1.15	Review of Economic Studies	1.35

Reviewing the journal titles in the right-hand column, the single most important determinant of a high h-index in comparison to JIF seems to be the extent to which the journal publishes policy oriented papers that are highly cited in working papers and policy documents. Publishing a large number of papers and being cited in conference papers and non-ISI indexed journals provide secondary reasons for a high h-index. Overall, the h-index might therefore more suitable to measure a journal's wider economic or social impact rather than its impact on an academic audience only.

As indicated above there are many journals, especially in Finance & Accounting, Marketing and General Management & Strategy that are not ISI-indexed. So how do these journals compare with journals that are ISI-indexed? As expected, journals that are ISI-indexed in general have a significantly higher h-index (23.5 versus 11.5; t = 15.002, p < 0.000).

But are there any non-ISI indexed journals with a relatively high h-index? In order to assess this I divided the journals by h-index into 4 equal groups. The quartile cut-off points for the h-index were 11, 16 and 24. Journals that ranked in the two top 50% (16 and above) in terms of h-index, but are not ISI-listed are listed in Table 4.

Table 4: Non-ISI indexed journals with a high h-index

Journal Title	h-index	Published in:
European Journal of Political Economy	28	Europe
International Journal of Project Management	27	Europe
ACM Transactions on Computer Human Interaction	26	USA
Journal of Knowledge Management	26	Europe
Empirical Economics	24	Europe
Accounting Horizons	23	USA
European Management Journal	23	Europe
Journal of Empirical Finance	23	Europe
European Journal of Marketing	22	Europe
Journal of Environmental Management	22	Europe
Journal of Financial Services Research	22	USA
Review of Finance	22	Europe
European Financial Management	21	Europe
Journal of Business Finance & Accounting	21	Europe
Accounting, Auditing & Accountability Journal	20	Europe
Business Strategy & the Environment	20	Europe
International Journal of Physical Distribution & Logistics Management	20	Europe
McKinsey Quarterly	20	USA
Academy of Management Learning & Education	19	USA
Electronic Markets	19	Europe
European Journal of Work and Organizational Psychology	19	Europe
Human Resource Management Journal	19	Europe
Journal of Industrial Ecology	19	USA
Journal of International Development	19	Europe
Management Accounting Research	19	Europe
Economics of Innovation and New Technology	18	Europe
German Economic Review	18	Europe
Industry and Innovation	18	Europe
International Business Review	18	Europe
Applied Financial Economics	17	Europe
Critical Perspectives on Accounting	17	Europe
Electronic Commerce Research	17	USA
Information Technology and People	17	Europe
International Journal of Retail & Distribution Management	17	Europe
Journal of Business Logistics	17	USA
Journal of Consumer Marketing	17	Europe
Journal of Financial Research	17	USA
Journal of Services Marketing	17	Europe
Journal of Supply Chain Management	17	USA
Managing Service Quality	17	Europe
Asia-Pacific Journal of Management	16	Asia
Business & Society	16	USA
European Accounting Review	16	Europe
Human Resource Management Review	16	Europe
Information and Organization	16	Europe
International Journal of Quality & Reliability Management	16	Europe
Journal of Business & Industrial Marketing	16	Europe
Journal of Computational Finance	16	USA
Journal of International Management	16	Europe
Journal of Public Economic Theory	16	USA

Journal of Travel Research	16	USA
Knowledge and Process Management	16	Europe
Management Decision	16	Europe
National Institute Economic Review	16	Europe

Journals with a high h-index that are not ISI listed occur in all disciplines, but are more frequent in the sub-disciplines identified above as having low ISI coverage. However, the single most distinguishing shared characteristic of these journals seems to be that they are published from Europe (usually by Blackwell, Elsevier, or Emerald) and generally have a European editor and a large proportion of non-US academics on the editorial board. Overall, nearly 75% of the non-ISI indexed journals with a high h-index are European journals.

I do not wish to imply that the ISI selection process is biased against non-US journals. Without knowledge of the actual number of European versus US journals submitted for possible inclusion in the database, it is impossible to assess this. European editors might display a self-selection bias and not submit their journals for ISI listing. Of course one reason for this could be the perceived bias against non-US journals. A similar debate is raging with regard to the representation of non-US authors in US-based journals.

15.4   DISCUSSION AND CONCLUSIONS

In this chapter I systematically compared the ranking of journals based on the traditionally used Thomson ISI JIF and the new Google Scholar based h-index. I have shown that any divergence between the two can generally be explained by either limitations in the way the JIF is calculated or by the more limited coverage of the ISI citation base.

I do acknowledge that our alternative metric disadvantages review journals with a small number of highly cited papers, but I conclude that in the field of Economics and Business in general, the Google Scholar based h-index provides a credible alternative for ranking journals. It addresses some of the statistical limitations underlying the JIF and is more suitable to measure a journal's wider economic or social impact rather than its impact on an academic audience only.

As such I argue that the Google Scholar h-index might provide a more accurate and comprehensive measure of journal impact and at the very least should be considered as a supplement to ISI-based impact analyses. However, even though an assessment of journal impact based on the journal's Google Scholar h-index might be more accurate and comprehensive than relying only on an ISI-based impact analysis, I would like to express strong caution against a single-minded focus on journal impact in evaluating individual scholars' research output.

Whilst journal impact can certainly be used as **one** of the criteria to evaluate research output, reducing the evaluation to **one single** number is unlikely to provide a complete picture of a scholar's real impact. Recently, many studies have established that highly-cited articles get published in journals that are not considered top journals in the field and a substantial proportion of the articles published in top journals fail to generate a high level of citations (see e.g. Starbuck, 2005, and Singh, Haddad & Chow, 2007).

Hence using journal proxies to evaluate the impact of individual articles can lead to substantial attribution errors. Unfortunately, the impact of individual articles is not generally known until quite some after their publication, making this measure more appropriate for decisions on for instance promotion or appointment to full professorial positions, than for tenure decisions.

15.5   REFERENCES

1. Harzing, A.W.K. (2007). **Journal Quality List**, 28th Edition, http://www.harzing.com/
2. Harzing, A.W.K. & Wal, R. van der (2008). **Google Scholar as a new source for citation analysis?**, *Ethics in Science and Environmental Politics*, 8(1): 62-71, published online January 8, http://www.int-res.com/articles/esep2008/8/e008pp5.pdf.
3. Singh, G., Haddad, K.M., & Chow, C.W. (2007). **Are articles in top management journals necessarily of higher quality?** *Journal of Management Inquiry*, 16(4): 319-331.
4. Starbuck, W.H. (2005). **How much better are the most-prestigious journals? The statistics of academic publication**. *Organization Science*, 16(2): 180-200.

Figure 1: *JIF versus h-index for all journals*

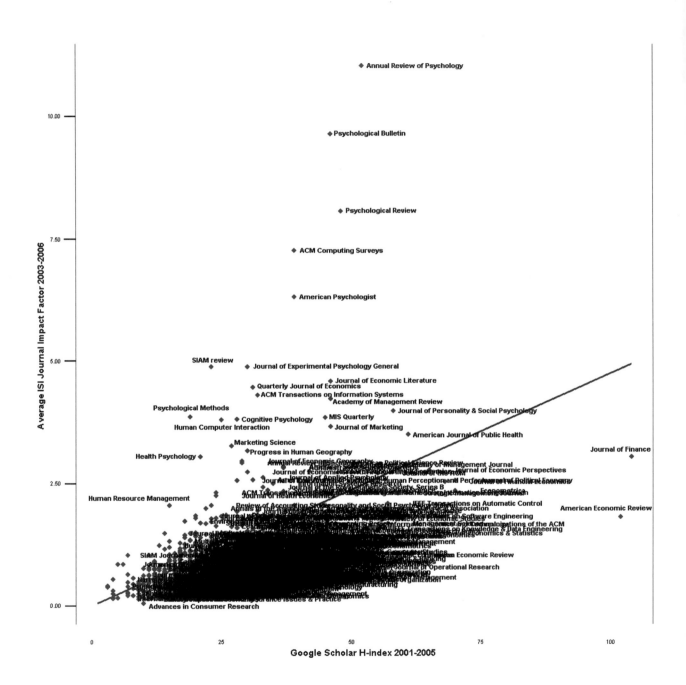

Figure 2:   *JIF versus h-index, Psychology journals and other outliers excluded*

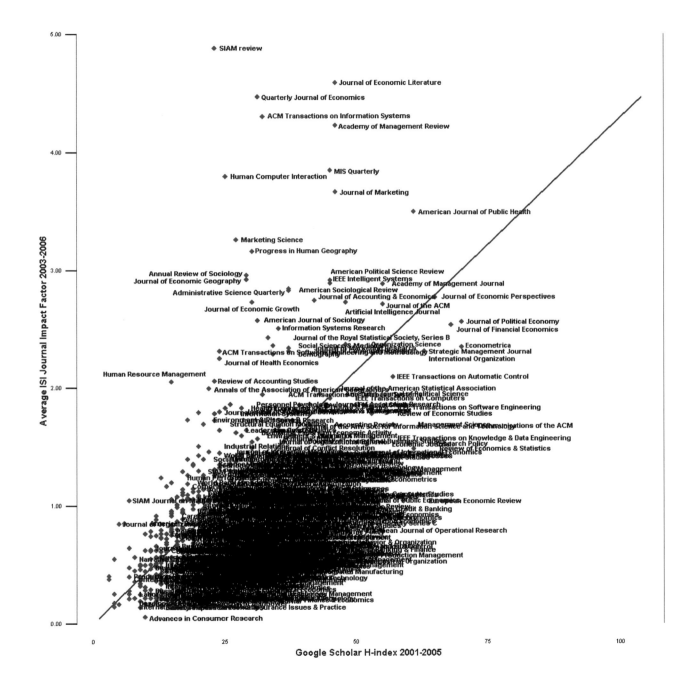

Figure 3: JIF versus h-index for Economics journals

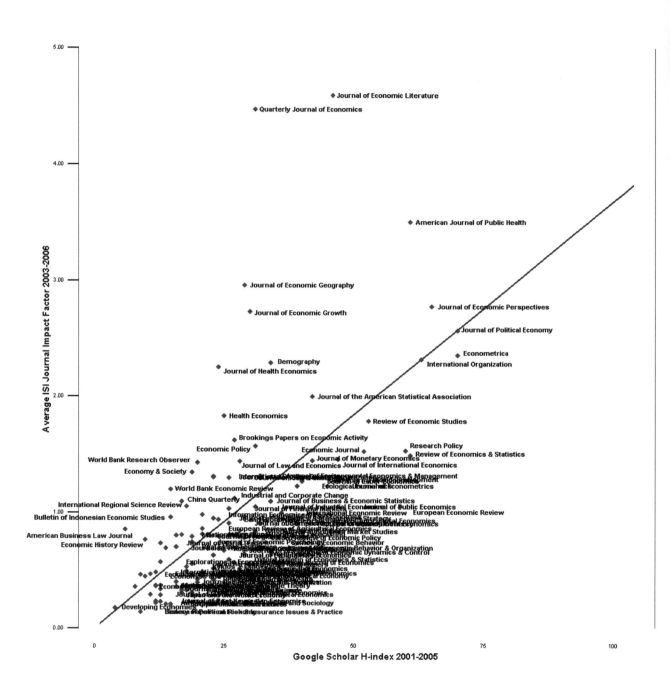

Figure 4: JIF versus h-index for Finance & Accounting journals

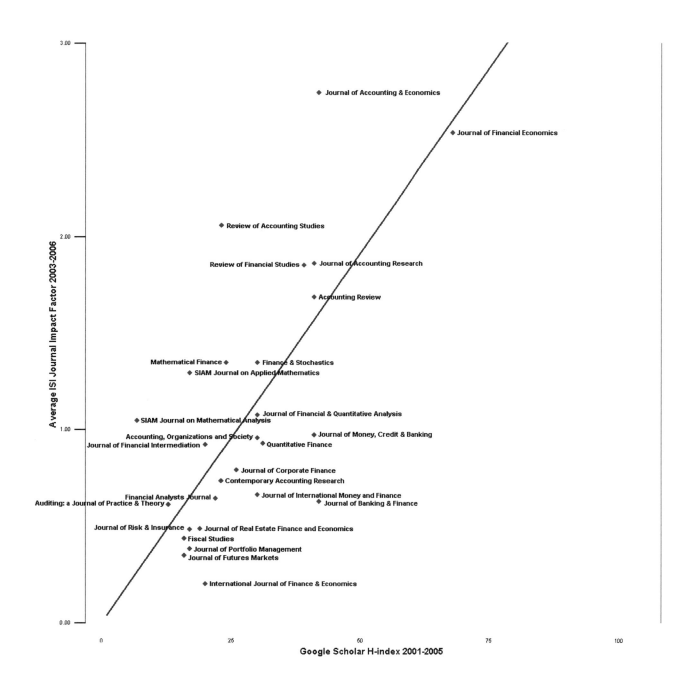

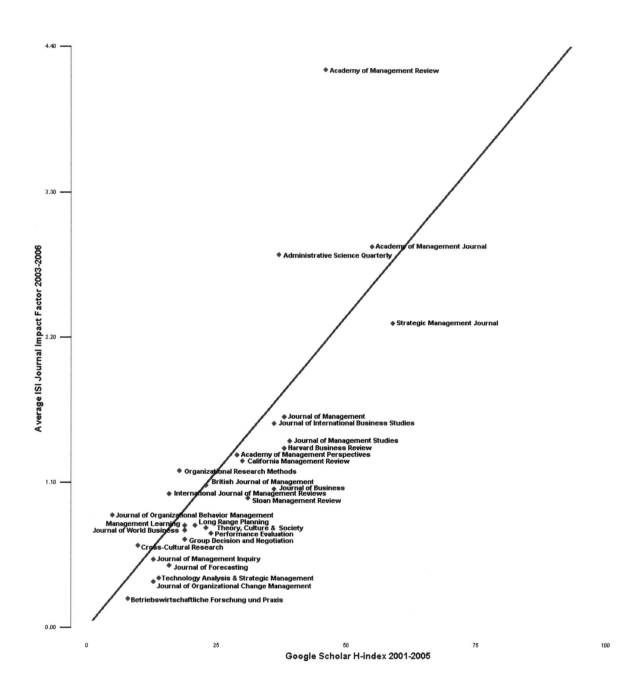

Figure 5: *JIF versus h-index for General Management & Strategy journals*

Average ISI Journal Impact Factor 2003-2006

4.40

3.30

2.20

1.10

0.00

◆ Academy of Management Review

◆ Academy of Management Journal
◆ Administrative Science Quarterly

◆ Strategic Management Journal

◆ Journal of Management
◆ Journal of International Business Studies

◆ Journal of Management Studies
◆ Harvard Business Review
◆ Academy of Management Perspectives
◆ California Management Review
◆ Organizational Research Methods
British Journal of Management
◆ Journal of Business
◆ International Journal of Management Reviews
◆ Sloan Management Review
◆ Journal of Organizational Behavior Management
Management Learning ◆ ◆ Long Range Planning
Journal of World Business ◆ ◆ ◆ Theory, Culture & Society
◆ Performance Evaluation
◆ Group Decision and Negotiation
◆ Cross-Cultural Research
◆ Journal of Management Inquiry
◆ Journal of Forecasting
◆ Technology Analysis & Strategic Management
Journal of Organizational Change Management
◆ Betriebswirtschaftliche Forschung und Praxis

0   25   50   75   100

Google Scholar H-index 2001-2005

Figure 6:   *JIF versus h-index for Management Information Systems and Knowledge Management journals*

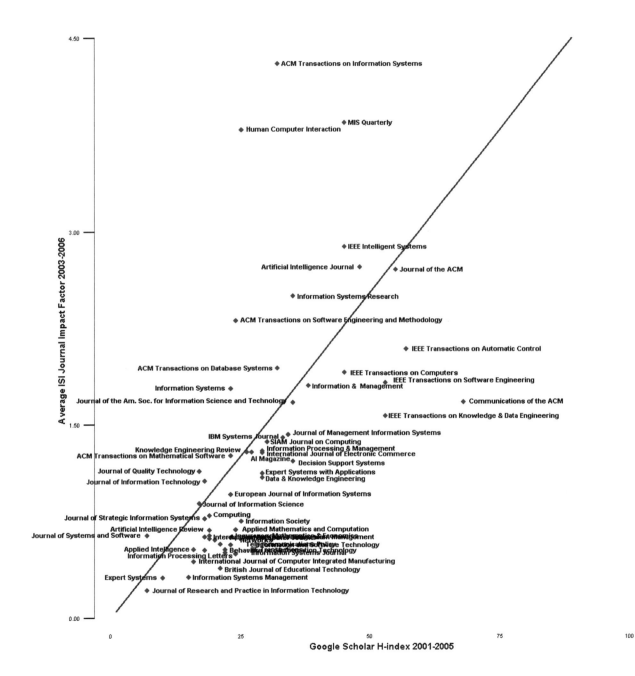

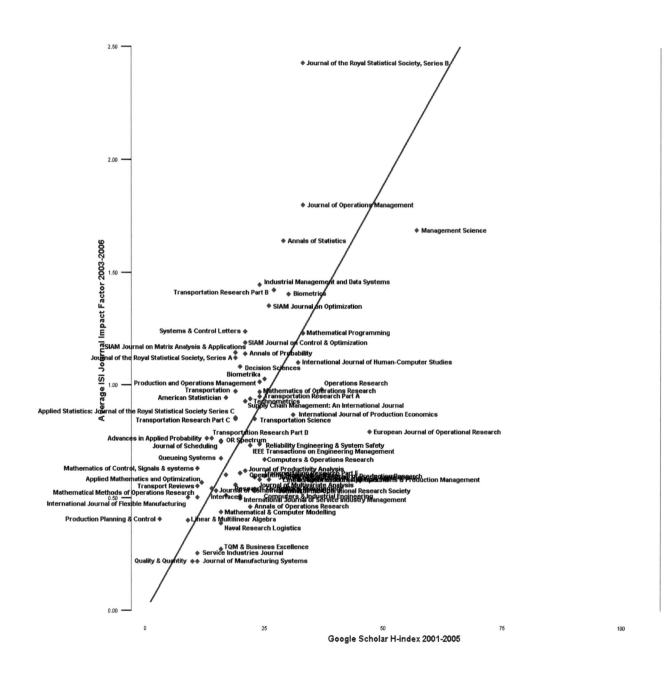

Figure 8:   *JIF versus h-index for Marketing journals*

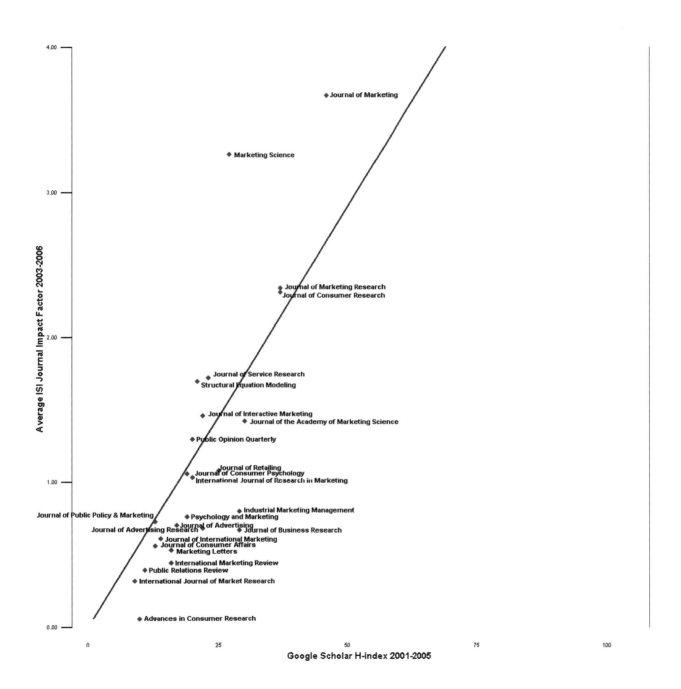

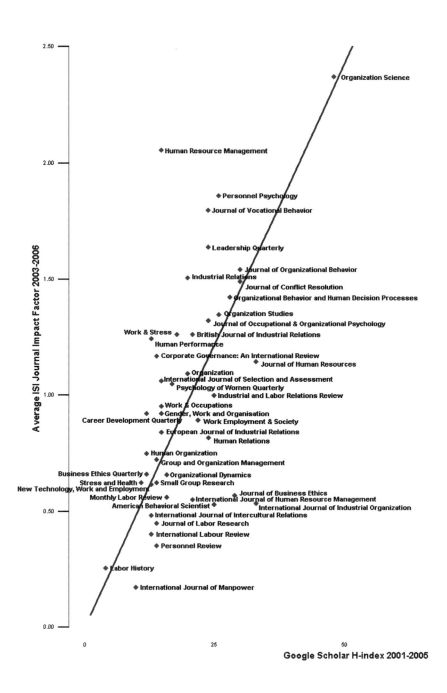

Figure 9: *JIF versus h-index for Organizational Behavior/Studies and Human Resource Management-/Industrial Relations journals*

CHAPTER 16:
AUTHOR CITATION ANALYSIS ACROSS DISCIPLINES

16.1   INTRODUCTION

Citation analysis is an increasingly common way to evaluate research impact. However, there seems to be a general lack of understanding of how different data sources and citation metrics might impact on comparisons of academics between disciplines. This chapter analyses the citation records of ten full professors at the University of Melbourne (Australia) in a variety of disciplines to illustrate how different data sources and different citations metrics might lead to very different conclusions.

The ten professors were chosen at random, but they were all established professors in their fields. In many cases they had high level positions such as Head of Department, Director of a major research centre, Associate Dean Research, Dean of a School or Faculty, or Deputy Vice Chancellor. One should therefore not necessarily consider their performance to reflect typical norms scores in their disciplines. There might be many excellent professors with lower research impact scores.

In addition, I do not claim that the academics used as an example in this chapter are fully representative of their disciplines. There are many performance differences even within the same discipline. However, the results presented in this chapter are fairly typical of the results I have gathered in nearly four years of research in citation analysis. This includes anecdotal knowledge gathered in responding to the many requests for assistance in using Publish or Perish, a citation analysis program using Google Scholar data.

16.2   DATA SOURCE COMPARISONS: CITATIONS ACROSS DISCIPLINES

Three different data sources for citation analysis are investigated in this chapter:

- Thomson Reuters Web of Science: Generally known as ISI Web of Science or ISI. This is the traditional source of citation data, established by Eugene Garfield in the 1960s. Many universities still use this as their only source of citation data. It has complete coverage of citations in the more than 10,000 journals that are ISI listed, going back to 1900. It is generally updated once or twice a week. Although its worldwide coverage has been improving recently, it still has a North American bias in many disciplines. It charges commercial rates for access.
- Scopus: Introduced by Elsevier in 2004, Scopus aims to be the most comprehensive Scientific, Medical, Technical and Social Science abstract and citation database containing all relevant literature, irrespective of medium or commercial model. It covers nearly 18,000 titles from more than 5,000 publishers. It also claims worldwide coverage; more than half of Scopus content is said to originate from Europe, Latin America and the Asia Pacific region. It is updated daily and charges commercial rates for access.
- Google Scholar: Introduced by Google in 2004, Google Scholar has become a very popular alternative data source, not least through the fact that access is free and citation analysis programs

such as Publish or Perish make bibliometric analysis easy. Some academics are skeptical about its wider coverage. However, studies (e.g. Vaughan and Shaw (2008) have found most of the citations to be scholarly. After a relatively slow start Google Scholar coverage is increasing, although Google still does not provide a list of its sources. Google Scholar is updated several times a week. For a more detailed analysis about Google Scholar as a source for citation analysis see Harzing & van der Wal (2008).

Table 1 reports the number of citations for our ten University of Melbourne professors. Definitions of data coverage of the citation data sources can be found underneath the table. As indicated above, most universities still use ISI as their primary or even only source of citation data. I will therefore first compare citation records for Scopus and Google Scholar with ISI citations records. Subsequently, I will compare the two different types of search functions in both ISI (General/Cited By search) and Scopus (General/More search).

Table 1: Number of citations for different disciplines using different data sources (May 2010)

Field	ISI General Search	ISI Cited by Search	Scopus General Search	Scopus "More"	Google Scholar Author
Cell Biology	2323	2334	1749	1765	2412
Computer Science	861	1130	1234	2445	6393
Mathematics	737	765	543	706	742
Pharmacology	6467	6725	3059	3173	5754
Physics	2508	2540	1950	2242	3153
Sciences	2579	2699	1707	2066	3690
Business	362	837	640	960	2245
Cinema Studies	43	269	6	6	1094
Education	144	781	273	944	4756
Linguistics	56	253	67	265	1803
Political Science	132	446	156	668	2540
Social Sciences	147	517	228	709	2485

- ISI General search = citations **IN** ISI-listed journals **TO** publications ISI-listed journals.
- ISI Cited by search = citations **IN** ISI-listed journals **TO** all publications (incl. non ISI-listed journals, books, conference papers, white papers, government reports). Please note that even in the "cited by" search function ISI **ignores** citations for second and further authors for non-ISI publications.
- Scopus General search = citations **IN** Scopus-listed journals **TO** publications in Scopus-listed journals.
- Scopus More = citations **IN** Scopus-listed journals **TO** all publications (incl. non-Scopus listed journals, books, conference proceedings, white papers, government reports). Unlike the ISI Cited By search, the Scopus More search is not additive, i.e. in order to establish an academic's total Scopus citations, one needs to add up the results from the Scopus General search and the Scopus More search.
- Google Scholar = citations **IN** all publications (incl. academic journals that are not ISI or Scopus listed, books, conference proceedings, white papers, government reports) **TO** all publications (incl. academic journals that are not ISI or Scopus listed, books, conference proceedings, white papers, government reports).

The difference in citation records between ISI versus Scopus varies hugely by discipline. For the academics working in the Sciences, Scopus generally finds fewer citations than ISI, with the exception of our Computer Scientist. For the academics working in the Social Sciences and Humanities Scopus generally finds more citations than ISI, with the exception of the Cinema Studies academic.

SCIENCES

As is readily apparent from Figure 1, the pattern of reduced citation scores for the Scientists is most pronounced for the Pharmacologist who sees his citations reduced by more than 50%. His most cited article has 919 citations in ISI, but only 248 in Scopus. The simple reason for this is that Scopus only includes citations from 1996 onwards. In fact, Scopus and ISI provide a virtually identical number of citations for this article from 1996 onwards. As this particular academic has been publishing for more than 40 years, his citation record in Scopus is very incomplete.

The Cell Biologist, Mathematician and Physicist also experience drops of around 25%, even though they have only been publishing for around 25 years. Again, this is caused by the fact that Scopus does not include citations before 1996 and all of these academics published some articles before this date. Comparison of individual articles published **after** 1995 shows virtually identical citation records in ISI and Scopus. If anything, Scopus tends to show a marginally higher number of citations for these articles.

Figure 1: Number of citations for ISI and Scopus General Search: Science disciplines

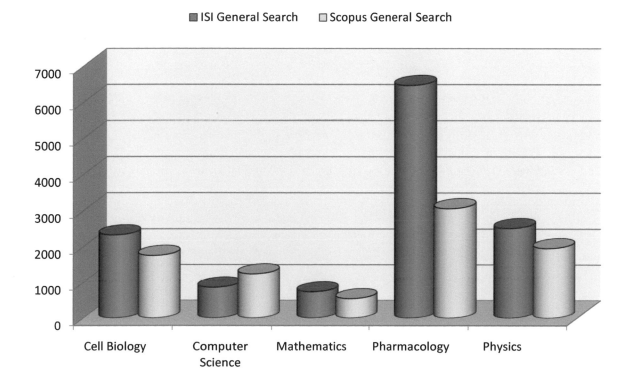

In contrast, our Computer Scientist sees his citations **increase** by 43% in Scopus. There are several reasons for this. First, although this academic has been publishing for 31 years, many of his most cited articles were published after 1995. Hence Scopus' restricted data coverage is not a problem. Second, the Computer Scientists benefits from the broader data coverage of Scopus in his field. Whilst ISI lists only 62 articles for him, Scopus lists around 100 articles. This difference did not occur for the other Science academics.

SOCIAL SCIENCES AND HUMANITIES

For four of our academics working in the Social Sciences and Humanities (Business, Education and Linguistics), Scopus finds more citations than ISI. As shown in Figure 2, this pattern is pronounced for the Business academic who sees her citations increase by 77%. As she only started publishing in 1995, the lack of citation coverage before 1996 is not a problem. Moreover, Scopus lists an additional 10 articles for her in journals that are not ISI-listed, but **are** included in the Scopus database. This includes her most highly cited article. In addition, because Scopus has a wider journal coverage in Business than ISI, citations for all her articles tend to be at least 10%, but sometimes 50% higher than citations in ISI.

A similar pattern is found for the academic working in Education. He even sees his citations increase by 90%, largely because Scopus lists more of the journals he has published in, but also because Scopus citations to articles listed in both databases are 20-100% higher than ISI citations. The Linguist and the Political Scientist only show a modest increase by 18-20% as for them better journal coverage in Scopus is counterbalanced by a reduction in pre-1996 citations. However, for the journal articles that are listed in both sources, Scopus generally provides 20-80% more citations than ISI. Hence journal coverage in four of the Social Sciences and Humanities fields seems much broader in Scopus.

Figure 2: Citations for ISI and Scopus General Search: Social Science and Humanities disciplines

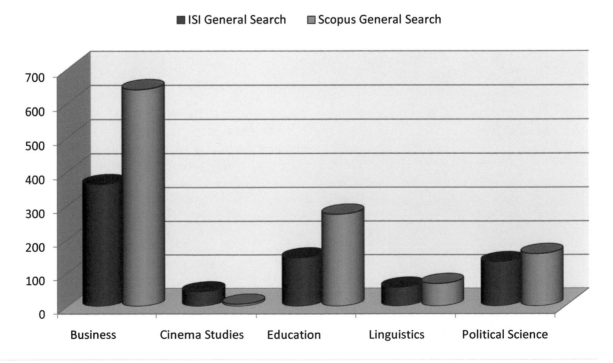

The Cinema Studies academic is worst off when using the Scopus database as nearly all of her journal publications date from before 1996, and the journals she has published in do not have pre-1996 coverage in Scopus. However, the only article by this academic that **is** included in Scopus has more citations than in ISI.

CONCLUSION

Comparing ISI and Scopus as a source for citations provides mixed results. In general, Scopus provides a higher citation count than ISI, **both** in the Sciences and in the Social Sciences and Humanities. In the Sciences, this increase in only marginal (except for Computer Science), whilst in the Social Sciences and Humanities, this increase is substantial.

Scopus appears to have a much broader journal coverage for the Social Sciences and Humanities than ISI and hence provides a fairer comparison. Whilst in ISI academics working in the Sciences have on average 17.5 times as many citations as the academics working in the Social Sciences and Humanities, in Scopus this difference is reduced to 7.5 times.

However, for the time being Scopus is hindered by its lack of coverage before 1996. This means that for most established academics in the Sciences, Scopus will lead to lower lifetime citation counts than ISI. In the Social Sciences and Humanities, a substantially increased citation count is likely for academics who have published the majority of their highly cited work after 1996.

16.2.2   GOOGLE SCHOLAR VERSUS ISI AND SCOPUS GENERAL SEARCH

As can easily be verified in Table 1, Google Scholar is the most democratic of the three data sources in that it provides the highest level of citations for all ten academics in our sample, with the exception of our Pharmacist.

SCIENCES

Even for the Pharmacist in our sample, Google Scholar only underestimates his citations by 10% and does much better than Scopus in this respect. The underestimation is most likely caused by Google Scholar's weaker coverage of older materials, which are not always available on the web. Since our Pharmacist has been publishing for over 40 years, some of his older work might not be covered in Google Scholar. This assumption is confirmed if I compare ISI and Google Scholars citations to his work in the last decade only. For the last decade alone, citations to his work in Google Scholar are twice as high as ISI citations.

As Figure 3 shows, overall, academics working in the Sciences do not show very significant differences between their ISI and Google Scholar citation scores. For the Pharmacist they are 10% lower, for the Mathematician and Cell Biologist they are only 1-3% higher. For the Physicist, citations in Google Scholar lie 25% above ISI citations.

As before, the Computer Scientist is the exception to this rule. In his case, Google Scholar citations are no less than 7.5 times as high as ISI citations. As for Scopus, this is partly caused by the much broader journal coverage of Google Scholar. However, in this particular case, a very significant chunk of the Google Scholar citations (more than 40%) are citations to a book that – as discussed below – is completely ignored in ISI.

Figure 3: Citations for ISI and Scopus General Search compared to Google Scholar: Science disciplines

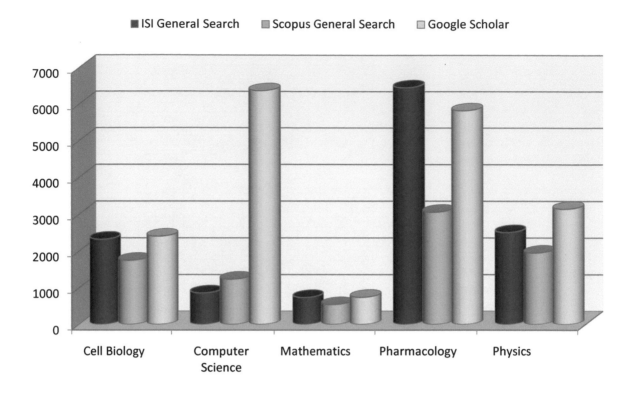

We have seen above that Scopus citation scores for the Scientists were generally lower than their ISI citation scores. Therefore, it is not surprising that their Google Scholar citation scores are substantially higher than their Scopus citation scores. For the Cell Biologist and the Mathematician Google Scholar citation scores are one third higher than Scopus citation scores, for the Physicist this is two thirds, whilst the Pharmacist has nearly twice as many citations in Google Scholar than in Scopus.

For the Computer Scientist Google Scholar provides five times as many citations as ISI, again reflecting the very significant number of book citations. So overall, although Google Scholar still has a slightly lower coverage of older publications than ISI, it is doing much better than Scopus in this respect.

SOCIAL SCIENCES AND HUMANITIES

As is readily apparent from Figure 4, for the academics working in the Social Sciences and Humanities, the differences between Google Scholar on the one hand, and ISI or Scopus on the other hand are much larger than for academics working in the Sciences. When comparing Google Scholar and ISI citation scores, the Business academic has six times as many citations in Google Scholar than in ISI. However, this difference is dwarfed by the increases for the Political Scientist (15 times), the Cinema Studies Academic (25 times), the Linguist (32 times) and the Educationalist (33 times). It is clear that for academics working in the Social Sciences and Humanities, a focus on citations to ISI listed publications only, severely underestimates their citation impact.

Figure 4: Citations for ISI and Scopus General Search compared to Google Scholar: Social Science and Humanities disciplines

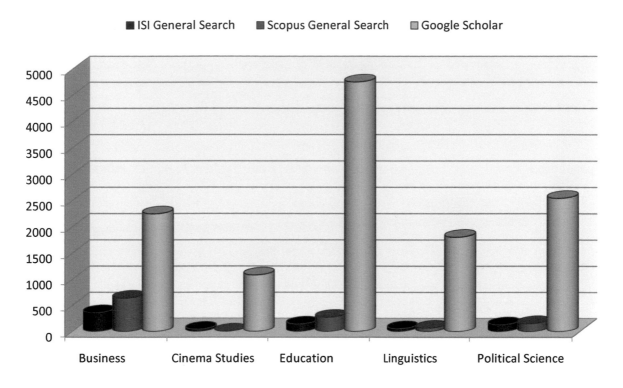

With regard to the differences between Google Scholar and Scopus, the Social Science and Humanities academics again follow a different pattern from most of the Science academics. Whilst for the Science academics differences between Google Scholar and Scopus are slightly larger than between Google Scholar and ISI, for academics in the Social Sciences and Humanities, they are slightly smaller, but still substantial in absolute terms. Differences run from 3.5 times as many citations in Google Scholar for the Business academic to 27 times as many for the Linguist. The Cinema Studies academic shows a 180 fold increase in citations, but that is caused entirely by the very incomplete coverage of her publications in Scopus.

CONCLUSION

Comparing Google Scholar on the one hand and ISI and Scopus on the other hand provides mixed results. For the academics working in the Sciences, Google Scholar's advantage over Scopus is larger than over ISI (except for the Computer Scientist). For the academics working in the Social Sciences and Humanities, this pattern is reversed in that Google Scholar's advantage over ISI is larger than over Scopus. However, in virtually all cases Google Scholar provide the highest citation count, reflecting its broader coverage in terms of sources compared to both ISI and Scopus and its longer coverage in time compared to Scopus.

Publication patterns in the Social Sciences and Humanities include a heavy emphasis on books and many of the journals in these fields are not listed in either ISI or Scopus. Publication patterns in Computer Science include a heavy emphasis on conference proceedings. Google Scholar therefore provides a much fairer assessment of citation impact for academics working in these disciplines. It includes citation in and to books, book chapters, government reports, conference proceedings, as well citations to and in academic journals not listed in ISI or Scopus.

So whilst in the ISI database academics working in the Sciences have on average 17.5 times as many citations as academics working in the Social Sciences and Humanities, in Google Scholar this difference is reduced to a mere 1.5 times. In addition, three of the Social Scientists (Business, Education & Political Science) have citation records that are higher than or comparable with three of the Scientists (Cell Biology, Mathematics, Physics).

16.2.3   ISI CITED BY VERSUS ISI GENERAL SEARCH

As indicated above, the *ISI Cited By* search function includes citations to non-ISI listed journals, books, book chapters and conference papers in addition to citations to ISI-listed journals (as in the *ISI General* search function). The difference between the *ISI Cited By* search and the *ISI General* search varies enormously between the various disciplines.

As is apparent from Figure 5, for four of our five academics working in the Sciences, there is virtually no difference between their citation records in the two different types of ISI searches. Their citation records increase only marginally by 0.5% to 4.0%. The simple reason is that in these four disciplines most journals are ISI listed and most academics only publish in journals. In fact, in these four cases the only **additional** citations in the *ISI Cited By* search function were caused by "stray citations", i.e. citations to ISI-listed journals that included either minor misspellings or referred to articles in press, and hence were not correctly merged into the master record by ISI data entry staff.

Figure 5: Citations for ISI General and ISI Cited By Search: Science disciplines

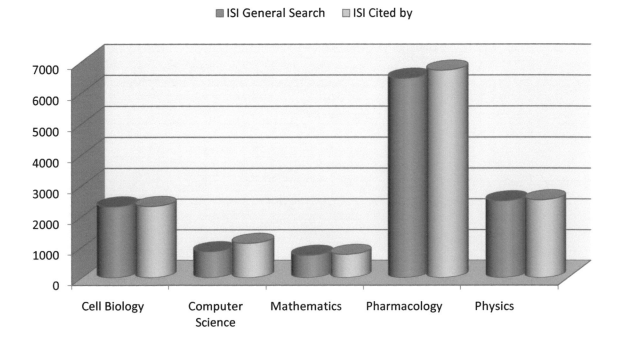

The fifth academic, who works in Computer Science, shows a fairly typical citation pattern for Engineering & Computer Science. He has a non-negligible number of additional citations in the *ISI Cited By* search function, increasing his overall ISI citation record by 31%. In fact, this still seriously underestimates his citation record **in** ISI-listed journals as it does not include the 700-odd ISI citations to a book for which he is the second author. As indicated above, ISI ignores citations to the second and further author for non-ISI publications. If these were included the Computer Science academic would see his publication record double between the two different types of ISI searches.

Figure 6: Citations for ISI General and ISI Cited By Search: Social Science and Humanities disciplines

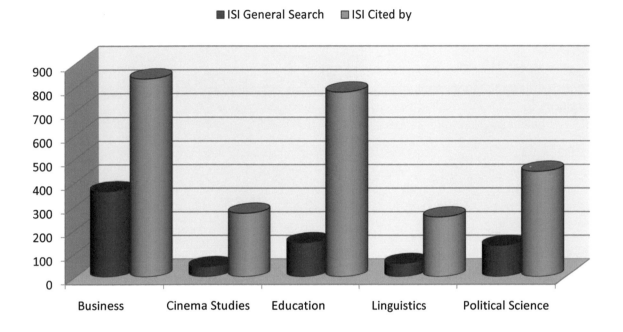

In contrast, as shown in Figure 6, our five academics working in the Social Sciences and Humanities show very large differences between their citation records in the two types of ISI searches. This difference ranges from having nearly 2.5 times as many citations in the *ISI Cited By* search function for the Business and Political Science academic, around 4.5 times as many citations for the Linguist, and 5.5-6 times as many citations in the *ISI Cited By* search function for the Education and the Cinemas Studies academic.

Consequently, the differences in citation records between the Sciences on the one hand and the Social Sciences and Humanities on the other hand are much larger in the *ISI General* search function than in the *ISI Cited By* search function. In the former case, academics in the Sciences on average have 17 times as many citations as the academics in the Social Sciences and Humanities, whilst in the latter case this is reduced to 5 times as many citations.

16.2.4   SCOPUS MORE VERSUS SCOPUS GENERAL SEARCH

Scopus has two search options that are very similar to their ISI equivalent, with the *Scopus General* Search function only including citations to Scopus-listed journals and the Scopus More function including citations to a wider range of publications. The difference between the two types of Scopus search functions still varies substantially between the various disciplines, but the differences are not as large as for the two types of ISI search functions.

Figure 7: Citations for Scopus General Search and Scopus More Search: Science disciplines

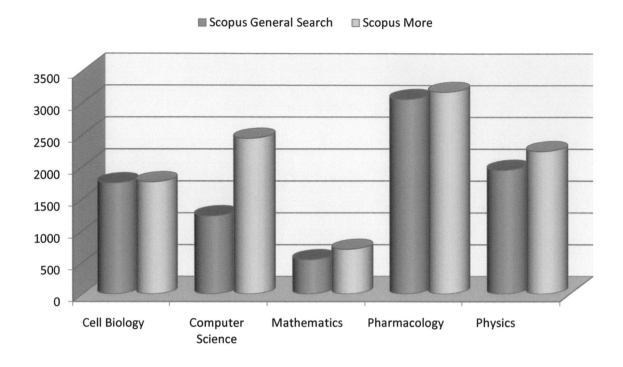

As Figure 7 shows, for two of our five academics working in the Sciences (Cell Biology and Pharmacology), there are very modest differences (1-4%) between their citation records in the two different types of Scopus searches. As for ISI, these were almost entirely caused by "stray citations", i.e. citations to Scopus listed journals that included either minor misspelling or referred to articles in press and hence were not correctly merged into the master record by Scopus data entry staff.

For the Physicist and the Mathematician, the increase is a bit more substantial with 15%-30% additional citations when adding the citations under Scopus *More*. For the Physicist and the Mathematician these differences are caused by not only by stray citations, but also by Scopus not correctly matching some relatively highly-cited Scopus-listed works to master records.

The Computer Scientist sees his citations double when adding the citations under Scopus More. In addition to stray and incorrectly matched records, this difference is caused largely by citations to a book (not included in the General search). Overall two thirds of the additional citations are citations to a single book.

As Figure 8 shows, differences are generally larger for our academics in the Social Sciences and Humanities, but again vary between the sub-disciplines. The Business academic only gathers 50% more citations, whilst the Education academic, the Linguist and the Political Scientist gather 3 to 4 times as many citations when adding the results of the Scopus More search. The Cinema Studies academic performs very poorly overall in Scopus, which seems to have a serious problem with coverage in this area.

Figure 8: Citations for Scopus General Search and Scopus More Search: Social Science & Humanities

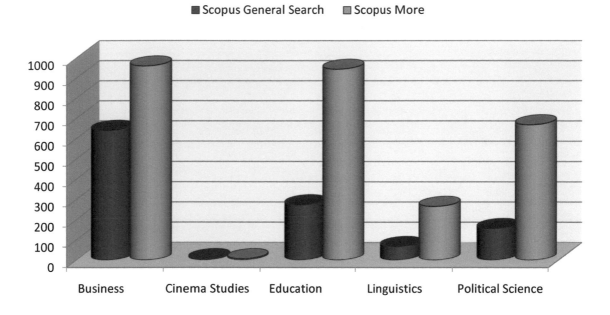

Consequently, the differences in citation records between the Sciences on the one hand and the Social Sciences and Humanities on the other hand are much larger in the *Scopus General* search function than in the *Scopus More* search function. In the former case, academics in the Sciences on average have 7.5 times as many citations as the academics in the Social Sciences and Humanities. In the latter case this is reduced to 3.5 times as many citations.

16.3   METRICS COMPARISONS ACROSS DISCIPLINES

Above I have discussed the impact of different data **sources** on the citation records of our sample of academics in the Sciences and Social Sciences and Humanities. Let's now look at different **metrics** for our ten professors, using the same database (Google Scholar). Table 2 provides a summary of the citation metrics. Below I will discuss each of them in turn.

16.3.1   H-INDEX

Proposed by J.E. Hirsch in his paper *An index to quantify an individual's scientific research output*, ar-Xiv:physics/0508025 v5 29 Sep 2005. It aims to provide a robust single-number metric of an academic's impact, combining quality with quantity. A scientist has index h if h of his/her Np papers have at least h citations each, and the other (Np-h) papers have no more than h citations each. Hence an academic with an h-index of 20 has 20 papers with at least 20 citations each.

Our ten professors differ substantially in their h-index, with the Pharmacist having an h-index that is more than three times as high as the Cinema Studies academic. On average the professors in the Sciences have a higher h-index (28) than the professors in the Social Sciences and Humanities (21). However, there are individual Social Sciences academics with h-indices equal to or higher than some of the Science academics.

Table 2: Citation metrics across fields

Field	Citations	h-index	# of authors	Hi-index	Hc-index	Hirsch's m	Indiv m
Cell Biology	2412	24	3.90	15	15	0.92	0.58
Computer Science	6393	34	2.57	22	22	1.10	0.71
Mathematics	742	15	2.95	8	8	0.63	0.33
Pharmacology	5754	39	3.08	23	18	0.93	0.62
Physics	3153	30	2.66	18	23	1.15	0.69
Sciences	3690	28	3.03	17	17	0.95	0.59
Business	2245	24	1.62	19	21	1.50	1.19
Cinema Studies	1094	12	1.14	12	9	0.36	0.36
Education	4756	28	1.51	25	25	1.00	0.89
Linguistics	1825	21	1.96	18	12	0.88	0.62
Political Science	2540	22	1.90	18	14	0.85	0.69
Social Sciences	2485	21	1.63	18	16	0.93	0.75

16.3.2   NUMBER OF AUTHORS

This metric calculates the average number of co-authors for the academic's entire body of work by dividing the total number of authors by the total number of papers. As is readily apparent from Figure 9, there is a fairly substantial difference between the Sciences and the Social Sciences and Humanities.

Figure 9: Average number of authors per paper in different disciplines

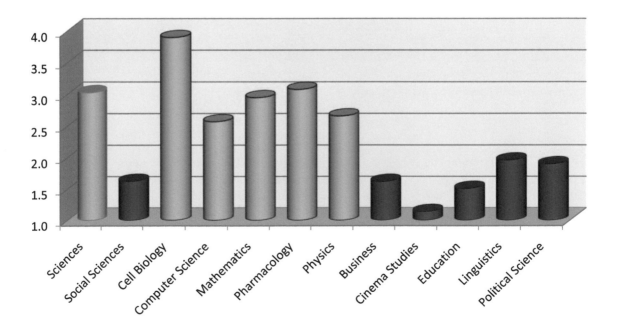

In the Sciences, papers on average have 3 authors (i.e. 2 co-authors), whilst in the Social Sciences and Humanities papers on average only have 1.6 authors (i.e. 0.6 co-author). However, there are substantial differences even within these broader categories. The Computer Scientist on average only has 1.5 co-author, whilst the Cell Biologist on average has nearly three co-authors. The Cinema Studies academic publishes virtually only single-authored work, having only 0.1 co-author on average, whilst the Linguist and the Political Scientist on average have nearly 1 co-author.

16.3.3   INDIVIDUAL H-INDEX

The Hi-norm corrects for the number of co-authors. I use the Publish or Perish alternative rather than the Batista et al. (2006) option. The latter divides the standard h-index by the average number of authors in the articles that contribute to the h-index.

The PoP alternative **first** normalizes the number of citations for each paper by dividing the number of citations by the number of authors for that paper, then calculates the h-index of the normalized citation counts. This approach is much more fine-grained than Batista et al.'s; I believe that it more accurately accounts for any co-authorship effects that might be present and that it is a better approximation of the per-author impact, which is what the original h-index set out to provide.

We have seen above that the number of co-authors in the Sciences is generally larger than the number of co-authors in the Social Sciences and Humanities. Hence, we would expect differences between disciplines to be smaller for the individual h-index than for the general h-index. Figure 10 shows that this is indeed the case.

Figure 10: H-index compared with the Individual h-index for different disciplines

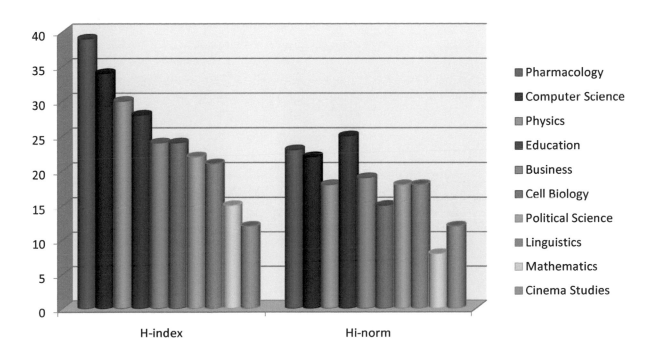

At 28 the average h-index in the Sciences is one third higher than the average h-index in the Social Sciences and Humanities at 21. However, the average Hi-norm for the two groups is virtually identical: 17 for the Sciences and 18 for the Social Sciences and Humanities.

16.3.4 CONTEMPORARY H-INDEX

The Hc-index corrects for the recentness of the citations, with recent citations carrying more weight. It was proposed by Antonis Sidiropoulos, Dimitrios Katsaros, and Yannis Manolopoulos in their paper *Generalized h-index for disclosing latent facts in citation networks*, arXiv:cs.DL/0607066 v1 13 Jul 2006. It adds an age-related weighting to each cited article, giving (by default; this depends on the parameterization) less weight to older articles.

The weighting is parameterized; the Publish or Perish implementation uses gamma=4 and delta=1, like the authors did for their experiments. This means that for an article published during the current year, its citations account four times. For an article published 4 years ago, its citations account only one time. For an article published 6 years ago, its citations account 4/6 times, and so on.

As the number of years that our academics have been active varies from 16 to 42, we would expect differences between them to be smaller for the Hc-index than for the h-index. Figure 11 shows that this is indeed the case. Our pharmacologist has been active for 42 and has the highest h-index. However, much of high highly-cited work was published a long time ago and his Hc-index is less than half of his regular h-index.

In contrast, the Business and Education academic have been active only 16 and 28 years and have recently published work that is highly cited. Hence their Hc-indices are nearly 90% of their h-indices. Differences between the Sciences and the Social Sciences and Humanities are smaller for the Hc-index (17 versus 16) than for the h-index (28 versus 21).

Figure 11: H-index compared with the Contemporary index for academics in different disciplines

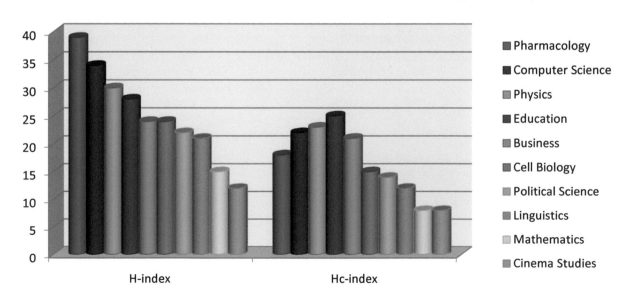

Proposed by J.E. Hirsch in his paper *An index to quantify an individual's scientific research output*, ar-Xiv:physics/0508025 v5 29 Sep 2005. It is calculated by dividing the h-index by the number of years the academic has been active. The latter is defined as the number of years that have passed since publication of the first paper. The Individual m is calculated by dividing the individual h-index by the number of years the academic has been active.

In his article Hirsch proposes norm scores for m for Physicists. He suggests that academics with an m of 1 can be considered to be *successful* academics, whilst academics with an m of 2 or 3 can be considered respectively as *outstanding* or *truly unique* individuals. To put this into context, consider that a popular physicist such as Stephen Hawking has an m of "only" 1.59. I would therefore suggest that we should consider an m of around 1 to reflect excellence rather than simple success in terms of research impact.

As can be seen in Table 2 and Figure 12, on average academics in both general fields have a very similar Hirsch's m index, with 0.95 for the Sciences and 0.93 for the Social Sciences and Humanities. This suggests that on average professors at the University of Melbourne should be considered to display excellence in terms of research impact.

Figure12: Hirsch's m and Individual m for academics in different disciplines

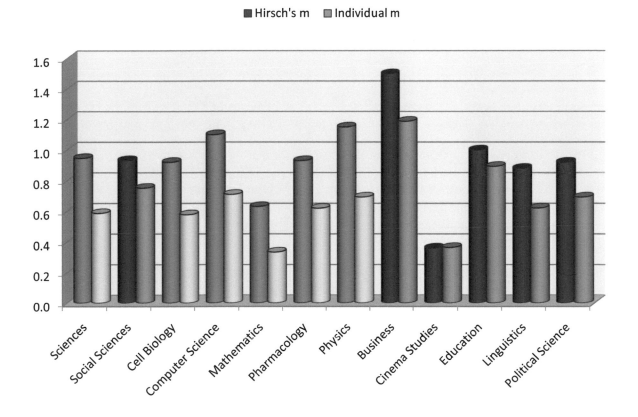

In fact, most of the individual academics hover around the m=1.0 mark, with only the Mathematician and the Cinema Studies academics scoring substantially lower and the Business academic scoring substantially higher. The latter case might be slightly anomalous as this academic has only been active for 16 years. She might not be able to maintain this level of performance over the next decades.

Looking at the individual m-index, which corrects for the number of co-authorships we see that on average academics in the Social Sciences and Humanities perform better than academics in the Sciences as their individual m-index is only 20% lower than their m-index, whilst academics in the Sciences experience nearly a 40% drop.

16.4   CONCLUSION

As a Social Scientist, my single biggest concern with the focus on research metrics is that ISI citations drawn from the ISI General search function (and their derivatives, such as the ISI h-index) are still the most commonly used metric. As the analysis in this chapter shows, this seriously disadvantages academics in both Engineering/Computer Science and the Social Sciences and Humanities as it underestimates citations records in these fields.

We started out our story with our professors in Science out-performing our professors in the Social Sciences and Humanities to a staggering extent, by having 17 times as many ISI citations. At the end of our story, we find that when using the most comprehensive data source and correcting for the number of co-authors and the length of the academic's publishing career, academics in the Social Sciences and Humanities on average out-perform academics in the Sciences.

The underestimation of research impact in the Social Sciences and Humanities might be even more pronounced in terms of research effort. A typical article in the Social Sciences and Humanities is 20 pages long and often requires three time-consuming rounds of revisions before it is accepted for a major journal. A typical paper in Medicine/Sciences is only 2-5 pages long and requires fewer revisions before it is accepted for a journal.

In addition, many academics in the Social Sciences and Humanities publish books that might run to 500 pages (still counting for only one publication). In fact, all of our Social Science and Humanities academics had published at least two books, which were generally amongst their most-cited works. Hence, even when one corrects for the number of co-authors, it is still not fair to compare the number of publications across disciplines.

On the other hand, one could argue that research in the Sciences generally requires larger amounts of funding. Hence academics in the Sciences might be forced to spend a large part of their time writing up grant applications rather than writing up articles, thus limiting their output.

So the inescapable conclusion is that one should not attempt to compare research performance across disciplines. However, I argue that the current emphasis on research metrics and the fact that most University administrators only know the ISI General search function seriously disadvantages the Social Sciences and Humanities. This chapter has established that with the correct benchmarks academics in the Social Sciences and Humanities perform at least as well, if not better, than academics in the Sciences.

So to cut a long story short:

- Academic performance in terms of citation impact can differ enormously depending on the data source and metrics used.
- It is not normally appropriate to compare citation records across disciplines. If one **has** to do so, Google Scholar is the most appropriate data source.
- The Hi-index and Hc-index (or Hirsch's m or Individual m) are more appropriate metrics to compare academics across disciplines and career stages than the traditional h-index.
- Academics in the Sciences out-perform academics in the Social Sciences and Humanities by a factor of 17.5 if one considers the traditional performance indicator: ISI General Search citations.
- Academics in the Social Sciences and Humanities out-perform academics in the Sciences when using a more comprehensive data-source and correcting for career stage and the number of co-authors.

16.6   REFERENCES

- Batista, P.D.; Campiteli, M.G.; Konouchi, O.; Martinez, A.S. (2006) **Is it possible to compare researchers with different scientific interests?** *Scientometrics*, 68(1): 179-189.
- Harzing, A.W.K.; Wal, R. van der (2008) **Google Scholar as a new source for citation analysis?**, *Ethics in Science and Environmental Politics*, 8(1): 62-71
- Hirsch, J.E. (2005). **An index to quantify an individual's scientific research output**, arXiv:physics/0508025 v5 29 Sep 2006.
- Vaughan, L.; Shaw, D. (2008) **A new look at evidence of scholarly citations in citation indexes and from web sources**, Scientometrics, 74(2): 317-330.

APPENDIX 1: LICENSE AGREEMENT

The Publish or Perish software is copyrighted. Its use and distribution is subject to the following license agreement. Unless otherwise noted, the Publish or Perish software and documentation were written by Tarma Software Research Pty Ltd. Copyright © 1990-2010 Tarma Software Research Pty Ltd. All rights reserved. The main source of information for the citations is Google Scholar, a service provided by Google. Tarma and Google are not affiliated. This program is provided courtesy of Harzing.com.

END USER LICENSE AGREEMENT

CAREFULLY READ THE FOLLOWING LICENSE AGREEMENT. YOU ACCEPT AND AGREE TO BE BOUND BY THIS LICENSE AGREEMENT BY CLICKING THE BUTTON LABELED "I ACCEPT" THAT IS DISPLAYED BELOW. IF YOU DO NOT AGREE TO THIS LICENSE, CLICK THE BUTTON LABELED "CANCEL" AND THE SOFTWARE WILL NOT BE INSTALLED.

LICENSE GRANT

"You" means the person or company who is being licensed to use the Software. "We," "us" and "our" means Tarma Software Research Pty Ltd. "Software" means the files distributed by us and our authorized representatives as Publish or Perish.

We hereby grant you a nonexclusive license to use the Software for private non-profit use. "Non-profit use" means that you do not charge or accept compensation for the use of the Software or any services that you provide with it.

The Software is "in use" on a computer when it is loaded into temporary memory (RAM) or installed into the permanent memory of a computer, for example a hard disk, CD-ROM or other storage device.

If the Software is permanently installed on the hard disk or other storage device of a computer (other than a network server) and one person uses that computer more than 80% of the time, then that person may also use the Software on a portable or home computer.

TITLE

We remain the owner of all right, title and interest in the Software and related explanatory written materials ("Documentation").

ARCHIVAL OR BACKUP COPIES

You may copy the Software for back up and archival purposes, provided that the original and each copy is kept in your possession and that your installation and use of the Software does not exceed that allowed in the "License Grant" section above.

THINGS YOU MAY NOT DO

The Software and Documentation are protected by Australian copyright laws and international treaties. You must treat the Software and Documentation like any other copyrighted material, for example a book. You may not:

- copy the Documentation,
- copy the Software except to make archival or backup copies as provided above,
- modify or adapt the Software or merge it into another program,
- reverse engineer, disassemble, decompile or make any attempt to discover the source code of the Software,
- place the Software onto a server so that it is accessible via a public network such as the Internet, or
- sublicense, rent, lease or lend any portion of the Software or Documentation.

TRANSFERS

You may transfer all your rights to use the Software and Documentation to another person or legal entity provided you transfer this Agreement, the Software and Documentation, including all copies, updates and prior versions to such person or entity and that you retain no copies, including copies stored on computer.

LIMITED WARRANTY

We warrant that for a period of 30 days after delivery of this copy of the Software to you:

- the media on which this copy of the Software is provided to you will be free from defects in materials and workmanship under normal use, and
- the Software will perform in substantial accordance with the Documentation.

To the extent permitted by applicable law, THE FOREGOING LIMITED WARRANTY IS IN LIEU OF ALL OTHER WARRANTIES OR CONDITIONS, EXPRESS OR IMPLIED, AND WE DISCLAIM ANY AND ALL IMPLIED WARRANTIES OR CONDITIONS, INCLUDING ANY IMPLIED WARRANTY OF TITLE, NONINFRINGEMENT, MERCHANTABILITY OR FITNESS FOR A PARTICULAR PURPOSE, regardless of whether we know or had reason to know of your particular needs. No employee, agent, dealer or distributor of ours is authorized to modify this limited warranty, nor to make any additional warranties.

SOME COUNTRIES OR STATES DO NOT ALLOW THE LIMITATION OR EXCLUSION OF LIABILITY FOR INCIDENTAL OR CONSEQUENTIAL DAMAGES, SO THE ABOVE LIMITATION MAY NOT APPLY TO YOU.

LIMITED REMEDY

Our entire liability and your exclusive remedy for breach of the foregoing warranty shall be, at our option, to either:

- return the price you paid, or

- repair or replace the Software or media that does not meet the foregoing warranty if it is returned to us with a copy of your receipt.

IN NO EVENT WILL WE BE LIABLE TO YOU FOR ANY DAMAGES, INCLUDING ANY LOST PROFITS, LOST SAVINGS, OR OTHER INCIDENTAL OR CONSEQUENTIAL DAMAGES ARISING FROM THE USE OR THE INABILITY TO USE THE SOFTWARE (EVEN IF WE OR AN AUTHORIZED DEALER OR DISTRIBUTOR HAS BEEN ADVISED OF THE POSSIBILITY OF THESE DAMAGES), OR FOR ANY CLAIM BY ANY OTHER PARTY.

SOME COUNTRIES OR STATES DO NOT ALLOW THE LIMITATION OR EXCLUSION OF LIABILITY FOR INCIDENTAL OR CONSEQUENTIAL DAMAGES, SO THE ABOVE LIMITATION MAY NOT APPLY TO YOU.

TERM AND TERMINATION

This license agreement takes effect upon your use of the software and remains effective until terminated. You may terminate it at any time by destroying all copies of the Software and Documentation in your possession. It will also automatically terminate if you fail to comply with any term or condition of this license agreement. You agree on termination of this license to destroy all copies of the Software and Documentation in your possession.

CONFIDENTIALITY

The Software contains trade secrets and proprietary know-how that belong to us and it is being made available to you in strict confidence. ANY USE OR DISCLOSURE OF THE SOFTWARE, OR OF ITS ALGORITHMS, PROTOCOLS OR INTERFACES, OTHER THAN IN STRICT ACCORDANCE WITH THIS LICENSE AGREEMENT, MAY BE ACTIONABLE AS A VIOLATION OF OUR TRADE SECRET RIGHTS.

GENERAL PROVISIONS

1. This written license agreement is the exclusive agreement between you and us concerning the Software and Documentation and supersedes any prior purchase order, communication, advertising or representation concerning the Software.
2. This license agreement may be modified only by a writing signed by you and us.
3. In the event of litigation between you and us concerning the Software or Documentation, the prevailing party in the litigation will be entitled to recover attorney fees and expenses from the other party.
4. This license agreement is governed by the laws of the State of Victoria, Australia, and the federal laws of Australia.
5. You agree that the Software will not be shipped, transferred or exported into any country or used in any manner prohibited by the United States Export Administration Act or any other export laws, restrictions or regulations.

APPENDIX 2: COMMAND REFERENCE

Publish or Perish commands can be reached through the main window (click on the appropriate button) or through the main menu (hit F10, or Alt+*first letter*, or click with the mouse).

Command	Description		Shortcut
Save As BibTeX...	Saves the currently checked citations in BibTeX format, encoded as Unicode UTF-8.		
Save As CSV...	Saves the currently checked citations in comma-separated format, encoded as Unicode UTF-8.		Ctrl+S
Save As EndNote...	Saves the currently checked citations in EndNote Import format, encoded as Unicode UTF-8.		Ctrl+Shift+S
Save As RIS...	Saves the currently checked citations in Reference Manager (RIS) format, encoded as Unicode UTF-8.		
Exit	Exits the program.		Alt+F4

EDIT MENU

Command	Description		Shortcut
Cut	Copies the currently selected text to the Windows clipboard, then deletes the text from the text field.		Ctrl+X
Copy	Copies the currently selected text to the Windows clipboard.		Ctrl+C
Paste	Paste any text on the Windows clipboard into the text field.		Ctrl+V
Delete	Delete the currently selected text from the text field.		Del
Copy Statistics	As Text	Copy the current statistics (only) as text to the Windows clipboard, from where they can be pasted into another application.	
	As CSV	Copy the current statistics (only) in CSV (Comma-Separated Value) format to the Windows clipboard, from where they can be pasted into another application.	
	As CSV with Header	Ditto, but prepends a comma-separated line that describes each of the fields on the subsequent data line.	
	For Excel	Copy the current statistics (only) in tab-separated format to the Windows clipboard, from where they can be pasted into another application, in particular into spreadsheet programs such as Microsoft Excel or OpenOffice Calc.	
	For Excel with Header	Ditto, but prepends a tab-separated line that describes each of the fields on the subsequent data line.	

Copy Results	As Text	Copy the current citation analysis data as text to the Windows clipboard, from where they can be pasted into other applications. This command combines the statistics (as per **Copy Statistics>As Text**) with the actual citations (as per **Save As CSV**).	Ctrl+Shift +C
	As CSV	Copy the current citation analysis data in CSV (Comma-Separated Value) format to the Windows clipboard, from where they can be pasted into another application.	
	As CSV with Header	Ditto, but prepends a comma-separated line that describes each of the fields on the subsequent data lines.	
	For Excel	Copy the current citation analysis data in tab-delimited format to the Windows clipboard, from where they can be pasted into another application, in particular into spreadsheet programs such as Microsoft Excel or OpenOffice Calc.	
	For Excel with Header	Ditto, but prepends a tab-separated line that describes each of the fields on the subsequent data lines.	
Split Citations		Splits the selected merged citations into their original items.	
Check/ SelectAll		Checks all citations in the Results list and recalculates citation statistics.	Ctrl+A
Check Selection		Checks all citations that are currently selected (i.e., highlighted) and recalculates the citation statistics.	Num +
Uncheck All		Unchecks all citations in the **Results** list & recalculates citation statistics.	Ctrl+U
Uncheck 0 Cites		Unchecks all citations in the **Results** list with 0 citations and recalculates the citation statistics. This is useful to exclude spurious references that Google Scholar sometimes returns.	Ctrl+0
Uncheck Selection		Unchecks all citations that are currently selected (i.e., highlighted) and recalculates the citation statistics.	Num -
Properties		Opens the properties dialog box for the currently selected item. This current applies only to the Query folder and Query items on the Multi-query pane, and has the same effect as clicking the **Edit...** button in that pane.	

VIEW MENU

Command	Description	Shortcut
Next Page	Displays the next query page (in the sequence author impact, journal impact, general search, multi-query).	Ctrl+PageDown
Previous Page	Displays the previous query page (in the opposite order as above).	Ctrl+PageUp
Author Impact Analysis	Displays the Author impact analysis page	
Journal Impact Analysis	Displays the Journal impact analysis page	

General Citation Search	Displays the General citation search page
Multi-Query Center	Displays the Multi-query center page
Open Article in Browser	Opens your web browser and displays the currently selected article or its abstract. This command is only available for articles for which Google Scholar returned an article URL.
Open Citations/ Related in Browser	Opens your web browser and displays a Google Scholar web page that contains the citations to the currently selected article. If the article has no citations, a web page with related articles is displayed instead, if available.

TOOLS MENU

Command	Description	Shortcut
Check for Updates	Contacts the Publish or Perish web site to see if any software updates are available. If so, you will be asked if you want to download and install these updates.	
Check for Announcements	Contacts the Publish or Perish web site to see if any new announcements are available. If so, they will be downloaded automatically and displayed in the announcements panel. The Publish or Perish software executes this command automatically once a day if the software is running.	
Send Feedback	Opens your email client and starts an email message to pop@harzing.com in which you can provide feedback about the program.	
Report Error	Generates an error report about the most recently encountered query error, then opens your email client and starts an email message to pop@harzing.com in which you can describe the problem.	
Preferences	Opens the General preferences and Queries preferences property sheets that allow you to edit some general program settings.	

HELP MENU

Command	Description	Shortcut
Contents	Opens this help file on the About Publish or Perish page.	F1
What's New	Opens the What's New? help page	
Publish or Perish Home Page	Opens your web browser and displays the Publish or Perish page on the Harzing.com web site.	
Publish or Perish FAQ	Opens your web browser and displays the Publish or Perish Frequently Asked Questions page on the Harzing.com web site.	
About Publish or Perish	Opens the **About Publish or Perish** dialog box that displays the program's version and some other information.	

APPENDIX 3:
POP-UP MENU RESULTS PAGE

Command	Description
Split Citations	If the currently selected results line consists of merged items, undoes the merge. The original items are shown again in the list. This command is only available for merged items.
Open Article in Browser	Opens the currently selected article in your web browser. This command is only available for some items (depending on the information that Google Scholar provided) and may actually open the abstract rather than the full article.
Open Citations/Related in Browser	Opens the Google Scholar web page that lists the referencing articles for the current item, if available. In absence of that, opens the Google Scholar "related" web page, if available.
Copy Statistics as Text	Copies the citation metrics (from the upper text field) to the Windows clipboard in plain text format. You can then paste this text into other applications.
Copy Statistics as CSV	Copies the citation metrics (from the upper text field) to the Windows clipboard in CSV (comma-separated value) format. You can then paste this into other applications for further processing.
Copy Statistics as CSV with Header	Does the same as the previous command, but precedes the statistics with an extra line that contains the names of the fields, also in comma-separated format.
Copy Statistics for Excel	Copies the citation metrics (from the upper text field) to the Windows clipboard in tab-separated format. You can then paste this into other applications for further processing, and in particular into spreadsheet applications such as Microsoft Excel, OpenOffice Calc, and SoftMaker's PlanMaker.
Copy Statistics for Excel with Header	Does the same as the previous command, but precedes the statistics with an extra line that contains the names of the fields, also in tab-separated format.
Copy Results as Text	Copies the results (from the lower list) to the Windows clipboard in plain text format. You can then paste this text into other applications.
Copy Results as CSV	Copies the results (from the lower list) to the Windows clipboard in CSV (comma-separated value) format. You can then paste this into other applications for further processing.
Copy Results as CSV with Header	Does the same as the previous command, but precedes the statistics with an extra line that contains the names of the fields, also in comma-separated format.
Copy Results for Excel	Copies the results (from the lower list) to the Windows clipboard in tab-separated format. You can then paste this into other applications for further processing, and in particular into spreadsheet applications such as Microsoft Excel, OpenOffice Calc,

	and SoftMaker's PlanMaker.
Copy Results for Excel with Header	Does the same as the previous command, but precedes the statistics with an extra line that contains the names of the fields, also in tab-separated format.
Check/Select All	Checks all items in the results list. Alternatively, press Ctrl+A.
Check Selection	Checks all selected (i.e., highlighted) items in the results list.
Uncheck All	Unchecks all items in the results list. Alternatively, press Ctrl+U.
Uncheck 0 Cites	Unchecks all results that have 0 citations. Alternatively, press Ctrl+0 (that's zero, not Oh).
Uncheck Selection	Unchecks all selected (i.e., highlighted) items in the results list.
Save As BiBTeX...	Saves the currently checked citations in BibTeX format, encoded as Unicode UTF-8.
Save As CSV...	Saves the currently checked citations in comma-separated format, encoded as Unicode UTF-8.
Save As End-Note...	Saves the currently checked citations in EndNote Import format, encoded as Unicode UTF-8.
Save As RIS...	Saves the currently checked citations in Reference Manager (RIS) format, encoded as Unicode UTF-8.

APPENDIX 4: EXPORT FORMATS

BIBTEX FORMAT DETAILS

The BibTeX format is defined in a variety of locations with varying level of detail; we have used Bib-TeX.org and Wikipedia.

Publish or Perish writes all BibTeX format files as plain text Unicode files, encoded as UTF-8 with the UTF-8 BOM (0xEF 0xBB 0xBF) at the start of the file. As of Publish or Perish version 2.2, if a field contains embedded '\' or '&' characters, they are escaped by prefixing them with another '\' to avoid misinterpretation as commands or control codes.

For each citation entry, Publish or Perish creates one of the following BibTeX entries:

BibTeX entry	Used for	Notes
@article	Journal articles	Used if the Publication field is present.
@book	Book	Used if the Publication field is empty, but the Publisher field is present.
@misc	Various	Used if none of the above applies.

For each BibTeX entry, Publish or Perish generates a citation key in the format *popxxxx* and then uses the following subset of the available BibTeX tags:

Tag	Used for	Notes
author	Author names	Set to the **Authors** field of the entry. If the field contains more than one author, Publish or Perish inserts " *and* " between names as per BibTeX requirements.
title	Title	Set to the **Title** field of the entry.
Journal	Journal name	Set to the **Publication** field of the entry if present, else omitted.
publisher	Publisher	Set to the **Publisher** field of the entry if present, else omitted.
url	UR	Set to the (hidden) **ArticleURL** field of the entry if present, else omitted.
year	Date	Set to the **Year** field of the entry is present, else omitted.
note	Notes	Set to *x cites: CitationsURL* if the entry has one or more citations, else omitted.

CSV FORMAT DETAILS

The CSV (Comma Separated Value) format is a defacto format defined by various sources; see for example this Wikipedia entry. Publish or Perish applies all required transformations: quotes around fields that contain embedded spaces or commas, quote doubling for fields with embedded quotes, etc.

To import a CSV file into Microsoft Excel, Access, OpenOffice Calc, or similar programs, choose the following settings in the receiving program:

- **File type:** *Text CSV*, or *Comma Separated Value*, depending on the receiving program
- **Character set:** *Unicode (UTF-8)*
- **Separated by:** *Comma* (only; uncheck any other separators)
- **Text delimiter:** " (i.e., the straight double quote)

Publish or Perish writes all CSV format files as plain text Unicode files, encoded as UTF-8 with the UTF-8 BOM (0xEF 0xBB 0xBF) at the start of the file. The first line in the file lists the fields; the remaining lines contain the citation entries, one per line. Missing fields result in an empty CSV field "". The following field names are used:

Tag	Used for	Notes
Cites	Number of citations	Set to the **Cites** field of the entry.
Authors	Author names	Set to the **Authors** field of the entry.
Title	Title	Set to the **Title** field of the entry.
Year	Year of publication	Set to the **Year** field of the entry.
Source	Journal name	Set to the **Publication** field of the entry.

Publisher	Publisher	Set to the **Publisher** field of the entry.
ArticleURL	URL	Set to the (hidden) **ArticleURL** field of the entry.
CitesURL	Notes	Set to the (hidden) **CitationsURL** field of the entry.
GSRank	Google Scholar ranking	Set to the **Rank** field of the entry. This is simply the order in which Google Scholar returned the results (1=first, 2=second, etc.). Typically, earlier ranked entries indicate more relevant query results. This field was introduced in Publish or Perish version 2.2; for results obtained with earlier versions, it is set to 0.

ENDNOTE IMPORT FORMAT DETAILS

The EndNote Import data exchange format is defined by Thomson ResearchSoft for use by its EndNote program; the format specification can be found in the help file of EndNote itself.

Publish or Perish writes all EndNote Import format files as plain text Unicode files, encoded as UTF-8 with the UTF-8 BOM (0xEF 0xBB 0xBF) at the start of the file. It uses the following subset of the available End-Note Import tags:

Tag	Used for	Notes
%0	Type of entry	Set to *Journal Article* if the **Publication** field is present, else to *Book*.
%A	Author names	Publish or Perish generates one **%A** line per author in the **Authors** field.
%T	Title	Set to the **Title** field of the entry.
%B	Book title	Set to the **Publication** field of the entry if present, else omitted.
%I	Publisher	Set to the **Publisher** field of the entry if present, else omitted.
%U	URL	Set to the (hidden) **ArticleURL** field of the entry if present, else omitted.
%D	Date	Set to the **Year** field of the entry if present, else omitted.
%1	Miscellaneous	Set to *x cites: CitationsURL* if the entry has one or more citations, else omitted.

RIS FORMAT DETAILS

The RIS data exchange format is defined by Thomson ResearchSoft for use by its Reference Manager and EndNote programs, among others; their web site contains the official definition.

Publish or Perish writes all RIS format files as plain text Unicode files, encoded as UTF-8 with the UTF-8 BOM (0xEF 0xBB 0xBF) at the start of the file. It uses the following subset of the available RIS tags:

Tag	Used for	Notes
TY	Type of entry	Set to *JOUR* if the **Publication** field is present, else to *BOOK*.

A1	(Primary) Author names	Publish or Perish generates one **A1** line per author in the **Authors** field. It also reformats each author's name as *LastName, Initials* as required by the RIS specification. Because the Google Scholar authors list is not always 100% accurate, this may occasionally lead to misinterpreted names.
T1	(Primary) Title	Set to the **Title** field of the entry.
T2	(Secondary) Title	Set to the **Publication** field of the entry if present, else omitted.
PB	Publisher	Set to the **Publisher** field of the entry if present, else omitted.
UR	URL	Set to the (hidden) **ArticleURL** field of the entry if present, else omitted.
Y1	Date	Set to **Year///** if the **Year** field of the entry is present, else omitted. The trailing "///" characters are required by the RIS date format specification.
M1	Miscellaneous	Set to *x cites: CitationsURL* if the entry has one or more citations, else omitted.
ER	End of record	Marks the end of the entry

APPENDIX 5: MESSAGE REFERENCE

MSG_QUERY_EXECERROR

```
Error <code> while performing query:
<message>
```
Indicates that some kind of error occurred while the query was performed.
Click **OK** to dismiss the message.

COMMON ERROR CODES

Code	Description	Comments
13	The data is invalid.	The Google Scholar response contained no recognizable data. This can be due to a change in the Google Scholar output format; please report to pop@harzing.com if you suspect that this is the case. Before reporting, please do the following: 1. Check if an updated version of PoP is available on the Harzing web site: http://www.harzing.com/pop.htm You can also use the Help > Check for Updates command from the main menu. 2. After installing the update, if any, repeat the query using the **Lookup Direct** button. This retrieves fresh data from Google Scholar, which might help to resolve the problem. If nothing else helps, then please lodge an error report to pop@harzing.com by using the Help > Report Error command from the main menu. This generates an error report (a plain text file) called *PoPError.txt* that you should at-

tach to your email to the Publish and Perish support address. We need the information in the error report for an accurate diagnosis.

1169	There was no match for the specified key in the index.	The Google Scholar response contained no entries. This can be due to a query that did not match any papers, or because Google Scholar refused access due to an excessive number of prior queries. In the former case, change the query parameters. In the latter case, retrying the query after an hour or two might resolve the situation.
1223	The operation was canceled by the user.	You pressed the Cancel button while the query was in progress.
1341	The server is currently disabled.	Google Scholar refused access due to an excessive number of prior queries. Retrying the query after an hour or two might resolve the situation.
8250	The server is not operational.	Google Scholar refused access due to an excessive number of prior queries. Retrying the query after an hour or two might resolve the situation.
8257	No results were returned.	The Google Scholar response contained no data at all. This is typically caused by a local access problem, for example interference by anti-virus tools. Switch off your anti-virus tool temporarily and retry the query using **Lookup Direct** to see if that resolves the problem. If nothing else helps, then please lodge an error report to pop@harzing.com by using the Help > Report Error command from the main menu. This generates an error report (a plain text file) called *PoPError.txt* that you should attach to your email to the Publish and Perish support address. We need the information in the error report for an accurate diagnosis.

MSG_MAX_RESULTS

```
Warning: Results limit reached.
The query returned count results, which is the maximum that Google
Scholar allows.
This may affect the query coverage. Click Help for more information.
```

Indicates that your query returned the maximum number of results that Google Scholar allows (1000; sometimes a few less). Your query may have more matches, but the remainder are not available. As a result, some potential matches may be omitted from the list of results. Generally speaking, the missing results are deemed by Google Scholar to be less relevant than the ones that were returned. In terms of citations, these are usually articles with few (or no) citations.

The omission may or may not be significant: most high-level citation metrics such as the h-index and g-index are fairly robust and are unlikely to be affected. However, if you are looking for one or more specific results, then these might be missing from the results list.

SUGGESTED REMEDY

If you feel that the query results don't include the information you were looking for, then you should try to narrow down the search by adding further search criteria. For example, you could use the **Year of publication between ... and ...** fields to limit your query to a few years.

MSG_UPDATE_AVAILABLE

```
A new version of Publish or Perish is available:
<version>
Do you want to download and install this version?
```

Indicates that the update check found a new version of Publish or Perish and offers to download and install it.

Click **Yes** to download and install the new version, or **No** to keep the currently installed version

MSG_UPDATE_ERROR

```
Error <code> while updating the software:
<message>
```

Indicates that some kind of error occurred while the software was updated.

Click **OK** to dismiss the message. In some cases, you might have to re-install the Publish or Perish software.

COMMON ERROR CODES

Code	Description	Comments
126	The specified module could not be found.	No software update information was available for Publish or Perish.
12029	No Internet connection was available.	Check that your computer is connected to the Internet and that any intervening firewalls and proxy servers allow you access to the Publish or Perish web site.

APPENDIX 6: POP-UP MENU MULTI-QUERY CENTER LIST VIEW

Command	Description	Shortcut
Lookup	Performs all selected queries. If possible, the queries are satisfied from the local Publish or Perish cache; this saves time and reduces the load on Google Scholar. If no cache entry for a query exists or the entry is older than the maximum cache age, then the query is forwarded to Google Scholar. After the results are received from Google Scholar, the local cache is automatically refreshed. **Tip:** You can change the maximum cache age in the Preferences - Queries dialog box, which is accessible through the File > Preferences command. **Warning:** If you have more than a few queries selected when you issue this command, then Google Scholar may start refusing the lookup requests because of an excessive number of requests. In that case you must wait a few hours before retrying the queries, preferably with fewer queries selected.	Ctrl+L
Lookup Direct	Sends all selected queries directly to Google Scholar, bypassing the local Publish or Perish cache. This may be useful if you suspect that Google Scholar may have newer information available than is available through the local cache. When the results are returned from Google Scholar, the local cache is automatically refreshed. **Note:** It is not useful to perform multiple direct lookups for the same query shortly after another; this merely increases the load on Google Scholar and increases the chance that your computer may be temporarily denied access by Google Scholar. We recommend that you only use the **Lookup Direct** function as a last resort. **Warning:** If you have more than a few queries selected when you issue this command, then Google Scholar may start refusing the lookup requests because of an excessive number of requests. In that case you must wait a few hours before retrying the queries, preferably with fewer queries selected.	Ctrl+Shift+L
New Query	Creates a new query. It will be placed in the the parent folder of the currently selected query.	
Import Query	Imports external query data into Publish or Perish. This command is currently only partially implemented.	
New Folder	Creates a new query folder under the current folder.	
Save As BibTeX...	Saves all currently selected queries results in BibTeX format, encoded as Unicode UTF-8.	
Save As	Saves all currently selected queries results in comma-separated format,	Ctrl+S

CSV...	encoded as Unicode UTF-8.	
Save As End-Note...	Saves all currently selected queries results in EndNote Import format, encoded as Unicode UTF-8.	Ctrl+Shift+S
Save As RIS...	Saves all currently selected queries results in Reference Manager (RIS) format, encoded as Unicode UTF-8.	
Copy Statistics as Text	Copies the citation metrics of all currently selected queries to the Windows clipboard in plain text format. You can then paste this text into other applications.	
Copy Statistics as CSV	Copies the citation metrics of all currently selected queries to the Windows clipboard in CSV (comma-separated value) format. You can then paste this into other applications for further processing.	
Copy Statistics as CSV with Header	Does the same as the previous command, but precedes the statistics with an extra line that contains the names of the fields, also in comma-separated format.	
Copy Statistics for Excel	Copies the citation metrics of all currently selected queries to the Windows clipboard in tab-separated format. You can then paste this into other applications for further processing, and in particular into spreadsheet applications such as Microsoft Excel, OpenOffice Calc, and SoftMaker's PlanMaker.	
Copy Statistics for Excel with Header	Does the same as the previous command, but precedes the statistics with an extra line that contains the names of the fields, also in tab-separated format.	
Properties	Opens the Properties dialog box for the first selected query.	Alt+Enter
Cut	Copies the currently selected queries to the Windows clipboard and delete them from their current positions. You can then paste them into a different folder.	Ctrl+X
Copy	Copies the currently selected queries to the Windows clipboard. You can then paste them into a different folder.	Ctrl+C
Paste	Pastes the folder or query on the Windows clipboard into the current folder.	Ctrl+V
Delete	Deletes the currently selected queries. Be careful if you use this command; once deleted, a folder or query cannot be retrieved. (You can, however, re-create the query and rely on the Publish or Perish cache to quickly retrieve the previous results.)	Delete

CPSIA information can be obtained
at www.ICGtesting.com
Printed in the USA
LVIC071513300613
340864LV00005B